THE MOVIES

THE MOVIES

A complete guide to the directors, stars, studios and movie genres

DON SHIACH

LORENZ BOOKS

This edition is published by Lorenz Books

Lorenz Books is an imprint of Anness Publishing Ltd
Hermes House, 88–89 Blackfriars Road, London SE1 8HA
tel. 020 7401 2077; fax 020 7633 9499
www.lorenzbooks.com; info@anness.com

© Anness Publishing Ltd 2003

This edition distributed in the UK by The Manning Partnership Ltd
6 The Old Dairy, Melcombe Road, Bath BA2 3LR
tel. 01225 478 444; fax 01225 478 440; sales@manning-partnership.co.uk

This edition distributed in the USA and Canada by National Book Network
4501 Forbes Boulevard, Suite 200, Lanham, MD 20706
tel. 301 459 3366; fax 301 429 5746; www.nbnbooks.com

This edition distributed in Australia by Pan Macmillan Australia
Level 18, St Martins Tower, 31 Market St, Sydney, NSW 2000
tel. 1300 135 113; fax 1300 135 103; customer.service@macmillan.com.au

A CIP catalogue record for this book
is available from the British Library.

Publisher: Joanna Lorenz
Managing Editor: Judith Simons
Project Editor: Felicity Forster
Designer: Peter Bailey–Proof Books
Proofreader: Charles Phillips
Production Controller: Wendy Lawson

1 3 5 7 9 10 8 6 4 2

CONTENTS

FOREWORD

It is difficult to believe that back in the 1950s, when the movie business was hit hard by the advent of television and other competing mass entertainments, the death of the movies – or, at least, of the habit of going to the movies – was confidently forecast by many an expert. Fifty years ago, very few would have predicted, as we entered the new millennium, that cinema would be very much alive and well and a multi-billion-dollar enterprise across the globe. Certainly, the film business has changed enormously in the last few decades, as most people now see their movies in their own homes via satellite and cable television, videos and DVDs rather than in a cinema. But somehow the magic of movie-going lives on. Blockbuster movies can make enormous profits for their producers not only from box-office receipts around the world, but also from sales and rentals of videos and DVDs and the revenue from showings on television. New cinema technology

ABOVE *Gainsborough melodramas such as* The Wicked Lady *were the cinematic equivalent of bodice-rippers in books, but they made stars of British actors such as James Mason and Margaret Lockwood.*

will further transform the way we have movies delivered to us. For example, the days of celluloid distribution are surely numbered: soon movies on first release will be "pumped into" thousands of cinemas by cable distribution. All in all, the rumour circulating back in the 1950s about the death of the cinema proved to be much exaggerated.

It seems, too, that each new generation falls in love with the products of old Hollywood, the British film industry at its peak, as well as the great works of European cinema, revelling in Astaire–Rogers musicals such as *Top Hat* and *Carefree*, the great MGM musicals, suffering with Margaret Lockwood and James Mason in those laughable Gainsborough melodramas such as *The Wicked Lady* and *Jassy*, laughing with Buster Keaton or Cary Grant in Hollywood comedies such as *The Navigator* and *Bringing Up Baby*, solving murder mysteries with *The*

Thin Man and partners, weeping at *Casablanca* or empathizing with Jean Gabin or Marcello Mastroianni in great European classics such *La Grande Illusion* or *8½*. Old movies will never die; they will eternally resurface on television until the last moments of human history.

Hollywood in its heyday, with its excesses and absurdities, its real achievements and its crass failures of taste and artistic judgement, has gone forever. But the movie business regularly regenerates itself, discovering new and unexpected forms. The Hollywood studio system has long since disappeared, but new stars (not only star actors but star directors, producers and screenwriters) are constantly being created by a business that devours and spits out talents, or even non-talents, who prove their worth by making a buck for the owners. New niche markets for different types of movies are always being identified and catered for: the teen movie, the over-40s movie, the gross-out comedy, the adult cartoon movie, the special effects extravaganza and many more. Movies are very big business, and enormous riches await those, like

ABOVE *Fan magazines were eagerly read and stars such as the young Joan Bennett were promoted on their covers as iconic beauties.*

ABOVE Bringing Up Baby *was one of the most successful of the type of madcap, irrational comedies that came to be known as "screwball".*

ABOVE *The movie villain of all movie villains, Darth Vader, in the* Star Wars *movies. George Lucas, the guiding creative hand behind the series, became a major Hollywood player because of the success of the first movie in 1977.*

ABOVE *8½ (1963) was Fellini's reflections on his own career as a director after having made eight and a half movies. For Fellini fans this is a key film of the Italian master.*

Steven Spielberg, George Lucas or James Cameron, who tap into the public consciousness. Movies are spectacle, they are dreams, they are a view of reality and unreality, a world

ABOVE *For many people, it is movies such as* Casablanca, *a prime example of a "bad good movie", that define the magic and enduring appeal of the cinema.*

of fantasy, an escape, a Utopia. They inhabit a separate universe of their own. Cinema, for better or worse, was the dominant art form of the 20th century and may well be the same in the 21st century as well. Even the fiercest detractors of this mass entertainment would have to admit that movies touch the lives of more

people on this planet than books, music or theatre do. There is no escaping them.

This book attempts to encapsulate something of the appeal of the movies. By its very nature, it has had to be a selective process; after all, no two movie fans would agree on a list of favourite stars, most important directors or best movies. Hollywood and its products figure most prominently because the history of movies is largely the history of the American film industry, although that is not to deny the importance of other major film-producing nations. Indeed, more certainly does not always mean better, as is all too obvious from some of the lamentable excesses of the Hollywood machine. The American film industry now dominates the world film market to an extent that the old Hollywood moguls such as Louis B. Mayer and Jack Warner only dreamt about. This is not altogether a healthy aspect of contemporary cinema. The French defend their native film industry from the swamping effects of American movies. I wish other countries such as Britain would follow suit.

If you are reading this, you are almost certainly a movie fan – maybe even a movie buff. You belong to a

universal club with millions of members across the globe, all in love with a technological medium that has harnessed the stuff of which dreams are made. Whenever people get together and spend time reminiscing, at some stage the topic of favourite movies will come up. Many of our most common cultural references are related to movies. The USA even elected a former minor movie star as one of its presidents. Hollywood, indeed, has a lot to answer for, as well as plenty to be proud of. So, as Dorothy Parker once put it:

OH, COME MY LOVE AND
JOIN WITH ME,
THE OLDEST INFANT INDUSTRY.
COME SEEK THE BOURNE
OF PALM AND PEARL,
THE LOVELY LAND OF
BOY-MEETS-GIRL.

COME GRACE THIS
LOTUS-LADEN SHORE,
THE ISLE OF
DO-WHAT'S-DONE BEFORE.
COME CURB THE NEW AND
WATCH THE OLD WIN,
BUT WHERE THE STREETS ARE
PAVED WITH GOLDWYN.

7

THE HISTORY OF THE MOVIES

THE MOVIE industry entered the new
millennium in fairly robust health
despite many gloomy forecasts that the
movie-going experience was on its last legs.
Most of us nowadays do indeed see most movies
through television, videos and DVDs, but
the tradition of "going to the pictures" has not
disappeared entirely. The cinema started out
as a shared experience and let us hope that it
continues to be one. In this section we trace the
development of the movie-going experience.

LEFT *The famous chariot race from the 1959 version of Ben-Hur.*
Charlton Heston beat Stephen Boyd in a race that was fixed.

INTRODUCTION

The film industry has existed for well over a hundred years now and, of course, has been transformed in ways that could not possibly have been foreseen from the perspective of the early days of the 1890s. The history of the cinema reflects the changing economic, industrial/post-industrial and sociological structures of a whole century. The entertainment business, of which the movies are such an important part, has grown to staggering proportions such that it plays a central role in the business life of many nations. If we all ceased going to the movies or stopped watching them on television, video or DVD, then the economy of the world would be in serious trouble.

What is essential to remember about the film industry is that it is an industry and movies are the result of a technological and industrial process that no other art form requires. Indeed, it is the fact that films are produced through this technological process that allows cultural snobs to look down on movies as cultural artefacts. Cinema has always had to contend with this kind of disparagement from people who prefer theatre or literature, and the fact that movies need really big bucks from investors before they can be made also allows movie-haters to sneer. How can anything worthwhile emerge from an industry where the dread hand of commerce controls the process, they ask? Well, somehow or other, good movies do get made, as well as lots of commercial dross.

From the early days of cinema, serious followers of this new technological art had to plough a largely lonely furrow in their admiration for the movies. Even as the movies enter the second century of their existence, there are still many people who will willingly sit through all kinds of second-rate nonsense in the theatre and think they are watching something worthwhile because it is, after all, the theatre, while dismissing the movies as mindless entertainment. But these are the dwindling minority. Movies have had to fight long and hard to be taken as seriously as books, theatre, art objects and music but, for the most part, that battle has been won. The once-derided pastime for the moronic masses has achieved much in its domination of the arts. How, then, did the cinema reach this pre-eminent position in the cultural life of millions of people around the world?

THE HUMBLE BEGINNINGS

The international film market we know today grew from the kinetoscope: a simple machine comprising a cabinet and a length of film on a spool. The customers inserted a coin, the light shone and the film was projected on to the back of the cabinet. From our 21st century perspective, it doesn't seem much of a show, but it must have seemed like magic then.

Movies have always been perceived as an American product but, in fact, European inventors played crucial roles in the development of the cinematic apparatus: for example, William Friese-Green in England, Georges Demeny in France, and Ottomar Anschutz and Max Skladanowsky in Germany. In the 1890s the pioneers were French: the Lumière brothers, Gaumont and Pathé.

ABOVE *An advert for the Lumière brothers' shows in Paris. To a turn-of-the-century audience, these Lumière extravaganzas had more than a touch of magic about them, an expectation the brothers skilfully exploited.*

However, it was in America that the public showing of early movies rapidly grew. Kinetoscope parlours were opened in 1894 in the principal cities of America. Perhaps it is not absolutely accurate to say that cinema began with the kinetoscope, because the essence of the cinematic experience is its communal nature (while retaining privacy for the individuals sitting in the darkness of the cinema as they see their dreams appear before them). Thus, the cinema was really born with the invention of a projector that could throw a series of moving images on to a screen. The Latham brothers and W.K.L. Dickson invented the Panoptikon projector, which took movies out of the kinetoscope

cabinet, and in September 1895 in Paris the Lumière brothers showed a paying audience films that they themselves had produced in their Lyons factory.

In the USA, musical theatres began to present movies as part of their variety bills. Film companies were formed – the Biograph and Vitagraph companies, for example. In 1902 the first motion picture theatre, the Electric, was opened in Los Angeles. Early cinemas were called "nickelodeons" because you paid a nickel (five cents) to see the show. By 1907 there were approximately 3000 such nickelodeons across America. The cinema was on its way to becoming

ABOVE *A contemporary artist's impression of a kinetoscope parlour in America. Note the respectable ambience and the genteel decor that seek to reinforce the notion that such establishments are quite "proper" for ladies and gentlemen.*

big business and despite dips in public favour, for example during the Depression of the 1930s and advent of the television age in the 1950s, it would never be anything other than a major industry thereafter.

THE NARRATIVE FILM

New York was at this time the centre of American film-making; Hollywood was still a suburb of Los Angeles that was kind to oranges. However, in 1903 the Edison factory produced a landmark in cinematic history – the first true narrative film, *The Great Train Robbery*. At the Biograph Studios in New York a few years later a young actor, Lawrence Griffith, replaced a sick director on a one-reeler, *The Adventures of Dollie*, and

launched the career of D.W. Griffith, film director. If the young Griffith had had any pretensions at this stage of his career to being a "serious artist", then he must have had to lay them aside, because between 1908 and 1913 he directed 450 motion pictures. The vast majority of these movies have not survived because they were disposable merchandise, produced to seduce the punters into the movie houses and then disposed of. The nickelodeons

RIGHT AND BELOW *The emblems of the Vitagraph and Essanay Studios.*

at this time were very hungry monsters with a bottomless appetite for 15- or 30-minute features to set before an eager mass audience. Films were cranked off the assembly line one after the other. Several movies would be shot cheek-by-jowl on crowded stages in the early studios. After all, there was no dialogue to speak, no sound effects to be recorded. These were the silents.

LEFT *It's a long, long way to* Dances with Wolves, *but* The Great Train Robbery *(1903) was not only the first full-length narrative film but also the first western to have them queueing round the block.*

THE PATH TO *THE BIRTH OF A NATION*

By 1912 "proper" cinemas, as opposed to nickelodeons or halls, were fairly common and admission prices had doubled. Commensurate with this increase in admission prices was the increased length of the movies shown: one- and two-reelers of 15 or 30 minutes had given way to four- and five-reelers. Motion pictures were moving up in the world. One of the first entrepreneurs to realize this was Adolph Zukor, who founded the Famous Players Film Company.

ABOVE *Yes, this was the humble beginning of the major studio, Warner Brothers. Even today, Hollywood and Los Angeles have a certain air of impermanence about them, but these premises look like they would not have survived a strong wind, let alone the mildest of Californian earth tremors.*

Gradually, he and other entrepreneurs seduced famous stage actors away from the stage and on to the screen.

However, American films had hot competition from abroad. For example, the Italian-made *Quo Vadis?*, an eight-reel epic, ran for 22 weeks in New York.

Hollywood began to replace New York as the centre of film-making. The reasons were several: independent producers went west to escape the clutches of the Motion Picture Patents Company, a trust (including the Vitagraph and Biograph companies) formed to enforce a monopoly on film-making patents; the suburbs around Los Angeles were relatively undeveloped and furnished excellent natural resources for film-making on the cheap (sun, desert, mountains, nearby urban locations); and, crucially, the area was also a source of far cheaper labour than could be found in New York.

In 1914 the Jesse Lasky Feature Play Company was formed. Lasky's brother-in-law, Samuel Goldfish, later Goldwyn, joined the company, as did another famous Hollywood name, Cecil B. De Mille, who directed their first feature *The Squaw Man* in a barn. In the same year Paramount Pictures was formed to release the pictures of

ABOVE *A publicity still for* The Birth of a Nation *(1915) – hopefully, the only film in movie history to project in its publicity the Ku Klux Klan as the heroic defenders of Christian civilization. The movie caused a furore, but at the same time made Griffith's reputation as a major innovator in terms of film technique. And, yes, it made megabucks at the box office too.*

the Famous Players Company. Production, distribution and exhibition were the three battlegrounds for the early companies.

In 1915 arguably the most famous silent movie of all, *The Birth of a Nation*, was released. A 12-reel epic about the civil war and its aftermath, the movie, directed by D.W. Griffith, was the first film to be granted "road show" status. It was a huge box-office hit all over the world and won critical praise from sources which had hitherto scorned the movies as "dreams for the masses".

The Birth of a Nation also aroused great controversy and opposition, particularly from black people. From our historical perspective, we can see just how horrendously racist it was in its ideology. The Ku Klux Klan were represented heroically as the defenders of civilized values, and carpetbaggers and rapacious "negroes" as the villains of the piece. However, Griffith's advanced film techniques – close-ups, crosscutting, the staging of elaborate crowd and battle scenes – indicated that the cinema had made a huge technical advance.

AMERICAN DOMINATION OF THE WORLD MARKET

By the end of World War I the American film industry had effectively established itself as the dominant cinema, although the film industries of the Soviet Union, Germany, France and Scandinavia would challenge Hollywood in the 1920s in terms of the artistic use of the medium. Directors such as Fritz Lang, Sergei Eisenstein, Friedrich Murnau, Abel Gance, Jean Renoir,

ABOVE *D.W. Griffith directed* Hearts of the World *at the request of the British government who wanted a propaganda film to boost morale. Griffith duly obliged.*

Mauritz Stiller and Carl Dreyer made films that very few American film-makers could match. However, to ruthless movie executives films are pure business. Studios had the power to impose their products wherever films were shown commercially.

Their own huge domestic market gave American film-makers an enormous advantage over other countries. Studios could make film

after film in the sure knowledge that American box-office revenues alone would produce substantial profits. Foreign revenues were the icing on the cake. Exhibitors all around the world were clamouring for products to show, and the USA produced far more films than anywhere else.

The businessmen who owned the studios realized that there were three crucial areas of the film business they

had to control if they were to establish a virtual monopoly in the marketplace: production, distribution and exhibition. Of these, the real money was to be made in distribution and exhibition, so all the major Hollywood studios were intent on setting up their distribution arms and buying as many cinemas in prime locations as they could. As the distributors of their own films, they could charge a substantial rental (usually between 30 and 40 per cent of box-office receipts) to cinemas not owned by themselves. As the owners of their own cinemas, they were

showing their own products and all revenues came back to the parent company. Most of the early movie moguls came into film production via other business activities as diverse as theatre ownership and scrap-dealing, and they brought a hard-nosed, ruthless, market-orientated approach to the enterprise of making movies for a mass audience.

The American film industry was also very efficient at publicizing its wares. The studios were adept at creating an aura of glamour and excitement around movies, and stars were the main carriers of this aura. The production of glamour was aided and abetted by newspapers and magazines in all the developed countries of the world. Thus, when Douglas Fairbanks and Mary Pickford came to Europe after the end of the World War I, they were greeted by enormous numbers of people wherever they went. Movie stars were the new royalty, and a huge publicity machine, partly wielded by the

ABOVE *Mary Pickford was more than just a pretty face. When her film career waned, she proved her worth as a movie mogul.*

13

ABOVE *Douglas Fairbanks was a major swashbuckling star of the silent era.*

Hollywood studios and partly by other media with vested interests in aiding this publicity, made sure they would retain that aura for years to come.

It was not only stars that projected this aura. Important movie-makers such as Griffith and De Mille were quickly recognized by the producers as "brand names" to sell their product. However, it was stars such as Fairbanks, Valentino, Garbo, Ronald Colman, Vilma Banky, Theda Bara and many others that the producers ultimately banked on to bring the customers in – the stars, and the easily recognizable type of product movie-goers were drawn to see again and again: westerns, exotic romantic dramas, swashbucklers, slapstick comedies, thrillers, cops-and-robber thrillers and musicals.

By the early 1920s, the American film industry had settled on the formula that would stand it in good stead (with troughs along the way) over the next decades: provide a steady diet of mainly undemanding, populist entertainments manufactured by assembly-line production methods with the stars that people loved and the content that customers would identify as the type of picture they preferred to see. Art was not part of the equation; if art happened by accident in the process of making a motion picture, that was beneficial to the prestige of the industry as long as it didn't put off the paying customers.

ABOVE *Two of the silent screen's biggest stars, Ronald Colman and Vilma Banky in a typical romantic melodrama of the 1920s. The vast commercial success of the movies led to an explosion in the number of related publications that exploited this mass interest in the new art. This souvenir supplement issued by* Picture Show *magazine illustrates this.*

LEFT *Her acting abilities may be in dispute, but for her many fans, Greta Garbo remains the eternal goddess of the silver screen. Publicists worked very hard to create this illusion.*

14

THE MAGIC OF THE MOVIES

By the 1920s movies were very big business indeed. The average movie product was unsophisticated and direct in its appeal, whether it was a Chaplin or Mack Sennett comedy or a melodramatic tearjerker starring Gloria Swanson or Norma Talmadge. Film-makers went after family audiences because that was where the money was, so escapism was the order of the day. The showmen's belief was that the movies should offer harmless entertainment and not bother with "messages". Movies offered an escape from everyday problems: they transported you to exotic locations and embroiled you in romantic and dangerous exploits. Up there on the screen, you could watch the parting of the Red Sea (courtesy of Cecil B. De Mille), see Ramon Novarro win a chariot race in Ancient Rome, or witness the crucifixion of Christ in *The King of Kings*. Spectacle, mayhem and melodrama are the stuff of which dreams are made, and the movies sold dreams.

The Hollywood studios were the Dream Factories, manufacturing fantasy for the millions. Dream Factories required Dream Palaces in which these manufactured dreams could be experienced, and so exotic cinemas such as Grauman's Chinese Theater in Los Angeles, the Granada in humble Tooting in South London, or Radio City Music Hall in New York were built in the years to come to add an extra enticement to cinema-goers. Movies transported you to a different world, so it was appropriate that cinemas should have this other-worldly ambience, as well.

ABOVE *Charlie Chaplin's popularity continued well after he had ceased producing the comedies that made him famous. This is a Belgian poster for a "portamanteau" 1950s movie of some of the best Chaplin comedy routines. All over the world, Chaplin was probably the most instantly recognized movie icon.*

LEFT *Buster Keaton is many people's favourite silent-era comedian. His career virtually vanished with the coming of sound. Lovers of silent movie comedies are usually as diehard as traditional jazz fans — and just as purist.*

THE COMING OF SOUND AND THE DEPRESSION

Although movies had become established as a major entertainment form worldwide, by the mid-1920s audiences were beginning to decrease. Films such as *Ben-Hur* and *The Ten Commandments* still made a fortune for their makers, but for the run-of-the-mill product, audiences were becoming harder to find. Just as it looked as though cinema's advance might be checked, the cavalry, in the shape of Warner Brothers and Vitaphone, came riding over the horizon, bugles blowing, to the rescue. Movies with sound had already been tried in a series of Vitaphone shorts and a musical accompaniment and sound effects in the John Barrymore version of *Don Juan*, but the major studios had turned their backs on this technological innovation because of the cost of installing equipment. But the Warner brothers – Harry, Jack, Sam and Albert – took a chance on Vitaphone because they needed a new impetus if they were going to be able to force their way into theatre ownership, which was so crucial if you wanted to become a major player on the Hollywood stage. The brothers backed *The Jazz Singer* with Al Jolson blacking up, and it made millions. The end was nigh for silent movies and every studio in Hollywood clambered on the bandwagon that Warners had set in motion. The headstart they had in producing "talkies" catapulted Warner Brothers to major studio status and forced their rivals to catch up.

They talk! They sing! They have sound effects! Movie-makers turned to musicals to make the most of this new technological development. During

ABOVE *Ronald Colman was one silent screen star whose career survived into the sound era, but his co-star here, Lili Damita, was not so lucky when the "talkies" took over.*

the first couple of years of the talkies, the market was saturated with all-singing, all-talking, all-dancing musical extravaganzas like *The Hollywood Revue of 1929*, *Broadway Melody*, *The Desert Song*, *Show of Shows* and *Gold Diggers of Broadway*. Producers also turned to filming Broadway stage shows, which was easy and relatively cheap. However, the essence of movies is that they move, and so audiences soon tired of these stage-bound exercises. A surfeit of musicals also led to audience indifference. And the Wall Street Crash had heralded the start of the Depression – millions of people around the world were struggling to survive and had no extra money to indulge in the purchase of movie tickets. The movie industry faced an extremely hard task in enticing Depression audiences into the emptying cinemas.

ABOVE The Hollywood Revue of 1929 *was a precursor of MGM's great musicals. Its static production numbers and corny routines paved the way for more sophisticated fare less than a decade later.*

GANGSTERS, MOLLS AND CENSORSHIP

In the early part of the 1930s, Hollywood turned to sensationalist drama to attract customers back into the cinemas. Three gangster films made in 1931–32, *Little Caesar, The Public Enemy* and *Scarface*, were successes both commercially and artistically, but aroused opposition from pressure groups such as the American Legion and Daughters of the American Revolution. These films portrayed the underbelly of the American Dream, a distorted Horatio Alger morality tale of success. The methods used by Edward G. Robinson, James Cagney and Paul Muni in these movies to achieve power in their gangland underworld had more than a passing resemblance to the ruthless machinations of American big business, and this did not endear them to the establishment. Law enforcers were portrayed as at best incompetent and at worst corrupt and this, too, irritated those who cherished the idea of the

ABOVE *Edward G. Robinson found instant screen immortality when he played an Al Capone-type gangster in* Little Caesar. *He impersonated criminals convincingly and won himself a huge fan following.*

Republic as the land of opportunity for decent American citizens who played it by the rules.

The other ingredient used by producers to tempt customers back into the cinemas was sex. Although extremely mild by present-day standards, movies such as *Dishonored* and *Morocco* with Marlene Dietrich and *The Story of Temple Drake* with Florence Eldridge had puritans all over the country reaching for their writing pads to dash off a letter to their Congressman. Mae West's films, such as *Night After Night* and *She Done Him Wrong*, also produced strong reactions. Jean Harlow was another new star who courted, and gained, disapproval.

ABOVE *Jean Harlow became the "bad girl" of 1930s movies, symbolizing a type of brassy and unsubtle glamour.*

Hollywood studios sniffed the wind and recognized that, if they did not do something themselves, they might be faced with external censorship. In 1927 the Motion Pictures Producers and Distributors of America (MPPDA) had established a code to govern the making of motion pictures, but now this code was updated and an

ABOVE *James Cagney was another major star who impersonated gangsters on screen and won a huge fan following for doing so.*

17

office known as the Production Code Administration (PCA, but commonly called the Hays Office after MPPDA chief William Hays, then later the Breen Office) was given the responsibility for making sure that the studios obeyed it. All scripts had to be approved by the PCA before shooting started, and when the film was completed the PCA could insist on cuts by threatening to refuse its Seal of Approval. A film without the PCA Seal of Approval could not be shown in any cinema that came under the jurisdiction of the MPPDA. In fact, the major studios, which controlled the MPPDA, turned this situation to their own advantage, and used the Seal of Approval system to ward off competitors and independent producers. They not only controlled which films could be shown on the major circuits, but also had a stranglehold through the PCA on the content of American movies. The extreme puritanism of the PCA conveniently suited the studios' commercial needs. They were after an undemanding family audience, and used the code as their excuse to produce "harmless" and largely mindless movies that promoted "the American Way of Life".

Other genres that did well at the box office in the 1930s were horror films and musicals once again. A cycle of cheaply made flicks dealing with

ABOVE *More sophisticated comedy fare was served up by Cary Grant, Katharine Hepburn and James Stewart in* The Philadelphia Story.

the Dracula and Frankenstein myths made stars of Bela Lugosi, Boris Karloff and Lon Chaney Jnr. After its brief demise, the musical underwent a rebirth with a series of Warners "Depression" musicals directed by Busby Berkeley, the recipe for which was regimented battalions of sturdy chorus girls, Nuremberg Rally-type production numbers and opulent costumes and settings. More sophisticated were the series of Astaire–Rogers musicals with Art Deco settings and the effortless grace of the two stars. These musicals could safely be described as "harmless entertainment", an antidote to the grimness of the decade. It was also the decade of screwball and sophisticated comedies such as *His Girl Friday* and *The Philadelphia Story*. The Marx Brothers were at their peak and the Disney studios were hugely successful with colourful animated features such as *Snow White and the Seven Dwarfs*. In the midst of all this escapism, some films with a populist tone emerged to confront the social problems of the time: Frank Capra's *Mr Deeds Comes to Town* and *Mr Smith Goes to Washington*, Fritz Lang's *Fury*

and John Ford's *The Grapes of Wrath*. However, audiences continued to decline, despite the studios offering double bills to their customers and cinema-owners even offering free china and other give-aways to entice movie-goers.

In Britain, the Korda brothers were establishing a production company that would rival Hollywood studios with films such as *The Private Life of Henry the Eighth* and *The Four Feathers*. Britain was often in the vanguard of technical advance, such as the introduction of colour, and Michael Powell's movie, *The Thief of Bagdad* (1940) showed what British technicians could achieve under imaginative direction. However, as usual, most British cinema seemed to be stuck in the past. By contrast, French cinema, with talents such as Marcel Pagnol, Jean Renoir and Marcel Carné, produced memorable films such as *Marius*, *La Règle du Jeu*, *La Grande Illusion* and *Le Quai des Brumes*. Stalinist dictatorship had locked Soviet directors such as Eisenstein into serving the interests of the totalitarian state after the major achievement of *Battleship Potemkin*.

ABOVE *The Disney studio were pushing back the frontiers of animated film in full-length cartoons such as* Snow White and the Seven Dwarfs *(1937).*

WARTIME BOOM

Colour quickly caught on in the late 1930s, and on December 31, 1939, in Atlanta, Georgia, the première was held of the technicolor epic, *Gone with the Wind*, which would go on to be one of the box-office winners of all time. Once America had entered World War II, an economic boom followed. People had money to spend and audiences craved Hollywood's brand of escapism to help keep grim reality at bay. Musicals flourished once more, with stars such as Betty Grable, Judy Garland and Gene Kelly. The so-called "women's picture" took off, aimed at a predominantly female audience separated from lovers and husbands: *The Great Lie, Now Voyager* and *Mildred Pierce* were three of the more memorable of these melodramas. Orson Welles had

managed to make *Citizen Kane* and *The Magnificent Ambersons* before RKO and Hollywood realized they had a talented rebel on their hands. Humphrey Bogart became a megastar with *The Maltese Falcon* and *Casablanca*, which did Ingrid Bergman's career no

ABOVE *Bette Davis and Mary Astor co-starred in* The Great Lie, *one of the many "women's pictures" that Davis and others starred in during this period.*

ABOVE Gone with the Wind *premièred in Atlanta on December 31, 1939, and at the time it seemed the last word in spectacular screen action.*

harm either. The dark days of the war also saw the emergence of a group of films that critics later dubbed *"film noir"*. The wartime shortages of materials to build sets and the restriction on the use of lighting may have forced film-makers to employ shadowy lighting techniques and expressionist designs, but there was also something doom-laden in the air that lasted into peacetime and permeated classic *film noir* movies such as *The Dark Mirror, Crossfire, Double Indemnity* and *Out of the Past*. Britain, meanwhile, predictably produced morale-raising movies such

as *San Demetrio-London*, *In Which We Serve* and *The Way to the Stars*; for the home front, the industry produced morale-boosters such as *Two Thousand Women*. At times, it seemed that only John Mills and David Niven stood between the country and defeat. France under German occupation still managed to produce the odd master-piece, especially *Les Enfants du Paradis*.

The absolute peak year for audience attendance in America was 1946: there were 90 million admissions per week across the nation, a figure that the present-day industry cannot even remotely approach. Business would never be the same again, however, and from then on the film industry contracted.

There were two main causes of the decline in movie attendances. Firstly, in 1948 there was a great increase in the number of television sets sold in the USA; the relatively new phenomenon of television was now the cinema's greatest competitor. Television provided free enter-tainment in people's own homes – why bother to go out and pay good money to see a movie? World War II had interrupted the development of television as a mass medium, but now

in the immediate post-war years we were entering the television age.

A second most important factor in the decline of the American film industry was legislation passed by the US government to break up the virtual monopoly that the "Big Five" studios enjoyed within the industry. The 1948 Paramount Decree forced the studios to sell off their cinemas in the prime sites of the largest American cities. This was a body blow to the studios because, contrary to popular belief, it was in the spheres of exhibition and distribution that they made their real profits. Production was the third arm of the monopoly structure exercised by the studios, but the major studios made as many movies as they did primarily in order to service their own exhibition and

distribution arms. Now that incentive was being taken away from them by a government that had begun to move in this direction before the war had intervened.

The Anti-Trust Law, or the Paramount decree, in essence broke the studios' monopoly hold on all aspects of the film business. This, in tandem with a 50 per cent drop in audiences suffered by the industry in the 10 years after the peak of 1946, forced the break-up of the old studio system. "Old Hollywood" would, over the next 20 to 30 years, change into "new Hollywood", in which the names of Louis B. Mayer, Harry Cohn and other moguls became a distant reminder of the great old days.

ABOVE *World War II continued to fascinate British film-makers.* San Demetrio-London *was an Ealing Studios production. These movies were propagandist in their tone and appeal.*

ABOVE *The subject of racial prejudice was tentatively dealt with in Elia Kazan's* Pinky.

Because the studios no longer had the incentive to make 50 or 60 movies a year to service their own movie-houses, long-term contract stars, directors, writers and other workers were gradually released. The numbers of movies produced by the majors decreased dramatically.

ABOVE *Otto Preminger's* Anatomy of a Murder *(1959) dealt with sexual matters in a way that would have had 1930s censors up in arms and demanding cuts.*

Partly because of the television challenge, the power of the PCA, the industry's censor, was eventually challenged by film-makers such as Otto Preminger with *The Moon is Blue* and *The Man with the Golden Arm.* Hollywood, with its need to offer the public films that would drag them away from their television sets, found it politic to relax censorship and allow hitherto taboo subjects to be dealt with on screen. *Pinky, A Place in the Sun, Cat on a Hot Tin Roof, Picnic, Baby Doll* and *Anatomy of a Murder* were typical of these "outspoken" movies about "adult issues". The thinking was that television was serving up anodyne fare such as *I Love Lucy*, so let's offer the public more adult material that

ABOVE *William Holden and Kim Novak starred in* Picnic *(1955), considered to be quite steamy in its time.*

television, in its pursuit of the family audience, could not compete with. Hollywood also discovered that most of its audience were between 16 and

BELOW *A Place in the Sun (1951) starring Elizabeth Taylor and Montgomery Clift was one of the movies that dealt with adult subjects with a new frankness.*

21

25 years old, so movies deemed to appeal to this young audience were rapidly produced: *Rebel Without a Cause, The Wild One* and *Rock Around the Clock* were three such movies. The mass audience for movies had fragmented and Hollywood could no longer depend on income from movie-goers who regularly went to the cinema two or three times a week.

The 1950s was also the decade of pneumatic blondes, fantasy women created by men to pander to male chauvinism: Marilyn Monroe, Jayne Mansfield, Kim Novak, Diana Dors and Mamie Van Doren. Simultaneously new directors such as Sidney Lumet, John Frankenheimer and Martin Ritt learnt their craft in television studios and then transferred to the big screen. Alfred Hitchcock made some of his best films around this time, including *Rear Window, Vertigo, North by Northwest* and *Psycho.* Elia Kazan directed *On the Waterfront* and John Ford *The Searchers.* Alexander Mackendrick, after his successes with Ealing comedies such as *The Ladykillers* and *The Maggie,* went to Hollywood and made the classic *Sweet Smell of Success.* Declining audiences meant that Hollywood could not afford to take many chances on what it considered to be uncommercial material or unproven writers and directors but, despite this lack of risk-taking, some good movies continued to be made in America.

However, it was with technological innovation that Hollywood principally gambled in its attempts to win back mass audiences: CinemaScope, VistaVision, 3-D, Todd-AO, Cinerama and other formats. Between the years 1954 and 1956 audience figures did show some increase compared to the preceding years, but the attractions of wide-screen and three-dimensional effects were short-lived and audience figures began to "dive" once again. In the USA, many people had fled the inner cities for the safety of the suburbs and were reluctant to venture back into the city in the evening to

ABOVE *Alexander Mackendrick directed the most famous of all Ealing comedies,* The Ladykillers. *Mackendrick brought a misanthropic tone to the cosy world of Ealing comedy.*

23

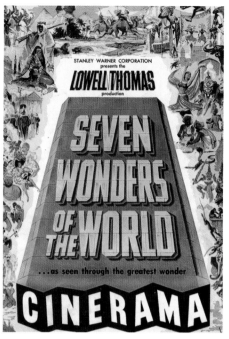

ABOVE *20th Century Fox used CinemaScope to attract movie-goers back into the cinemas.*

ABOVE AND ABOVE RIGHT *Cinerama was a curved-screen alternative to CinemaScope, but few feature films were ever shot using this process.*

see a movie when they had the television on tap in their front room. It would take time for the suburban shopping mall movie-houses and multiplexes to catch up with this sociological phenomenon.

In the late 1950s and early 60s, French cinema gained new impetus with the *Nouvelle Vague (New Wave)* movement, led by directors such as

François Truffaut, Jean-Luc Godard, Claude Chabrol, Louis Malle and Eric Rohmer. Ingmar Bergman directed a series of outstanding films in Sweden, including *The Seventh Seal* and *Wild Strawberries*. The international success of this "art cinema" testified to the fact that mass audiences were turning away from mainstream pictures, except in the case of epics such as

MGM's remake of *Ben-Hur* and De Mille's remake of his own *The Ten Commandments*. Italy had led the way after the war in establishing this "art" market with the Neo-realist school of directors, pre-eminent of whom were Vittorio De Sica and Roberto Rossellini. Now, in the mid- to late 50s, a new generation of Italian directors was coming to the fore, including Michelangelo Antonioni (*L'Avventura*) and Federico Fellini (*La Dolce Vita*, *La Strada*). After a decade of making *Carry On* and *Doctor* movies, Ealing comedies and endless war movies, something stirred in British cinema and pictures such as *Room at the Top*, *A Taste of Honey*, *This Sporting Life*, *Saturday Night and Sunday Morning* and *Billy Liar* helped to extend the range of British films. Japanese cinema was also making a world impact, principally through Akira Kurosawa's films *Seven Samurai* and *Rashomon*. Eastern European cinema, particularly the Polish, Hungarian and Czechoslovakian industries, provided an outlet for covert social criticism, and directors such as Andrzej Wajda and Milos Forman became familiar names on the art-house circuit.

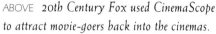

ABOVE *The war fable* Les Carabiniers *(1963), directed by Jean-Luc Godard, represented the Nouvelle Vague (New Wave) movement in French cinema.*

24

THE RISE OF THE AGENT AND THE PACKAGE DEAL

The butt of many a comedian's jokes, the agent, suddenly came to the fore in the power struggle in Hollywood. When the old studio system broke up, more and more films were made by independent producers who, however, had to make deals with the studios over distribution and, frequently, finance. The agents were ready to fill the vacuum that the demise of the studios as movie-making factories had left. Top agents, such as MCA and William Morris, could approach a studio with a

BELOW *New power-brokers Marlon Brando and Paul Newman confer. Major stars like these could now call the shots in new Hollywood.*

LEFT *Steve McQueen performs his own stunts in* The Great Escape, *something that would never have been allowed in old Hollywood.*

a package could ensure that a project would actually get off the ground.

The 60s, however, were not good years for Hollywood – at least until very late in the decade, when "youth" films such as *Easy Rider* and *The Graduate* emerged. Gone were the days of family pictures and the Louis B. Mayer ethos of "beautiful people in beautiful stories". Hollywood was now willing to make money from anything; and if youthful rebellion, after the heady days of 1968, was the fashion, then the new moguls were only too anxious to put youthful rebellion on screen.

In the 70s, a new generation of American directors arrived. Men such as Steven Spielberg, Martin Scorsese, Francis Coppola, Brian De Palma and George Lucas were steeped in Hollywood myths, and very often looked back to "old Hollywood" for their inspiration. Spielberg, for example, "raided" Disney films for *Close Encounters of the Third Kind* and *E.T.*, whilst Scorsese reinvented the MGM musical with *New York, New*

package deal that would consist of a screenplay by a well-known writer, a major star or two, an executive producer and a director – all of them under contract to the agency. The agents became the power-brokers of Hollywood. And although much was written about the end of the star system, a few major stars had more power than ever before. In the 1960s and 70s Barbra Streisand, Robert Redford, Jane Fonda, Marlon Brando, Dustin Hoffman, Steve McQueen, Paul Newman and others wielded immense power: their participation in

RIGHT *Steven Spielberg directed the block-buster* Jaws *(1975), which showed the new moguls that they could trust young directors with big-budget features.*

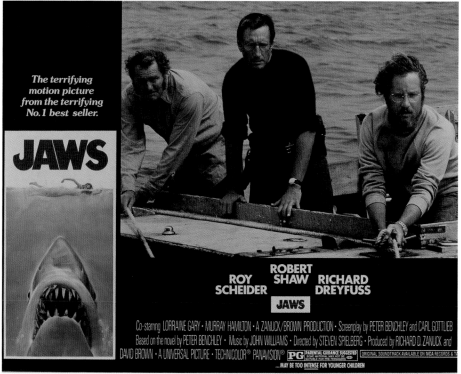

The terrifying motion picture from the terrifying No. 1 best seller.

JAWS

ROY SCHEIDER · ROBERT SHAW · RICHARD DREYFUSS

JAWS

Co-starring LORRAINE GARY · MURRAY HAMILTON · A ZANUCK/BROWN PRODUCTION · Screenplay by PETER BENCHLEY and CARL GOTTLIEB
Based on the novel by PETER BENCHLEY · Music by JOHN WILLIAMS · Directed by STEVEN SPIELBERG · Produced by RICHARD D. ZANUCK and
DAVID BROWN · A UNIVERSAL PICTURE · TECHNICOLOR® PANAVISION® · PG PARENTAL GUIDANCE SUGGESTED · ORIGINAL SOUNDTRACK AVAILABLE ON MCA RECORDS & TA
...MAY BE TOO INTENSE FOR YOUNGER CHILDREN

York and remade John Ford's *The Searchers* in *Taxi Driver*. These "movie brats" were not only brilliant film-makers. They also knew how to make movies that would become all-time box-office winners, such as *Jaws, Star Wars* and *Raiders of the Lost Ark*. Audience figures would never return to their 1946 peak, but mega-hits in the cinema could make more money than ever before for their makers, including directors and stars who were usually on a percentage of the box-office revenues.

One feature of the 70s was the emergence of "new" national cinemas. Films that were both entertaining and important started to emerge from countries as diverse as the Sudan and Argentina. One of the strongest was the Australian cinema, led by *Picnic at Hanging Rock, Mad Max* and *My Brilliant Career*. Australian directors

RIGHT *The success of the first* Rambo *movie (1982) generated two sequels (1985, 1988) starring Sylvester Stallone, who rapidly became a power-broker in the industry.*

Peter Weir, Bruce Beresford and Fred Schepisi went on to direct movies in America. The German cinema experienced something of a reawakening with the emergence of direc-tors such as Rainer Werner Fassbinder, Hans Werner Herzog and Wim Wenders. However, the British cinema was exper-iencing difficulty in maintaining a separate identity from the American industry, a situation that the French have never faced because they believe in an indigenous cinema and prove that by producing, on average, six times as many home-grown movies as the British do.

Cinema had become truly international by the 70s and 80s with directors such as Italy's Bernardo Bertolucci, France's Louis Malle and Germany's Wim Wenders making films in their native countries, Hollywood and elsewhere. The art film circuit was established, and if a film failed to find a wide release in the cinema, it could always get showings on some of the many television channels that were sprouting up in every country.

Video, and the fact that VCRs became part of almost every household, was the next challenge to cinema, but this time the businessmen behind the movie industry harnessed the new technology and turned it to their profit. For every one customer who sees a movie in the cinema, 12 now see it on video or DVD. In addition, the spread of cable and satellite television has added a new market for new and not-so-new films. Customers pay monthly premiums to watch new and old movies on channels dedicated to round-the-clock transmission of films. Or you can watch a new movie via pay-per-view. New movie productions are very often financed by cable companies such as HBO in America, or by television channels in Britain. But Hollywood in the 80s generally played it safe with winning formulas repeated ad nauseam, spawning endless sequels, and even "prequels". After all, just how many *Airplane!, Rocky* and *Halloween* sequels can the public accept?

COMPUTER TECHNOLOGY AND ANIMATION

No one can say with any certainty what the future holds for cinema. The accepted wisdom in Hollywood today is that "no one knows anything", meaning it is all a gamble because nobody can gauge public taste or how the industry will develop.

The importance of computerized technology to our society in general cannot be exaggerated. And the movie-making business has been and will continue to be transformed by that technology's ability to take over from humans some of the traditional skills associated with film-making. For example, when we think of the special effects created by specialists like Ray Harryhausen in the 1950s, 60s and 70s for movies such as *Jason and the Argonauts*, *One Million Years BC* and *The Golden Voyage of Sinbad*, the word "creaky" comes to mind. Compare

ABOVE Gladiator *employed state-of-the-art computer-generated special effects to flesh out its revenge story set in ancient Rome.*

those effects with the computer-generated effects of the *Jurassic Park* movies, the most recent *Star Wars* movies or *Gladiator*, and it can be seen how cinema technology is harnessing the advances in computer graphics to startling effect.

However, the "special effects" movies of the last 25 years, dating from 1977 when the first *Star Wars* was released with a resultant box-office harvest that has shaped Hollywood thinking ever since, seldom match their technical excellence with artistic worth. If we make a direct comparison of the Roman epics *Spartacus* (1960) and *Gladiator* (2000), is the latter with its computer-generated effects in the battle and gladitorial arena scenes in the same artistic league as the Kubrick-directed *Spartacus*, one of the few Hollywood epics that is not a no-brainer? *Spartacus* has a literate script by Dalton Trumbo, Kubrick's eye for

visual impact and is about more than just war and violence. The overrated *Gladiator* is basically a revenge western transcribed to Roman times, it isn't about anything very much, is directed by Ridley Scott and, for all its computer wizardy, fails to rise above the pedestrian. The point is that the technical advances of computerized graphics do not guarantee overall excellence – indeed, they very often guarantee the opposite because the special effects become the movie.

Two of the biggest box-office successes of recent years further illustrate this point: *Independence Day* (1996) and *Titanic* (1997). *Independence Day* made megabucks, but it is a spectacularly bad movie, inferior to many of the alien invasion movies of the 1950s (such as *The Day The Earth*

ABOVE The Day the Earth Stood Still *seemed in the forefront of cinematic special effects when it was released in the 1950s.*

ABOVE *The* Star Wars *movies ushered in a new era of special effects in Hollywood movies.*

Stood Still and *Invaders from Mars*) despite all the Oscar-winning special effects that were largely generated by computers. The script is laughable, the mock heroics of the Clinton-like president figure wholly implausible and the term "no-brainer" might well have been coined for this flick. They hardly come dumber than *Independence Day*, but *Titanic* certainly runs it close. Directed by James Cameron, and with the sinking of the Titanic spectacularly represented by state-of-the-art special effects, the movie itself is sunk by its third-rate "television special" script, its mawkishness, its stereotyped characterization and hackneyed storylines. It is almost as though the film-makers, having decided to film the Titanic disaster as

realistically and viscerally as possible, forgot the essential element of creating an adult and credible screenplay and decided just to go with what they had: a script that would not even pass muster for a television pilot.

Thus, computer-generated special effects cannot replace the need for scripts that escape banality or direction that is not merely at the service of the special-effects technicians. Not so long ago, there was industry talk about replacing actors such as Schwarzenegger and Stallone with their computer-generated "doubles". In other words, Arnie and Sly would not even have to be in one of their movies for there to be a Schwarzenegger or Stallone movie; the computer would do it for them. In those particular cases, perhaps the loss might not be that huge, but when stars can be replaced

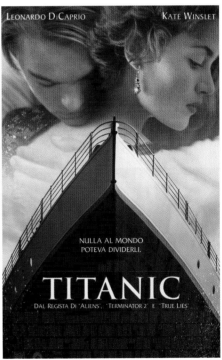

LEONARDO DiCAPRIO   KATE WINSLET

NULLA AL MONDO
POTEVA DIVIDERLI.

TITANIC

DAL REGISTA DI 'ALIENS', 'TERMINATOR 2' E 'TRUE LIES'

ABOVE Titanic *(1997) was a triumph of contemporary special effects, but lacked conviction in terms of story and characters.*

at will by their computerized doubles, then the industry needs to take a step back and consider what direction it is heading.

Another major technological advance of recent years has been in the field of animation, which is intimately linked with computerization. However, the end-products in animated films have been more encouraging. *Toy Story* and *Toy Story 2* have been much admired by people of all tastes and ages because the scripts are witty and intelligent, the graphics inventive and appealing, and the animation is at the service of the story. Other notable animated films of some worth have been *A Bug's Life*, *Antz*, *Stuart Little*, *Chicken Run* and *Shrek*. Disney have moved with the times with *The Lion King*, which took $220 million at the American box office and became the Disney Corporation's all-time biggest grosser. *Aladdin* and *Beauty and the Beast* also made huge profits,

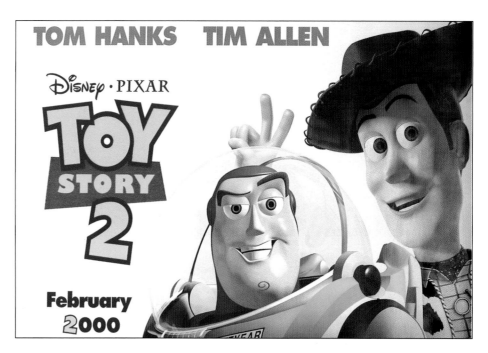

although they were seen as more traditional Disney fare. There has always been a large market for adult strip-cartoon comics, and contemporary animated movies are reaching that market, as television animated series such as *The Simpsons*

ABOVE *The producers of the* Toy Story *series lavished care on the quality of the scripts as well as the special effects.*

and *South Park* have also done, the latter series having been turned into a successful feature film.

THE FUTURE

The advances in cinematic technology have been so rapid in the last decade or so that it would be a brave person who forecasts future developments in not only how movies are made but also how they are seen by the mass audience. However, I think we can be certain that

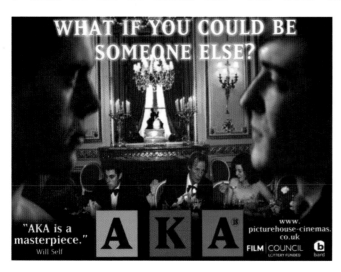

"interactive cinema" may evolve at some future date, similar to so-called interactive television in that the viewer, in theory at least, can intervene and shape the spectacle he or she is watching. In other words, Aldous Huxley's "feelies" from *Brave New World* may be just around the technological corner. We may all sit in our cinema seats and press the appropriate button to add special effects such as smells, sounds or visual motifs to the movie we are watching.

LEFT *AKA told its story on a screen that was split into three sections.*

Perhaps one day we will be able to alter storylines or movie endings to suit our own particular needs. Although there is no sign that cinema-going audiences are about to decline dramatically, there is always the possibility that people will retreat into their own homes to watch their movies, as more and more choice and control are handed over, in theory at least, to the customer.

Movies are now being shot on digital cameras, which reduces costs. It may be that this will be the path that independent film-makers in particular will have to follow. It is now possible for directors to shoot their films in one continuous take on digital cameras: no editing required – just an immense amount of pre-shooting rehearsal. Split-screen movies such as *AKA* (2002) may also have a future.

With the inevitable continuing spread of cable and satellite television and the emergence of top-quality DVD versions of movies (surely the days of videos are numbered), it is impossible to state categorically that cinema as we have known it will survive. The Hollywood film industry and its ownership change hands so rapidly nowadays, it is difficult to keep up with the latest deals and power-broking. Twenty-odd years ago, huge electronics firms such as Sony realized that they needed to control the production of movies to back the sales of their hardware.

When Sony subsequently bought Columbia, Harry Cohn, the long-time head of the studio and legendary movieland monster, must have been whizzing around in his grave. In a similar move, Rupert Murdoch's News International bought the 20th Century Fox studios to expand their control over different branches of the mass communication business. The old movies moguls such as Mayer and Zukor may have been tyrants and philistines at heart, but they could occasionally, given a nudge or two, recognize talent and they were at least involved in the day-to-day business of making movies. Contemporary owners of the major film production companies are generally not primarily movie people and seem much more

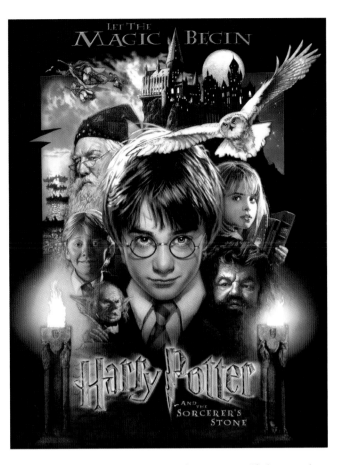

RIGHT *The* Harry Potter *movies depend largely on the effectiveness of their computer-generated effects.*

remote from the business of making pictures. An accusation made about contemporary Hollywood is that the accountants and the bankers are in charge and that explains why so many American films are the purest dross.

But it has really always been like this. There has always been a struggle between the people who want to make worthwhile movies and the entrepreneurs who just want to make millions.

There are not many producers around who would rather make *Citizen Kane* than a gross-out comedy such as *There's Something About Mary*. What will survive without doubt are movies themselves, however we choose to view them. But it is the fervent hope of this writer, and many others, I suspect, that people will continue to come together in movie houses to share the anticipation as the opening credits and the musical score jointly tell us that we are about to participate in that unique entertainment

LEFT Shrek *had a witty script and terrific special effects, and took the animated film to new heights.*

experience: the cinema. If the number of people actually going to cinemas shrinks significantly, then something irreplaceable will have gone from the business. The cinema-going experience is an important part of our communal culture.

However, too often cinema-going nowadays is not altogether a pleasurable experience – and for reasons not connected with the quality of the movies on offer. Cinemas now make as much money from their sales of grazing junk food as they do from ticket sales; the pervasive smells of hot dogs and popcorn, the rustling of sweetie bags, the crunching of crisps, not to mention talking, boorish behaviour and the ringing of mobile phones, threaten to make attendance at many local cinemas something of a trial. But when the movie is enthralling, when our minds and emotions are involved, and the audience shares that with you, then the cinema-going experience is like no other. Long may movie houses continue to prosper.

31

THE DIRECTORS

O RSON WELLES stated that movie directing was the most overrated profession in the world. In many ways, he was right. Some film directors are hacks who may have a certain level of technical know-how and the ability to command a film crew but who bring little else to the party. In some cases, a film's worth has little to do with the director. But other directors seem capable of producing images that mesmerize audiences. In this section we discuss the theory of "authorship". Whether or not the director can ever be seen as the "author" of a film, it is clear that some directors are a genuinely creative influence.

LEFT *Director Michael Curtiz with Errol Flynn and Olivia De Havilland, lighting cameraman, camera operator, sound recordist and make-up specialists shooting a scene for* Dodge City *(1939).*

INTRODUCTION

Movie-making is unavoidably and unarguably a collaborative exercise. In the very early days of Hollywood, it soon became apparent to the moneymen that an assembly-line form of production was the only economic way to meet the demands of making enough product to satisfy the weekly demands of the cinemas they themselves owned. Basically, those guys approached the business of turning out movies like Henry Ford did with motor cars. Never mind the quality; count the numbers. They recognized that there were several key personnel in this process, however – the directors, the cameramen, even the occasional writer, and perhaps the principal players. Loath as they were to allow these employees to feel themselves more important than the producers, the early moguls had to concede their central role in the movie-making process, and helped to build up their reputations as key selling points in the marketing of movies.

In those days, most movies were churned out one after the other on the stages and back lots of the studios. In the silent era, several movies would be

ABOVE Singin' in the Rain *represents the assembly-line methods of early Hollywood.*

filming on different parts of the same vast stages. Think of the scene in *Singin' in the Rain* when Gene Kelly as Don Lockwood, silent-screen star, reports for the first day of shooting on his new swashbuckler. As he walks towards the stage where his movie is to be shot, he passes various westerns and jungle adventures already in the process of being filmed. His partner, played by Donald O'Connor, asks him what this movie he is going to start is about and when Kelly/Lockwood tells him, O'Connor/Cosmo remarks that he doesn't know why the studio bothers to make a new movie when they could release an old Don Lockwood movie under a new title. The implication is that no one would really notice – when you've seen one movie, you've seen them all. It is a humorous comment on the assembly-line form of production that was dominant in early Hollywood.

With the advent of sound pictures, movies could not be shot so close to one another, but the principle of assembly-line production remained the same. The battle in Hollywood has always been between the producers and investors on the one hand, and the "artists", the creative people on the other, whether they be directors, actors, cameramen, set designers, costume designers or composers of soundtracks. Too often,

crass commercialism has won out and the quality of the movies has suffered, but occasionally, despite the best efforts of philistine producers, something worthwhile gets made.

So who are the really key movie-makers, given that is a technological art and that the production process is so complicated and multifarious? Is the analogy with motor car manufacture relevant? After all, who makes a car? The original designer? The engineers? The mechanics who

ABOVE *Laurence Olivier directed and starred in the 1948 movie version of* Hamlet.

put it together? The engine-builders? A presiding genius? The fact is that they all contribute, but some contributors are more important than others and are the key players in the process. Film directors can legitimately claim to be key players in the film-making process, but their claims are not always justified, by any means. Some absurd claims have been made for individual film directors (such as Jerry Lewis, for example, or some Hollywood hack like Budd Boetticher), but such absurdities do not mean that some directors can be classed as the authors of the films they make. In this section of the book, we will look at the role of the director and some of the directors who have claims to be the major creative hands in the making of "their" movies.

Director Alfred Hitchcock and star Bruce Dern sit and talk in a break from shooting Family Plot *(1976).*

MOVIE AUTHORSHIP

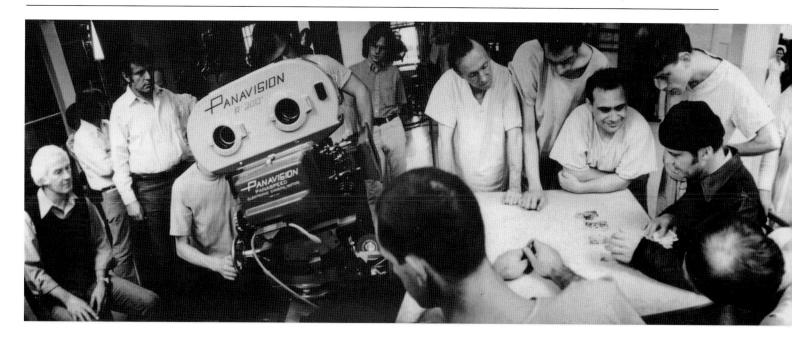

When we read a novel, we know who the author is. There are all sorts of arguments about authorship in literature. Post-structuralist theory has focused attention on the need to recognize the dependence of individual texts on other similar texts and suggested that it is not just the voice of the author that gives the text its meaning. The status of the author as the sole creator of the text and of any meaning it might contain has been put into serious question. Post-structuralists argue that we can ascribe any meaning to any text and should abandon the search for the meaning supposedly intended by an author.

Then, as the making of a movie is clearly a much more collaborative effort than the writing of a novel, is there any point in discussing the "authorship" of a movie? And if there is a point, who is this author? The screenwriter? Possibly the actors (some movie-goers still think the actors make up the lines as they go along)? The producer? The director? Perhaps even the film studio itself? Can we ever claim that there is one overall author of a finished commercial film?

The French movie critics in the 1940s and 50s were in no doubt. They looked at the commercial products of the Hollywood studios in particular and decided that the real authors of the movies they (the critics) liked were the directors of the films. They even went as far as to make a ranking list of directors who qualified for "auteur" status. A director was either one of these favoured with the accolade of "auteur" or he was a studio hack. There was no middle ground.

An "auteur" was a director who could claim to be the author of "his" films by creating a personal vision of the world within the film text. According to the auteur theory, these directors used the conventional elements of Hollywood film-making – the generic forms of the western or melodrama, the star system, the general mode of production, the conventional means of signifying meaning – to project an individual view of the world, whether it be a covert criticism of American society or some personal obsession.

Directors such as Alfred Hitchcock and Howard Hawks were cited as two of the "genius" directors who used conventional formats

ABOVE *Milos Forman oversees shooting on* One Flew Over the Cuckoo's Nest.

(Hitchcock with his thrillers, Hawks across a whole range of genres – westerns, screwball comedy, actioners, science fiction, musicals) to pursue their particular themes and obsessions. Suddenly, even relatively unknown Hollywood directors were elevated to auteur status. Little did "B" picture directors such as Joseph H. Lewis and Budd Boetticher realize when they were making cheaply produced gangster pictures and

ABOVE *A movie such as* The Quiet Man *(1952) would be seen as essential to Ford's canon, the product of his own personal vision.*

ABOVE *Martin Ritt gives direction to Sally Field while filming* Norma Rae (1979).

westerns respectively that they would one day be feted by European critics as artists with a coherent philosophy of life embedded in their movies.

Younger British critics in the early 1960s took up the auteur theory, mainly in the pages of *Movie* magazine, and discovered their own heroes. Indeed, the first edition of *Movie* had definitive lists of "great", "excellent", "talented" and merely "competent" directors. To qualify for the top rankings, a director had to have a coherent vision that informed most of the movies he made. Thus, not only Hitchcock and Hawks qualified, but also Fritz Lang, Otto Preminger, Orson Welles, John Ford, Vincente Minnelli, Nicholas Ray and numerous others. Most of these directors were surprised when such critics pointed out to them that a coherent vision of the world shone through their films.

Undoubtedly directors are key figures in the process of making movies, but how many can truly be counted as the major artistic influence? It is a mistake to imagine that most films "belong" to a director, especially when the assembly-line mode of production that operated in Hollywood is considered. In old Hollywood, more often than not, a director would have little or no control over script and casting. For

example, Orson Welles was in South America trying to set up his next movie when RKO edited his second movie, *The Magnificent Ambersons*, in such a way as to produce the last few minutes of the movie that supplied a clichéd happy ending that was a betrayal of the dark perspective of Welles's vision. Directors were finally employees of the studios, and producers were there to make sure they did what the studio required.

However, there were some free spirits who did manage to use the system to make the films they wanted to make. Orson Welles is the outstanding example of a talented director who, after having made two brilliant movies, was sidelined by Hollywood because he was too much of an individualist. Hitchcock, on the other hand, won for himself a great deal of freedom by becoming the producer of his own movies and working out a deal over distribution with various major studios. A director had much more control over how he made "his" film when he had some economic involvement in the production; otherwise the studios who were putting up the money could largely dictate to him. In this situation, for a director who wanted to "say something" in movies, it was a matter of imposing some personal angle or trait where he could. However, there were some directors (John Ford, Howard Hawks, Vincente Minnelli, for example) who had the confidence of the studios and producers and were given their head to a certain extent

because they delivered the product in a form that was not only artistically satisfying but also made big bucks for the studio at the box office.

Since the break-up of the Hollywood studio system, numerous film-makers have won themselves much greater freedom over how they make their films. The packaging of a movie project (a script, a bevy of stars, a director, producer and an independent company) is done by agents who then deal with the studios who may act merely as distributors or bankers. Directors such as Steven Spielberg, George Lucas, James Cameron, the Coen Brothers and Woody Allen have far greater artistic control over their movies than those who worked under the old system.

However, that kind of freedom is not always productive because a director can be just as self-indulgent and tedious as writers can. Someone should have perhaps laid a restraining hand on Fellini, for example, before he turned out indulgent tosh like *Juliet of the Spirits*. The studio system was undoubtedly stifling to many talents, but the fact is that it also trained directors to work within certain disciplines; work of a surprisingly high quality was often produced in a business dedicated to making money.

ABOVE *British director Nicolas Roeg jokes with Tony Curtis and Michael Emil during the shooting of* Insignificance (1985).

"OLD HOLLYWOOD" GREATS

ALFRED HITCHCOCK
(1899–1980)

Of all the Hollywood directors that the French critics "rediscovered" in the 1950s, Alfred Hitchcock was the auteur who received the most attention and praise. His forte was the suspense thriller and he rarely changed the formula, but he used the genre, consciously and often unconsciously, to work through his own fears and obsessions. However, his first responsibility, as he saw it, was to make the audience squirm. He was a master of audience manipulation, presenting our fears, lusts, nightmares and weaknesses in the movies he directed; but in the process he revealed more about himself than he thought he was doing.

Born in Leytonstone, London, in 1899, Hitchcock had a lonely and repressed childhood, which left him with emotional scars that he spent the rest of his life exposing on screen. He also had a Catholic upbringing, which left him with a fear of authority, a sense of guilt – especially about sex – and the expectation of punishment. All these obsessions regularly surface in his movies. His obesity also gave him a complex about his unattractiveness to women. He usually cast very personable actors in the leading roles in his movies (Cary Grant, James Stewart, Gregory Peck) and put cool blondes opposite them; these glamorous women, however, would be subject to screen humiliation and sometimes murder. Joan Fontaine was the subject of Cary Grant's murderous intentions in *Suspicion* (the studio insisted that Grant be cleared of suspicion at the end of the movie because it might have damaged his star image), Grant was beastly to Ingrid Bergman in *Notorious*, Ray Milland tried to murder Grace Kelly in *Dial M for Murder*, Kim Novak was thrown off a high tower (twice) in *Vertigo*, Janet Leigh was slaughtered in a shower in *Psycho*, Tippi Hedren was attacked by birds in *The Birds* and variously humiliated by Sean Connery in *Marnie*, and various women were raped and murdered in *Frenzy*.

ABOVE *Psycho and Hitchcock were attacked as depraved when the film was first released, but it has since been re-evaluated as one of the best-ever Hollywood movies.*

Hitchcock's favourite among his own movies was *Shadow of a Doubt*, starring Joseph Cotten as a charming uncle-figure who happened to have the distressing habit of bumping off widows for their money. No two fans would agree on Hitchcock's best films, but here is my choice: *Rebecca, Shadow of a Doubt, Notorious, Strangers on a Train, Vertigo, North by Northwest* and *Psycho. Blackmail, The Lodger, The Man Who Knew Too Much, Sabotage, The Thirty-Nine Steps* and *The Lady Vanishes* are perhaps the best of his British output before he went to Hollywood. *Suspicion, Spellbound, I Confess, Dial M for Murder, The Wrong Man, The Birds* and *Marnie* all have outstanding Hitchcockian scenes in them. His last movies, *Torn Curtain, Topaz, Frenzy* and *Family Plot* represent the world of his dotage.

Whether consciously or not, Hitchcock challenged the audience to consider themselves as voyeurs. He knew that we are fascinated by the process of watching – and the cinema makes voyeurs of us all. He played on our fantasies and made us feel guilty about what they reveal about ourselves. He could manipulate us to feel anxiety for the "wrong people": for example, after Norman Bates has murdered Marion Crane (Janet Leigh) in the shower scene in *Psycho*, albeit dressed as his mother, we watch anxiously as he cleans up the blood, remembers the newspaper containing the money in the bedroom at the last moment, stuffs the dead body into the boot of Leigh's car and drives to the swamp. When the car stops halfway down in the swamp, we want it to continue to submerge even though it contains the murdered body. Hitchcock has successfully transferred our sympathy from the victim to the murderer, manipulating our emotions in a manner that leaves us feeling distinctly uncomfortable. He was at the very least a master cinematic storyteller, but there are perhaps depths of meaning to his films that go beyond the conventional thriller.

37

JOHN FORD (1895–1973)

John Ford consistently denied any serious artistic purpose in his work, and hooted with laughter at the idea of any consistent philosophy permeating the movies he directed. But critics have marked him down as one of the great originals of the Hollywood scene; some see him as a poet of the cinematic image, and certainly some of his films contain stunning visual images and dramatic power. However, there are unarguably distasteful elements to them (racism in their representation of Native Americans, extreme conservative values including glorifying militarism and a gung-ho American patriotism, mindless violence, crude slapstick humour and a prevalent sexism). He is best known for his westerns: *Stagecoach*, *Drums Along the Mohawk*, *My Darling Clementine*, *Fort Apache*, *She*

> "DON'T EVER FORGET WHAT I'M GOING TO TELL YOU. ACTORS ARE CRAP."
> *JOHN FORD*

Wore a Yellow Ribbon, *Rio Grande*, *Wagonmaster*, *The Searchers* and *The Man Who Shot Liberty Valance* are among his best known. His politics were a kind of maverick right-wing extremism, which may explain why he used stars with similar political beliefs, such as John Wayne and Ward Bond, so often in his movies.

John Ford's films generally deal with groups of men in situations where they have to show their courage and loyalty to one another. He could be extremely sentimental at times, especially in his "Oirish" movies such as *The Quiet Man* and *The Last Hurrah*. American Indians are portrayed as savages in almost all of the westerns until *The Searchers* (1956), but there is a belated attempt to redress the balance in the 1964 *Cheyenne Autumn*. At its best, Ford's work has a warmth and humanity about it (*The Grapes of Wrath*, *The Long Voyage Home*, *Young Mr Lincoln*); at its worst it celebrates a kind of mindless, brutal machismo (*They Were*

ABOVE *The Searchers (1956) is rated as one of the best westerns ever made and is a major opus of John Ford.*

Expendable, *Donovan's Reef*). Running through the body of his films is a romanticized militarism and a lament for an America that has vanished forever, a lawless frontier culture that was obliterated by the march of civilization and the law book.

BELOW *Henry Fonda as Abraham Lincoln in Ford's* Young Mr Lincoln, *a rather solemn biopic of the legendary American president.*

HOWARD HAWKS (1896–1977)

Hawks is a test case for the theory that certain directors have a consistent vision that shines through all the films they direct, because he was the archetypal journeyman director elevated to auteur status initially by the French critics and then later by supporters of the auteur theory. Born in Indiana, Hawks directed movies across a wide range of genres: actioners (*Barbary Coast, Only Angels Have Wings, To Have and Have Not, The Big Sky*), westerns (*Red River, Rio Bravo, El Dorado*), screwball comedies (*Twentieth Century, Bringing Up Baby, His Girl Friday*), gangsters (*Scarface*), private eye thrillers (*The Big Sleep*), science fiction (*The Thing*), musicals (*Gentlemen Prefer Blondes*) and epics (*Land of the Pharaohs*).

> "WHEN YOU FIND OUT A THING GOES PRETTY WELL, YOU MIGHT AS WELL DO IT AGAIN."
> *HOWARD HAWKS*

He is quoted as saying, "For me the best drama is one that deals with a man in danger," and that holds true for most of his movies. How much overall control he had over the content of his movies remains in doubt, however, and how much he deserves auteur status remains a matter of judgement. I think it is safe to say that his reputation has declined since the heady days when the French among others claimed him as a cinematic genius.

ABOVE *Howard Hawks directed Bogart in* The Big Sleep. *At one point he found the plot so complicated that he had to telephone writer Raymond Chandler to explain it; Chandler couldn't help out. The movie is more about style than narrative coherence, and macho cool rather than love between men and women.*

THE TALENTED JOURNEYMEN

FRANK CAPRA (1897–1991)

Many would claim that Capra belongs in the first rank of American directors for the body of "populist" films he made in the 1930s and 40s in which he celebrated the essential decency of the common man and the virtues of American democracy. Capra's populism consisted of his taking the side of the little guy against the battalions of big business and organized politics. A simplistic philosophy and wish-fulfilling happy endings are found in *Mr Deeds Goes to Town* (Gary Cooper inheriting wealth and going to New York to help poor farmers), *You Can't Take It with You, Mr Smith Goes to Washington* (James Stewart sorting out the political machine), *Meet John Doe* and *It's a Wonderful Life* in which Stewart again saves small-town America from perdition. As well as these movies, Capra directed Harlow in *Platinum Blonde*, Gable and Colbert in *It Happened One Night*, Ronald Colman in *Lost Horizon* and Tracy and Hepburn in *State of the Union*. His later films were entirely forgettable: *Riding High* and *Here Comes the Groom* with Crosby, and *A Hole in the Head* with Sinatra. *It's a Wonderful Life* is undoubtedly one of the favourite Hollywood movies for many people, and its sentimentality and whimsy are hard to resist.

ABOVE It's a Wonderful Life *(1946) is a perennial favourite, defying critical rigour.*

ABOVE *Frank Capra directs Bing Crosby on the set of* Here Comes the Groom *(1951).*

MICHAEL CURTIZ (1888–1962)

Curtiz was Hungarian by birth and had a substantial career in European films before he came to Hollywood to direct some of the most famous pictures of the 1930s and 40s. He directed Errol Flynn in *Captain Blood*, *The Charge of the Light Brigade*, *The Perfect Specimen*, *The Adventures of Robin Hood*, *The Private Lives of Elizabeth and Essex*, *Dodge City*, *Virginia City*, *The Sea Hawk* and *Sante Fe Trail*. He showed he had a feeling for romance and *film noir* in the classic *Casablanca* and *Mildred Pierce*. He directed Cagney in *Yankee Doodle Dandy*, Claude Rains in the *film noir* *The Unsuspected* and Elvis Presley in *King Creole*. He also made real turkeys

ABOVE *Director Michael Curtiz, on the ground, watches leading man Errol Flynn turn on the charm in the western* Dodge City. *Curtiz directed Flynn in nine movies.*

such as *The Egyptian*, *The Jazz Singer* (the 1953 version) and *The Vagabond King*. Primarily associated with Warner Brothers, Curtiz was the quintessential journeyman director, turning his directorial hand to most genres; however, very few critics, even the most obsessive of French auteurists, have made a case for Curtiz's "vision". Curtiz helped to give some of the movies he directed a certain visual style, but beyond that, he had little to contribute.

ABOVE *Cecil B. De Mille's 1956 version of* The Ten Commandments.

ABOVE *George Cukor directed Joan Crawford in this melodrama,* A Woman's Face *(1941).*

GEORGE CUKOR (1899–1983)

Cukor came to be known as a woman's director because of the sensitivity with which he handled top female stars and "women's pictures". He was also known for directing respectable screen adaptations of famous literary works such as *Little Women, David Copperfield, Romeo and Juliet* and *The Women*. Musicals included *A Star is Born, Les Girls* and *My Fair Lady*. Comedies were perhaps his forte: *The Philadelphia Story, Adam's Rib, Born Yesterday, The Marrying Kind* and *Pat and Mike*. He also directed Greta Garbo in *Camille*, Joan Crawford in *A Woman's Face*, Bette Davis in *The Actress* and Marilyn Monroe in *Let's Make Love*. Cukor's main talent may have consisted of his ability to adapt literary and theatrical influences to the cinema and to serve up middlebrow entertainment in various forms over a period of 40 years. He managed to survive as a gay man in "old Hollywood" without scandal breaking over his head.

WILLIAM WYLER (1902–81)

Wyler, of German origin, was known as a very hard taskmaster for actors. He took no nonsense from even the biggest stars such as Bette Davis, who was notoriously difficult in her heyday and whom he directed in *Jezebel, The Letter* and *The Little Foxes*, or Laurence Olivier, who in his youth displayed a disdain for Hollywood that did not sit well with the autocratic Wyler. To his credit, Olivier later paid tribute to Wyler's influence on him as a director and actor after he had directed him in *Wuthering Heights*. One of his most important movies was *The Best Years of Our Lives*, which examined the problems facing ex-GIs coming to terms with the post-war USA, and offered some liberal but simplistic solutions. Wyler was also entrusted with action pictures, notably *The Desperate Hours, The Big Country* and

ABOVE *Journeyman director Henry King (1888–1982) has his fans even when directing swashbucklers such as* Captain from Castile *with Tyrone Power.*

Ben-Hur. Charlton Heston, the star of *Ben-Hur*, is quoted as saying, "Doing a picture with Willie is like getting the works at a Turkish bath. You damn near drown, but you come out smelling like a rose." Melodramas directed by Wyler included *The Heiress, Carrie* and *The Children's Hour*, and he also directed Streisand in *Funny Girl*.

41

ABOVE *William Wyler directed the post-war drama* The Best Years of Our Lives *(1946), about the difficulties of ex-GIs and their families readjusting to peacetime.*

VINCENTE MINNELLI
(1903–86)

Minnelli was one of MGM's longest-serving directors. Indeed, in a career spanning 35 years, he made only three films out of 36 for studios other than MGM. This makes him an interesting test case as a director: as a resident studio director with some talent, how much control did he have over the movies he made?

Minnelli is best known for his musicals, but he has also acquired a reputation for the melodramas he directed in the 1950s. These include *The Cobweb, The Bad and the Beautiful, Some Came Running* and *Home from the Hill*. His best-known musicals are *Meet Me in St Louis, The Pirate, An American in Paris, The Band Wagon, Gigi* and *On a Clear Day You Can See Forever*. He is, in fact, known as the father of the modern movie musical and has other paternity claims as the father of Liza Minnelli, the product of his brief marriage to Judy Garland. His favourite film of the ones he directed himself was *Lust for*

42

Life in which Kirk Douglas played Van Gogh. Minnelli was revered by critics as a stylist and for his feeling for colour and design within the screen space. Yet he seldom or ever found his own projects to film, and never had final cutting rights over what he had shot. Indeed, some of his movies were partially reshot or completed by other directors (*An American in Paris, Gigi, The Seventh Sin*) and as one of MGM's most successful and highly-thought-of

LEFT *One of the most popular musicals Vincente Minnelli directed was* Gigi *(1958), adapted from a novella by Colette and a book by Alan Jay Lerner. The score was written by Frederick Loewe.*

directors, he was shunted from movie to movie without much time for reflection. Yet, despite all this, some critics still manage to discover a consistent vision of the world incorporated in his movies. If we accept that style is meaning, then Minnelli could be said to have a consistent philosophy in the movies he directed, but his supporters go beyond that to discover common thematic obsessions and narrative resolutions personal to the director. He certainly never thought of himself as the author of his movies and like other Hollywood stalwarts was very surprised when these claims were made on his behalf. He may not have been an intellectual director, but he "said" something through the application of his style.

BELOW *Minnelli directed one of the best movies about Hollywood,* The Bad and the Beautiful *(1952), which starred Kirk Douglas as a David Selznick-like producer.*

ABOVE *Fritz Lang, the German expressionist director of* Metropolis *(1927) found a new career in Hollywood. A western he directed with Marlene Dietrich,* Rancho Notorious *(1952), has become a cult movie.*

BILLY WILDER (1906–2002)

Another European expatriate of Austrian origin, Wilder specialized in rather sour comedy and noirish melodramas. He co-wrote, with Charles Brackett and then I.A.L. Diamond, many of the films he directed. As a writer, he collaborated on Garbo's *Ninotchka* and the Stanwyck–Cooper *Ball of Fire*. As a writer-director, his finest efforts were *Double Indemnity* (on which he collaborated with Raymond Chandler) and *Sunset Boulevard*. Other notable films include *Ace in the Hole*, *The Seven Year Itch*, *Some Like it Hot* and *The Apartment*. His later films became increasingly raucous and vulgar: *Irma La Douce*, *Kiss Me Stupid* and *Avanti!* Wilder was quoted as saying that the best direction is the one you don't see; certainly, he was no stylist and his main talent may have been as a writer and in his instinct for what worked on screen. He was clever enough to choose talented collaborators and when that collaboration worked, he was instrumental in making some of Hollywood's finest. But an auteur?

ABOVE *Billy Wilder directed* The Apartment, *which many people think superior fare to rather vulgar comedies such as* Some Like it Hot, The Fortune Cookie *and* Kiss Me Stupid.

Certainly not. He himself dismissed the auteur theory as intellectualizing nonsense. However, Wilder was involved in making some of Hollywood's best movies, which reinforces the argument that the overwhelming majority of movies are a genuinely collaborative effort.

GEORGE STEVENS (1904–75)

Stevens's best film as a director is probably *Shane*, the classic western, and yet he was not a western specialist. He made a name in the 1930s directing Hepburn in *Alice Adams* and again in *Woman of the Year*. His films tended towards the sentimental and the romantic, for example, *I Remember Mama* and *A Place in the Sun*. He directed Dean, Taylor and Hudson in the Texan epic *Giant* and was also responsible for *The Greatest Story Ever Told*. During World War II, he directed some of the most impressive footage of the conflict and the liberation of the Nazi concentration camps. Undoubtedly, Stevens had a sure instinct for manipulating the emotions of the cinema audience: *Shane* and *A Place in the Sun* are guaranteed to produce tears. It is, however, perhaps that talent to manipulate that defines his limitations as a director. He is an interesting test case for a Hollywood director: auteur or talented hack?

ABOVE *George Stevens directed Liz Taylor and Rock Hudson in the Texan epic* Giant *(1956). The movie is best known as James Dean's last movie before his death in a car accident in 1955.*

43

JOHN HUSTON (1906–87)

A talented director or a lucky son of a famous father who happened to get involved with some decent movies? Opinions divide over John Huston largely because there is little discernible pattern to his work. He himself is quoted as saying, "I fail to see any continuity in my work from picture to picture." One can see a pattern of a rather bogus male camaderie and machismo, however. There is a

direct some of the best of Hollywood movies: *The Maltese Falcon, The Treasure of the Sierra Madre, The Asphalt Jungle, The Misfits* and *Wise Blood*. However, he also directed some of the worst: *Moulin Rouge, Moby Dick, The Barbarian and the Geisha, The Bible...In the Beginning* and *Escape to Victory*. The jury is still out on *Prizzi's Honour* and *The Dead*.

> "WE CAN MAKE BAD PICTURES TOO. COSTS MORE BUT WE CAN MAKE 'EM."
> JOHN HUSTON

Huston was certainly no stylist in the sense that Orson Welles was. He himself disclaimed any thematic continuity in his movies, so what exactly was his contribution to the movies he directed? He was able, by all accounts, to bully a performance out of actors, had a fairly sure instinct for some of the projects he directed, and worked with able collaborators. That does not make him in any way the author of the movies he directed. As an actor in movies such as *The Bible...In the Beginning* and *Chinatown*, he tended to the "hammy" and in public interviews he came over as playing John Huston the legendary film director rather than emerging from behind that mask he wore. However, there is no doubting his staying power or his iconic status among old Hollywood directors. Undoubtedly, he was associated with some of the better movies Hollywood made in its heyday.

BELOW Joseph L. Mankiewicz (1909–93) was an important and talented writer-director. All About Eve, *about New York theatre people, is a much-admired movie.*

ABOVE John Huston had a hit with the first film he directed, The Maltese Falcon *starring Humphrey Bogart and Mary Astor.*

compelling portrait of Huston in Clint Eastwood's 1990 movie *White Hunter, Black Heart;* the movie centres around a Hollywood director shooting a movie in Africa that is clearly intended to be *The African Queen,* and the Huston-like character is obsessed with shooting big game resulting in the unnecessary death of an African servant. In the 1973 *The Way We Were,* the cowardly lefty Hollywood director (played by Patrick O'Neal) who caves into McCarthyite pressure is clearly based on Huston. Despite his personal and professional failings, Huston did

THE MAVERICKS

This section focuses on "maverick" directors who, for one reason or another, did not quite fit in with the Hollywood system, or who carved out for themselves a unique position within that system.

JOSEF VON STERNBERG (1894–1969)

Another Austrian expatriate director, Von Sternberg's career was closely associated with the films in which he directed Marlene Dietrich. Neither of their careers ever really recovered from their professional split, though Von Sternberg suffered more than the star he "created".

Von Sternberg was known as a stylist; indeed he is quoted as saying that he cared little for the stories of his films, only about how they were photographed and presented. That is just as well because movies such as *Shanghai Express, Morocco, Blonde Venus, The Scarlet Empress* and *The Devil is a Woman* teeter on the edge of being "high camp" rubbish and only the "look" of them saves them. Von Sternberg liked shooting through shutters and lattices, gauze and mists; he also decorated his sets elaborately to create a Hollywood concept of decadence. There is a campness about his most famous movies.

After his films with Dietrich, his career went into a downward spiral; he directed the unfinished *I Claudius* for Korda and then made very few films until his death in 1969. He once said, "The only way to succeed is to make people hate you. That way they remember you." It seems that people remembered Von Sternberg's autocratic ways only too well, because very few of them offered him a directing job in his declining years.

BELOW *Josef Von Sternberg directed Jane Russell in the strange, exotic melodrama Macao in 1952. Style was everything to Sternberg – much more important than story.*

ORSON WELLES (1915–85)

The enfant terrible of Hollywood in the 1940s, Welles first came to fame when he terrorized America with his documentary-style radio version of H.G. Wells's *The War of the Worlds*, convincing thousands of Americans that their country was being invaded by aliens. *Citizen Kane* (1941) then established his reputation as a director of movies; his story of a press baron, based on the life of William Randolph Hearst, was seen as innovatory in its use of deep-focus photography,

ABOVE *Martin Ritt (1914–90) made this study of male bravado,* Hud, *in 1963. Other notable films he directed include* Edge of the City *(1956),* The Spy Who Came in from the Cold *(1965) and* Norma Rae *(1979).*

ABOVE *Always battling against lack of money, Orson Welles made several Shakespearian movies.* Othello *has its pluses and minuses – but at least it got made.*

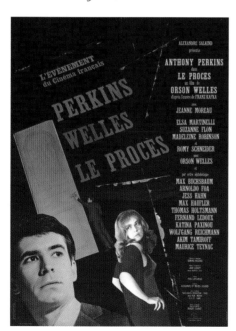

ABOVE *Orson Welles directed* The Trial *in 1962, a film adaptation of Kafka's famous novel. Shot in the old Gare D'Orsay station in Paris, it suffered somewhat from Welles's usual underbudgeting.*

overlapping sound, expressionistic sets and creative montage sequences. How much of the credit for these innovations should go to cameraman Gregg Toland and co-writer Herman J. Mankiewicz is still a matter of controversy. Welles's second film for RKO, *The Magnificent Ambersons*, was badly mauled by the studio, which added a spurious happy ending. Thereafter, Welles's relationship with the studios declined, and he was more often seen as an actor in films made by others, such as *Jane Eyre, Prince of Foxes, The Third Man, The Black Rose, Moby Dick, The Long Hot Summer* and *The Roots of Heaven*. Some of the later films he directed have authentic Welles touches to them, notably *The Stranger, Macbeth, Othello, The Lady from Shanghai, Touch of Evil,*

> "EVERYONE DENIES I AM A GENIUS BUT NO ONE EVER CALLED ME THAT IN THE FIRST PLACE."
> ORSON WELLES

> "DIRECTING FILMS IS THE MOST OVER-RATED PROFESSION IN THE WORLD."
> ORSON WELLES

The Trial, Chimes at Midnight and *The Immortal Story*. The usual adjective used about his later work is "flawed", but many of those flaws were caused by very low, even disappearing budgets. Welles said of himself, "I started at the top and worked down", and there is more than a grain of truth in that statement, including the implication that he may have brought many of his troubles upon his own head. However, *Kane* and *Ambersons* alone elevate him to the status of major director. Hollywood could not handle his maverick genius and he could not handle Hollywood.

NICHOLAS RAY (1911–79)

Ray became an icon for many European critics and film-makers – another figure, like Welles, identified

ABOVE *Nicholas Ray directed John Wayne and Robert Ryan in the tough war movie* The Flying Leathernecks *(1951).*

as a genius director partly destroyed by the studio system. His artistic background was with the left-wing Group Theatre, where he was a protégé of Elia Kazan. His first Hollywood film *They Live by Night* is probably his best; the story of the isolated and alienated young lovers (played by Farley Granger and Cathy O'Donnell) is given added impact by Ray's imaginative use of the screen space and his creative mise-en-scène. Ray clearly identified with the outsider and the young in American society, and this was again reflected in his direction of James Dean in *Rebel Without a Cause.* The institution of the family gets a rough ride in several of his films, notably in *They Live by Night, Rebel* and also in *Bigger Than Life,* where James Mason takes medical drugs and is transformed into an oppressive patriarch – his real self, the movie implies. Ray also made *In a Lonely Place,* a study of paranoia and violence

starring Humphrey Bogart as a Hollywood writer; this movie was perceived as being a comment on the paranoia engendered by the McCarthyite investigations into Hollywood in the late 40s and early 50s.

French critics in particular saw merits in later Ray films such as *Bitter Victory* and *Party Girl* that few other people could perceive, and they even found things to admire in two epics he

ABOVE *Nicholas Ray's* Rebel Without a Cause *made James Dean a screen icon for millions. It is the ultimate teen-angst movie.*

directed in the early 60s, *King of Kings* and *55 Days at Peking.* Wim Wenders, the German director, paid one last tribute when he made a film about Ray when the American was dying of cancer in 1979, *Lightning over Water.* This was a last defiant romantic gesture from a romantic director.

ELIA KAZAN (b. 1909)

Kazan, of Greek descent, worked in the 1930s as an actor with the left-wing Group Theatre in New York, but later he spectacularly re-nounced his radical past when he served as a friendly witness in front of the Congressional com-mittee investigating so-called communist infiltration into Hollywood in the 1940s and 50s. Kazan went so far as to "name names" of past Communist associates to the committee. His testimony

and also demonstrations inside and outside the auditorium where the Oscars ceremony was being held.

DOUGLAS SIRK (1900–87)

Of Danish origin, Sirk worked in the German Expressionist theatre of the 1920s before directing various European films and coming to Hollywood. His first major film was *Summer Storm* (1944), adapted from a Chekhov short story, then he made a series of comedies for Universal including *Has Anybody Seen My Gal?*, *Meet Me at the Fair* and *Take Me to Town*. However,

probably saved his own career, but at the expense of the careers of other Hollywood colleagues, who never forgave him.

Kazan's early films are far from personal: *A Tree Grows in Brooklyn, Gentleman's Agreement, The Sea of Grass* and *Pinky*. He described MGM, for whom he made *The Sea of Grass*, as an industrial compound run by businessmen. His first personal project was *A Streetcar Named Desire* with Marlon Brando and Vivien Leigh and, after his testimony to the Congressional committee, he concentrated on making movies which, to varying degrees, seemed to justify the stand he had taken. *On the Waterfront* justified "snitching" on your friends when it showed Terry Malloy (Brando) turning stool-pigeon on his erstwhile gangster pals; the movie was also a huge success and gave Kazan carte blanche to tackle any film project he wanted to and have final cut rights over the movies he made. He went on to make *East of Eden, Baby Doll, A Face in the Crowd, Wild River, Splendor in the Grass* and *The Last Tycoon*. In between

he made two films which he adapted from his own novels, *America America* and *The Arrangement*. In these films he represents his family's coming to the USA and experiencing the joys and tribulations of American capitalism. Kazan's main talents were his undoubted ability to direct actors and the emotional intensity he brought to his movies. Controversially, in 1998 he was awarded an honorary Oscar, a gesture that brought much vocal criticism from survivors of the McCarthyite persecutions in Hollywood

WARREN BEATTY
JEAN SEBERG

UNE PRODUCTION
ROBERT ROSSEN

Lilith

avec PETER FONDA · KIM HUNTER · ANNE MEACHAM · JAMES PATTERSON · ROBERT REILLY
Scénario de ROBERT ROSSEN · d'après le roman de J.R. SALAMANCA · Produit et Mis en Scène par ROBERT ROSSEN

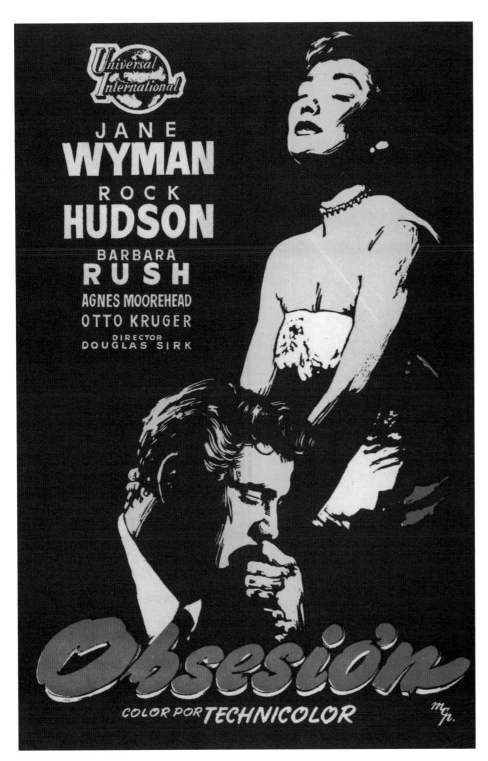

ABOVE *Douglas Sirk directed a series of melodramas for Universal-International in the 1950s and 60s.* Magnificent Obession, *starring Rock Hudson and Jane Wyman, was released in 1954.*

Sirk's reputation as an auteur – and he has numerous supporters as such – rests squarely on the melodramas he directed in the 1950s: *All I Desire, Magnificent Obsession, There's Always Tomorrow, All That Heaven Allows,* *Written on the Wind, The Tarnished Angels* and *Imitation of Life.* Supporters of Sirk's claims to seriousness say that he used the excesses of the melodramatic genre to criticize the era of Eisenhower's America in all its materialism and conformity. Detractors of these claims say that you can read anything you like into these excessively sentimental pieces of schlock if you really want to find an excuse for liking them. However,

there is little doubt that Sirk used ironic and distancing devices in his direction to draw attention to the social points he wanted to make. His left-wing credentials endeared him to many film critics in Europe, but some feminist critics, although admitting his films were more than just examples of kitsch, pointed out that they did tend to reinforce patriarchal structures while appearing to attack them. Another aspect of Sirk's directing is his use of colour, camera angles and reflecting surfaces such as mirrors. His melodramas often employ a fast editing technique and the effect is almost like a strip cartoon of imagery. A good example of this is the opening pre-credits sequence to *Written on the Wind*: Robert Stack drives his red sports car at speed, he arrives at the family mansion, a concerned face appears at the window, he enters the mansion and climbs the staircase, the leaves blow into the hall, there is a gunshot. It is, in its own way, a brilliant use of editing technique to build tension and reach the melodramatic heights to which these movies aspire.

STANLEY KUBRICK (1928–99)

After two minor, low-budget films, Kubrick, who had been a photographer with *Life* magazine, made *The Killing* (1956), a semi-documentary crime thriller which brought him much attention. *Paths of Glory*, an anti-war movie set in World War I trenches with Kirk Douglas as a French officer defending three men wrongfully accused of cowardice, established his reputation as a major director. The epic *Spartacus* continued his association with Kirk Douglas, and is usually seen as one of the few intelligent epics.

Kubrick's desire to film challenging material led him to direct *Lolita* in 1962, and he used the movie to paint a picture of an America that was aimless and materialistic. His black

Peter Sellers · George C. Scott
in Stanley Kubrick's

Dr. Strangelove

Or: How I Learned To Stop Worrying And Love The Bomb

the hot-line suspense comedy

LEFT Dr Strangelove (1964) is a hilarious satire on Cold War thinking and the American military. It still has much relevance today.

OPPOSITE Kubrick's 2001: A Space Odyssey (1968) is rated by many as by far the best of all space travel movies. It has its obscurities, but it remains a major work of this director.

Kubrick insisted on independence as a producer-director and his films were always notable, though he has been criticized for being too interested in his sets and staging of events at the expense of the characters. Certainly, since *Paths of Glory*, there was a distancing of emotional involvement, but he remained a great talent throughout his career.

comedy *Dr Strangelove* remains a very funny comment on the nightmare of the dangers of nuclear warfare and *2001: A Space Odyssey* in 1968 took the space film into new dimensions. *A Clockwork Orange* was controversially violent and aroused a storm of protest (Kubrick later withdrew it from circulation), but *Barry Lyndon* was largely damned with the faint praise of being beautiful to look at but not much else. It is, however, one of the greatly underrated movies of the 1970s. *The Shining* again aroused protests because of its violence, particularly towards women. *Full Metal Jacket* was Kubrick's Vietnam movie, and it is certainly among the best of the crop of movies about that American nightmare. The movie he had just completed before his untimely death in 1999, *Eyes Wide Shut* (starring Tom Cruise and Nicole

Kidman), however, is sadly an unworthy last legacy of a director who can truly be said to have been a major talent in the art of film-making.

ABOVE After the critical mauling A Clockwork Orange received on its release in 1971, Kubrick withdrew the movie from circulation for many years. Some critics see the movie as a major work, others as a kind of aberration from this endlessly inventive director.

THE DIRECTORS OF NEW HOLLYWOOD

JOHN CASSAVETES (1929–89)

Cassavetes was never a hugely successful director, but he made the movies he wanted to in his own personal style. He was a successful Hollywood actor (in *Edge of the City* and *Virgin Island*) before he turned to directing, but it was his experimental film *Shadows* (1961) that established his reputation for risk-taking: actors' improvisation, hand-held cameras, disjointed narrative and a refusal to portray human relationships sentimentally. He is quoted as saying, "When I started making pictures, I wanted to make Frank Capra pictures. But I've never been able to make anything but these crazy tough pictures. You are what you are." "These crazy tough pictures" include *Faces* (1968), *Husbands* (1970), *A Woman Under the Influence* (1974), *The Killing of a Chinese Bookie* (1976), *Opening Night* (1977), *Gloria* (1980) and *Love Streams* (1984). Only *Gloria* achieved any substantial commercial success. His wife, Gena Rowlands, starred in most of his films and he himself also acted in some of them. Other favourite male actors he used were Peter Falk and Ben Gazzara, who were his personal friends. Almost all of the films Cassavetes directed have real flaws in them, but there is a rawness and honesty that distinguishes them sharply from the standard Hollywood product. Tragically, he died in 1989 at the age of 60.

> "I NEVER KNOW WHAT MY MOVIES ARE ABOUT UNTIL I FINISH THEM."
> *JOHN CASSAVETES*

STEVEN SPIELBERG (b. 1946)

Spielberg is the world's most famous and successful living film director. He makes movies for the mass market and is phenomenally successful at it. *Jaws, Close Encounters of the Third Kind, E.T., Raiders of the Lost Ark, Indiana Jones and the Temple of Doom, Indiana Jones and the Last Crusade, Jurassic Park, Schindler's List* and *Saving Private Ryan* have made him a multi-millionaire and carved him a very powerful position within the American film industry. He is the most consistently successful of the "movie brats", that group of movie-obsessed young men who conquered Hollywood in the 1970s: George Lucas, Francis Coppola, Martin Scorsese, Brian De Palma, Peter Bogdanovich and Spielberg himself. He has garnered critical praise as well as commercial success.

Spielberg openly confesses his debt to Disney and the Saturday-morning serials, but his films are also in the tradition of Frank Capra populism – they are for the individual against bureaucracy and on the side the decent instincts of the ordinary people against the government that appears to act in their name. Witness the Richard Dreyfuss character in *Close Encounters* or the neighbourhood youngsters

LEFT *John Cassavetes'* Love Streams *(1984) displayed some of his strengths and weaknesses as a director: his on-the-edge intensity and his rambling, rather self-indulgent style of narrative.*

saving E.T. Spielberg's directorial touch used to be less certain in "adult" movies such as *The Color Purple* and *Always*, where the issues are more complex. However, the much admired and highly successful *Schindler's List* and *Saving Private Ryan*, with their massive and challenging subject matter, marked a new departure for him. In these films, both of which earned Spielberg Best Director Oscars, and despite their many faults, he could no longer be accused of an overly simplistic child's vision. *AI* (2001) was begun by Kubrick before he died

and completed by Spielberg. It is a film that lacks consistency. The opening sequences clearly show Kubrick's dark vision; the latter part is pure Spielberg – content sacrificed to visual effects and a whimsical sentimentality. However, Spielberg is a Hollywood phenomenon, not only

in terms of his success, but because he is a product of the very same movie culture which he now enriches. His faults as a director include a certain shallowness, the desire to please audiences at the expense of artistic integrity and the lack of real intellectual content.

ABOVE *Spielberg's* Saving Private Ryan *has an opening 20 minutes that communicates what war is really like more convincingly than almost any other war movie.*

BELOW *Spielberg's* Close Encounters of the Third Kind *(1977) represented aliens as benevolent beings.*

53

MARTIN SCORSESE (b. 1942)

Scorsese directed *Mean Streets* (1973) and *Taxi Driver* (1976), two of the seminal movies of the modern American cinema. Like the rest of the "movie brats", Scorsese is in love with cinema per se and his films persistently show his debt to old Hollywood. *Taxi Driver* is a very late *film noir*, *New York, New York* is in part a tribute to the MGM musical, *Raging Bull* owes something to *On the Waterfront* in its portrayal of the Jake La Motta protagonist, and *The Color of Money* is a late sequel to *The Hustler*. However, Scorsese brings his own personal obsessions to these movies: his ambivalence towards macho values, group and family loyalties, the concept of success and the price it demands. Several of his films have been criticized for their depiction of extreme violence, in particular *Mean Streets* (his first real success), *Taxi Driver, Raging Bull* and *GoodFellas*. The *Last Temptation of Christ* aroused great controversy amongst critics because of its perceived blasphemy.

Scorsese has consistently used his own experiences of growing up in the Little Italy section of New York as material in his films, and violence and Catholic guilt were intrinsic parts of that experience for him. He has a romantic trait and this comes out in *Alice Doesn't Live Here Any More* and *The Color of Money. King of Comedy* was

54

LEFT Taxi Driver *is a seminal movie of the 1970s. Directed by Martin Scorsese and scripted by Paul Schrader, it is a vivid and compelling vision of urban life in that era.*

a box-office failure but showed his talent for exposing through comedy the tawdry nature of the search for fame and success in modern America. In latter years, Scorsese seems to have run out of steam and *The Age of Innocence* (1993), *Casino* (1995) and *Bringing Out the Dead* (1999) smack of a director who has lost his way. *The Gangs of New York* (2002) returned to the themes of tribal loyalties and power-broking in the criminal world. Of all the so-called movie brats, Scorsese may turn out to be the most important as a maker of films that reflect their time. His films frequently make for uncomfortable viewing, partly because of the director's ambivalent attitude to his material, which, in turn, sets up insecurities in the spectator about how he or she should be reacting to the extreme emotions and violence represented on screen. The climax of *Taxi Driver* is a case in point: how do we react to the massacre of the bad guys by Travis Bickle (De Niro)? Raise a cheer or deplore such extreme vigilante actions? It is that kind of complexity that makes the best of Scorsese's movies memorable.

FRANCIS COPPOLA (b. 1939)

Coppola first made it in movies as a writer; his writing credits include *This Property is Condemned* and *Patton*. His first success as a director was *The Godfather*, which he also co-wrote, one of the key American movies of the 1970s. That was followed by the almost as impressive *The Conversation*, a movie about paranoia, betrayal and Nixon's America. *The Godfather Part II* (1974) was even more effective than the first part. Perhaps his most personal movie has been *Apocalypse Now*, an LSD picture of the Vietnam war. He sank a lot of the money he made out of the *Godfather* movies into this very expensive venture. He has, in fact, always been willing to risk his own capital, as shown when he founded his own studio, Zoetrope, in San Francisco and employed old Hollywood stalwart Gene Kelly and British director Michael Powell as associates, but this attempt to make films in a traditional studio-based set-up was doomed to failure. Movies such as *One from the Heart* and *Hammett* were more or less disasters at the box office, leaving Coppola relatively

BELOW The Godfather (*1972*) *established Francis Coppola as a major director. Here the local undertaker seeks a favour from Don Corleone (Marlon Brando), the New York-based head of a Mafia family.*

impoverished. He then made two teenage melodramas from S.E. Hinton novels, *The Outsiders* and *Rumble Fish*, which revived his fortunes, but failed to save the Zoetrope studios. *The Cotton Club* (1984) was a disaster, *Peggy Sue Got Married* (1986) a popular success but showed Coppola coasting, whilst *Tucker: The Man and His Dream* (1988) was disappointing. The third part of the *Godfather* trilogy followed in 1990: it has a stunning last 20 minutes, but it takes too long to reach that high dramatic point and cannot be compared in overall quality to the first two movies. *Bram Stoker's Dracula* (1992) lacked real conviction, whilst with *The Rainmaker* (1997) his career seemed finally to evaporate. Coppola's major achievements with the first two *Godfather* movies, *The Conversation* and *Apocalypse Now*, however, mean he has already won himself an important niche in Hollywood history. He has been a truly creative director, but like Orson Welles before him, has managed to dissipate his talent from a mixture of hubris, bad judgements and ill-luck.

BELOW *Oliver Stone wrote the screenplay of* Scarface *(1983), which was directed by Brian De Palma and starred Al Pacino. It is a very violent movie and was censured for that reason.*

OLIVER STONE (b. 1946)
As a writer, Stone was responsible for *Midnight Express, Scarface* and *Year of the Dragon*. He co-wrote and directed *Salvador*, a tough indictment of fascism in Latin America and America's covert support of it. Another film he wrote and directed, the Vietnam movie *Platoon*, won him an Oscar as a director; he had used his own experiences of the war as an ordinary "grunt" for his screenplay. *Wall Street* was another huge success for him as a director and writer; this time his target was greed and corruption among junk bond dealers, but the radicalism of the movie was watered down by pinning the blame on a few rotten apples rather than the system itself. This lack of political edge may be why Hollywood has taken Stone to its flinty bosom and showered further awards on his second Vietnam movie, *Born on the Fourth of July*, which showed a paraplegic Vietnam veteran winning through to become a public spokesman for his comrades.

However, *JFK* (1991), a long, rambling, and sometimes quite confusing but brilliant analysis of one of the many conspiracy theories surrounding John F. Kennedy's assassination, strengthened Stone's reputation for radicalism. Before that, he had made *The Doors*, a biopic about the rock star Jim Morrison. *Natural Born Killers* (1994) was wilfully misunderstood by many critics who criticized the movie for its violence, amorality and glamorization of young psychopathic killers. In fact, Stone intended it as an ironic statement about the media's obsession with crime and criminals and the way that the latter are turned into celebrities. The 1995 *Nixon* was a fascinating biopic of the former US president, which managed the dubious achievement of making you feel sorry for old Tricky Dicky. Stone's movies are usually a mixed bag: brilliance

ABOVE *Oliver Stone on the set of the 1993* Heaven and Earth. *Stone is one of the few important contemporary Hollywood directors prepared to break free from formulaic movie production, despite his sensationalist tendency.*

vying with indulgence and overstatement, intelligencecompeting with crassness and oversimplification. At the very least, they usually have a visceral quality that reflects the passions and energy of the director.

DAVID LYNCH (b. 1946)
The low-budget quasi-horror movie *Eraserhead* (1977) launched Lynch's career. He followed this with the more conventional *The Elephant Man* (1980) and then had a disastrous flop with the sci-fi bore *Dune* (1984). *Blue Velvet* (1986) and *Wild at Heart* (1990) re-established his credentials, while *Mulholland Drive* (2001) is considered by his fans to be a major opus of contemporary cinema. The *Twin Peaks* series on television won him a mass audience, but the movie sequel in 1992 was a mess. Indeed, there is a huge gap between the best and the worst of Lynch's work in the movies. For many, however, he is the most talented director working in contemporary Hollywood; for others, he is a pretentious and exploitative operator in the grey area between commercial schlock and art movies.

QUENTIN TARANTINO (b. 1963)

His many admirers compared the enfant terrible Tarantino with the young Orson Welles. His detractors, however, argue that his movies are all cool macho style and have little real significance. His detractors also assert that the films he has written and

ABOVE *Tarantino's* Reservoir Dogs *was shocking in its violence and sadism. Tarantino's ambivalence about torture and machismo makes for unsettling viewing.*

directed himself – *Reservoir Dogs* (1992), *Pulp Fiction* (1994) and *Jackie Brown* (1997) are basically splatter movies, selling designer violence to the mainly young and male masses. *Jackie Brown* – adapted from Elmore Leonard's novel *Rum Punch* – was a refreshing surprise, however. For a start, it has a much lower body count. Although it features Tarantino's trademark snappy dialogue, the characters have a depth and complexity missing from his earlier work. Pam Grier, whose star had waned since her 1970s "Blaxploitation" movies, clearly relishes a role that other actresses in their 40s would kill for. Only time will tell if Tarantino can abandon the cheap thrills of his early work and continue to produce

stories for thinking adults. He is undoubtedly talented, but appeals too often to the sadistic and the repressed violent, and possibly fascistic, impulses of the mass audience.

JAMES CAMERON (b. 1954)

Cameron made his directorial debut with the risible *Pirhana II: The Spawning* (1981). He first showed real promise with *The Terminator* (1984) – an unusually intelligent action movie. *Aliens* (1986), *The Abyss* (1989) and *Terminator 2: Judgment Day* (1991) all feature strong female characters, as well as what has become one of Cameron's hallmarks: ground-breaking use of state-of-the-art special effects. Cameron also works as a high-profile action screenwriter. His scripts include *Rambo: First Blood Part II* (1985) and *Strange Days* (1995). Cameron's detractors were certain that *Titanic* – at $200 million, the most expensive film ever made – would sink without trace. Instead, it became a box-office smash, winning 10 Oscars, including Best Director. *Titanic* is a

ABOVE *James Cameron directed the second of the* Alien *series with Sigourney Weaver as the intrepid Ripley.*

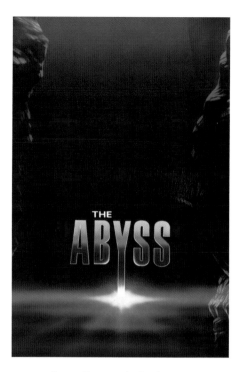

ABOVE *James Cameron had a huge success with* The Abyss, *an underwater sci-fi epic.*

visually stunning tribute to the doomed ship, but a movie should be more than just special effects. It is one of the worst Hollywood movies ever made, on a par with the horrendous *Pearl Harbor* (2000).

JOEL COEN (b. 1954) AND ETHAN COEN (b. 1957)

The Coen brothers started with the *film noir* thriller *Blood Simple* (1984) and have been making quirky, personal movies ever since. These include *Miller's Crossing* (1990), the very impressive *Barton Fink* (1991, one of the best movies about Hollywood ever made), *The Hudsucker Proxy* (1994), *Fargo* (1996), *The Big Lebowski* (1998) and *O Brother, Where Art Thou?* (2000), a modern version of Homer's *Odyssey*.

SPIKE LEE (b. 1957)

Lee is one of the few black directors to have reached major status within the Hollywood system. Movies such as *Do the Right Thing* (1989), *Mo' Better Blues* (1990), *Malcolm X* (1992) and *He Got Game* (1998) have garnered critical praise as well as large audiences.

RIGHT *Spike Lee not only directs, but also acts in a number of his own movies. Here he is with co-star Rosie Perez in* Do the Right Thing *(1989). Lee has sometimes been criticized for the sexual politics of his movies.*

RON HOWARD (b. 1954)

The 1984 *Splash!* was Howard's first real success and the banality of that movie set the tone for further success with *Cocoon* (1985), *Willow* (1988), *Backdraft* (1991), *Far and Away* (1992, starring Tom Cruise and Nicole Kidman), *Apollo 13* (1995) and *A Beautiful Mind* (2001).

TIM ROBBINS (b. 1958)

Robbins is better known as an actor, but he has directed three worthwhile movies: *Bob Roberts* (1992), in which he plays a phony country singer who uses his fame to run for office playing on the crude prejudices of his listening audience, *Dead Man Walking* (1995), a powerful indictment of capital punishment – a movie in which Sean Penn showed he really can act – and *The Cradle Will Rock* (1999), a movie version of the radical 1930s play first mounted by the left-wing Group Theatre.

MICHAEL MANN (b. 1943)

Michael Mann directed the first of the Hannibal Lecter movies, the 1986 *Manhunter* with Brian Cox as Lecter. He reaped the critical and commercial jackpot with the very effective adaptation of Fenimore Cooper's pre-Revolution in *The Last of the Mohicans* (1992). Basically, Mann is a storyteller of skill, as he showed once again in the overblown *Heat* (1995) and *The Insider* (1999).

ABOVE *The Last of the Mohicans (1992) gave Daniel Day-Lewis a marvellous part as Hawkeye, who performs heroics to rescue his love from the clutches of some very bad Native Americans indeed.*

"Houston, we have a problem."

RON HOWARD

APOLLO 13

LEFT *Perhaps Ron Howard's best movie was the impressive* Apollo 13 *(1995), about the real-life space mission that went badly wrong.*

57

THE DIRECTORS

INDEPENDENTS AND OUTSIDERS

MICHAEL CIMINO (b. 1943)

Is Michael Cimino merely a talented journeyman who happened to get lucky with subject, script and stars in *The Deer Hunter* (1978), one of the best films made in Hollywood in the 1970s? Before that, he had directed Clint Eastwood in the lightweight *Thunderbolt and Lightfoot* (1974) and after his huge success with the Vietnam movie, he became notorious for *Heaven's Gate* (1980), which reputedly ruined United Artists by costing millions over budget and taking minimal amounts at the box office. Since that debacle, Cimino has made the pedestrian *Year of the Dragon* (1985) and a remake of the old Bogart/Fredric March movie *The Desperate Hours* (1990).

JOHN SAYLES (b. 1950)

Sayles has been ploughing his particular furrow on the fringes of Hollywood for many years, making worthy, leftish movies about social issues. *Lianna* (1983) explored the theme of lesbianism long before mainstream Hollywood discovered designer lesbians. Sayles worked with radical cinematographer Haskell Wexler in the 1987 *Matewan* about coalminers' struggles in the 1920s and the following year he made *Eight Men Out*, a movie about the 1919 World Series baseball fix. The 1991 *City of Hope* deals with a more contemporary urban landscape narrative and as usual Sayles makes critical points about the injustices and hypocrisies of American life. *Lone Star* (1996) explored police corruption.

HAL HARTLEY (b. 1959)

Trust (1990) was perhaps Hartley's breakthrough movie, and since then he has established himself a comfortable niche in the independent, art-house circuit. *Simple Men* followed

ABOVE *Michael Cimino directed one of the best Vietnam movies* The Deer Hunter *(1978). Its central episode involves a very frightening game of Russian roulette.*

in 1992, then *Amateur* (1994), *Flirt* (1995) and *Henry Fool* (1997).

TODD SOLONDZ (b. 1959)

Solondz's reputation rests on two movies: *Welcome to the Dollhouse* (1995) and *Happiness* (1998). The former is a sharp and acerbic look at the constraints of family and suburban life on a teenage girl: it is definitely on the side of nonconformity and the nonjoiner. *Happiness* is rather an unpleasant and misanthropic movie that dwells with rather too much relish on perverse sexuality.

WHIT STILLMAN (b. 1952)

Stillman's characters are usually rich, Ivy League, sophisticated young men and women. Indeed, the characters in *Metropolitan* (1990) converse and interact with one another in such an intricate and urbane way that it comes over more as artifice than real. It is the same in the 1994 *Barcelona*: the characters he represents are so cool and cerebral that they seem to inhabit a different universe from mere mortals. The 1998 *The Last Days of Disco* is less etiolated, and some real pain filters through the sophistication, but his preppie world is beginning to pall somewhat and he will have to find a new impetus if he is to develop as a writer and director. His movies are intelligent, but somehow bloodless.

58

BRITISH DIRECTORS

CAROL REED (1906–76)

Carol Reed brought a liberal outlook to a conservative British film industry and made some of the most enduring of British films. His first major film was *The Stars Look Down* (1939) about coal miners. It starred Michael Redgrave as an idealistic coalminer's son who fights to win rights for the exploited miners. Reed also directed one of the great British movies, *Odd Man Out* (1947), which sympathetically portrayed an IRA gunman played by James Mason. *The Fallen Idol*, from a Graham Greene screenplay and

ABOVE *Carol Reed's* Odd Man Out *(1947) is a courageous British movie portraying an IRA activist in a sympathetic light.*

starring Ralph Richardson and Michèle Morgan, was expertly directed by Reed in 1948 and then he made his most famous film, *The Third Man*, with Orson Welles as the charming but criminal Harry Lime. *The Third Man* is generally thought to be one of the very best British movies ever made. *Outcast of the Islands*, adapted from the Conrad novel, was another distinguished film, although it is unfairly neglected nowadays. His later movies failed to match these successes, although *Oliver!* (1968) brought him a major international hit. Reed was one of the few British directors respected by the "movie brats" of Hollywood who admired his gifts.

MICHAEL POWELL (1905–90)

Working in collaboration with Emeric Pressburger, Powell directed some of the most colourful and interesting wartime and post-war British movies, including *The Thief of Bagdad* (1940), *The Life and Death of Colonel Blimp* (1943), *A Matter of Life and Death* (1946), *Black Narcissus* (1947) and *The Red Shoes* (1948). His films are distinguished by their elaborate design concepts, extravagant use of bright colour and a tendency towards lurid melodrama. He also made some awful movies such as *Oh, Rosalinda!* (1955), *Honeymoon* (1960) and *Age of Consent* (1969). A horror film made in 1960, *Peeping Tom*, was met by the almost total disapproval of critics and public, although Powell's reputation has been re-established and enhanced since then. Some of his earlier films are even more interesting than some of his much-praised later films: *The Edge of the World* (1937), *A Canterbury Tale* (1944) and *I Know Where I'm Going* (1945). Undoubtedly overrated as a

ABOVE *Rated by many as one of Michael Powell's best films,* The Red Shoes *(1948) incorporated a ballet sequence that exploited star Moira Shearer to the limit.*

director by people such as Martin Scorsese, Powell nevertheless was one of the most creative directors around in British cinema. At the very least, he tried to experiment in his films, and although his efforts are sometimes crass, he must be given credit for that.

ABOVE *Michael Powell co-directed* The Life and Death of Colonel Blimp *(1943), which reputedly was one of Churchill's favourite movies because it seemed to criticize the old guard of the military establishment.*

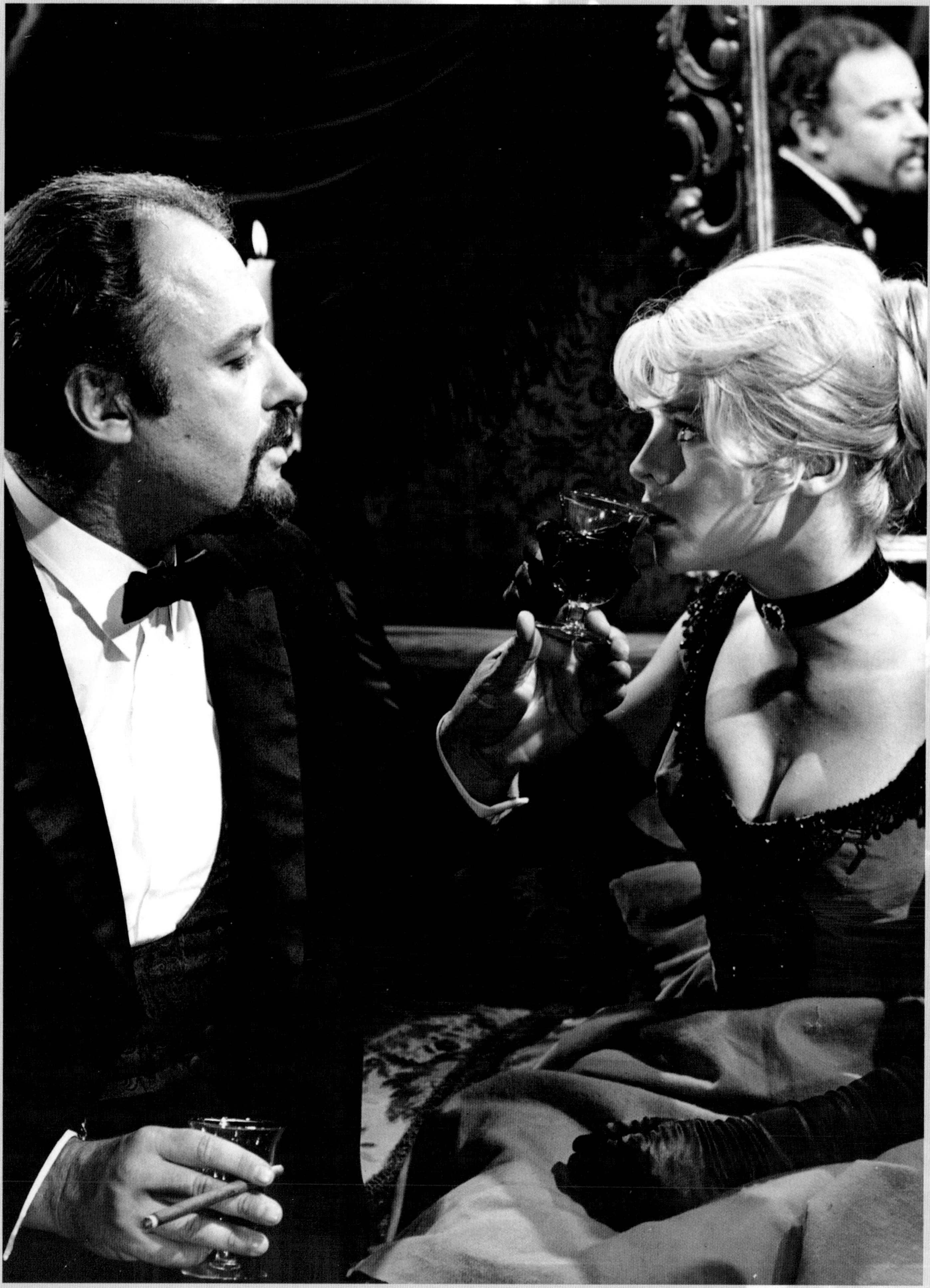

DAVID LEAN (1908–91)

Lean's first major success as a director was *Brief Encounter* (1946), that quintessential British tale of unconsummated illicit love set mainly in a railway station. There followed adaptations of two Dickens novels, which many think are Lean's best films: *Great Expectations* (1946) and *Oliver Twist* (1948). In the early 1950s he made *The Sound Barrier*, *Hobson's Choice* and *Summertime*, this last one starring Katharine Hepburn as a lovelorn spinster on holiday in Venice. He took a leap into the multi-million-dollar budget product with *The Bridge on the River Kwai* (1957), and from then it seemed that Lean could not make a small picture. *Lawrence of Arabia* (1962) and

OPPOSITE *David Lean directed* Doctor Zhivago *(1965), the highly successful epic film adaptation of Boris Pasternak's novel. Here Rod Steiger as the baddie seduces a fascinated Julie Christie.*

Doctor Zhivago (1965) were two major successes for him, but his penchant for epic scale and overblown scenes served him badly in *Ryan's Daughter* (1970), a simple Irish love story that he attempted to inflate to epic dimensions. Critical raspberries for that film encouraged him to give up directing until he made *A Passage to India* in 1984, which was also received coolly, and was the last film he directed.

Lean was a director with a banal visual imagination (the success of movies such as *Lawrence of Arabia* owed a lot to his cinematographer, Freddie Young), but he had a certain talent for story-telling in the cinema, which probably came from his experience as a film editor. However, many people rate his films as serious movies worthy of earnest consideration. My advice is to wallow in movies such as *Zhivago* for what they are: overblown, enjoyable epics! *Lawrence of Arabia* alone will probably mean that his reputation will last.

LINDSAY ANDERSON (1923–94)

Anderson was first a critic, and then was involved in the "Free Cinema" British documentary movement, making many shorts in the 1950s, including *O Dreamland*, *Thursday's Children* and *Every Day Except Christmas*. His first feature was *This Sporting Life* (1963), a film about the northern working class and rugby league. This was followed by *If...* (1968), which was a huge success. Later movies were prone to high-minded sententiousness and to making "state-of-the-nation" simplifications. These include *O Lucky Man!* (1973) and *Britannia Hospital* (1982). Anderson's radicalism seemed to be transformed into a kind of nihilistic conservatism, throwing some doubt over how deeply felt his

BELOW This Sporting Life *was directed by Lindsay Anderson and featured Richard Harris as an inarticulate rugby league player searching for emotional fulfilment in an affair with a widow played by Rachel Roberts.*

De quel côté serez-vous ?

if....

RICHARD ATTENBOROUGH (b. 1923)

Attenborough had a long career as an actor in British films before turning to directing. He seems to be David Lean's natural successor in the overblown stakes. His first directorial effort, *Oh! What a Lovely War*, managed to depoliticize the message of the original stage version, which prepared the way for *Young Winston* (1972), a film supposedly about the youthful adventures of Churchill. *A Bridge Too Far* and *Magic* did not add much to his directorial reputation, but *Gandhi* (1982) did, and he won an Oscar for it. *A Chorus Line* (1985) was an unusual project for him, but he was back on more familiar territory with *Cry Freedom* (1987), which dealt with the story of black South African campaigner Steve Biko. *Chaplin* (1992) failed at the box office and largely with the critics.

Recently, he has been more active as a jobbing actor than as a director. He has reached that venerable age when he is treated with reverence by the Establishment. As a young actor, Attenborough would crop up in British war movies usually playing the working-class coward who broke down under pressure, much to the chagrin of the Public School officers. Dickie has come a long way from those roles. He may have been a better actor than a director, and will be remembered for his performances in *Brighton Rock* (1947) and *10 Rillington Place* (1971).

major works were. He returned to the theatre in the latter part of his life. The last movie he directed was *The Whales of August* (1987) with Bette Davis and Lillian Gish, a mediocre end to an interesting career in the cinema. He was a notoriously difficult man, dogmatic, egotistical and irritable, but he was an undoubted talent.

ABOVE *If... (1968) is generally considered to be Lindsay Anderson's major cinematic work. Its mix of revolutionary politics, teenage angst and a good deal of feyness makes it enduringly interesting. Anderson was a great movie buff, and If... was very heavily influenced by the work of Jean Vigo, the French director of* Zéro de Conduite *and* L'Atalante.

LEFT Oh! What a Lovely War, *directed by Richard Attenborough, was adapted from a stage play with music. It evoked the horror of the World War I trenches as though performed by a pierrot troupe on Brighton Pier.*

ALAN PARKER (b. 1944)

It was the success of the 1976 *Bugsy Malone* that established Parker as a director, and this led to his directing *Midnight Express* (1978), which was a huge hit and won him an Academy Award nomination. He even survived directing *Fame* (1980) and went on to make a very personal film about a marriage break-up, *Shoot the Moon* (1982), which starred Albert Finney and Diane Keaton. *Birdy* (1985) and *Angel Heart* (1987) did not make many waves, and it took the controversial *Mississippi Burning* (1988) to put him back on the cinematic map; his critics accused him of making the FBI agents the real heroes of the struggle against violent racism in the American South. He had a huge popular success with *The Commitments* (1991), although *The Road to Wellville* (1994), the execrable *Evita* (1996) and the lachrymose *Angela's Ashes* (1999) scarcely enhanced his reputation. Parker is an expert manipulator of audience emotions, but his films are frequently exploitative and simple-minded.

ABOVE *Two new hopes of the 1970s for British cinema: Alan Parker, director, and David Puttnam, producer.*

KEN LOACH (b. 1936)

Loach has been directing feature films for more than 30 years, so he can scarcely be called an emerging director, but it is only since around 1990 that he has been given sufficient credit for making movies with social and political messages from a leftist point of view. His TV play *Up the Junction* (1967), *Poor Cow* (1967), *Kes* (1969) and *Family Life* (1971) were all classic Loach works in which he represented working-class life with warmth and sympathy (usually) without falling into patronizing sentimentality. The 1980s were not fruitful for Loach and he seemed to become the forgotten man of British cinema in the Thatcher era, but *Hidden Agenda* (1990) and *Riff-Raff* (1990) brought him back into the fold. *Land and Freedom* (1995), *Carla's Song* (1996) and *My Name is Joe* (1998) all

BELOW *Ken Loach directed a young David Bradley in* Kes, *which was about a working-class boy's attempt to escape the brutality of his everyday life by caring for a kestrel.*

confronted political issues head-on. *Sweet Sixteen* (2002), however, seemed unnecessarily nihilist and hopeless in tone and subject. At times, Loach's movies seem more worthy in intent than remarkable in execution, but as almost a lone radical voice in the British cinema, he has to be lauded.

ABOVE *Derek Jarman had a talent for the visual in the cinema, but did his movies amount to much more than that? This is a tableau from his movie* Caravaggio.

DEREK JARMAN (1942–94)

Jarman's first feature was *Sebastiane* (1976), followed by *Jubilee* (1978) and *The Tempest* (1979). *Caravaggio* (1986),

Edward II (1991) and the 1993 *Wittgenstein* enhanced his reputation for directing movies that stressed the importance of decor and visual effects. Jarman died of Aids in 1994.

RIDLEY SCOTT (b. 1937)

Scott graduated from the world of television commercials to direct feature films. After *The Duellists* (1977), a film adaptation of a Joseph Conrad story, he had the good fortune to direct *Alien* (1979), the success of which placed him in the big league of bankable directors. This was followed by *Blade Runner* (1982), a movie that displayed Scott's talent for

RIGHT *Ridley Scott's* Blade Runner *(1982) has become something of a cult movie for sci-fi fans. Certainly the sets and special effects are very impressive.*

ABOVE The Draughtsman's Contract *was a huge success for director Peter Greenaway. It is a movie that tries too hard to be "stylish".*

creating impressive and rich visual effects. However, what his movies lack is food for the brain as *Legend* (1985), *1492: Conquest of Paradise* (1992), *Gladiator* (2000) and *Black Hawk Down* (2001) prove. He also had a great success with *Thelma and Louise* (1991). There is no consistency in Scott's movies other than a kind of macho con-servatism, but he is highly rated by some critics and movie fans.

PETER GREENAWAY (b. 1942)

Greenaway had his first big movie success with *The Draughtsman's Contract* (1983). This was followed by *A Zed and Two Noughts* (1985), *Drowning by Numbers* (1988) and *The Cook, The Thief, His Wife and*

Her Lover (1989), all of them very arty or art-schooly. *Prospero's Books*, *The Baby of Macon* and *The Pillow Book* have continued to place emphasis on visuals rather than dramatic content.

MIKE LEIGH (b. 1943)

Leigh's movies often cover similar territory to Loach's but without the political conviction or warmth of the latter. His movies generally divide people into two camps: those who think he makes realistic and sometimes amusing films about the working- and lower-middle classes, and those who find his movies patronizing, smug, stereotyping and full of clichés. His first movie was *Bleak Moments* (1971), a very gloomy picture of social misfits in London guaranteed to make audiences feel smugly superior to these inadequate wretches. *Nuts in May* and *Abigail's Party* were popular successes on television, as Loach piled on the stereotypes and invited audiences to patronize these aspiring idiots. *Secrets and Lies* (1996) brought him to the attention of Hollywood, which Leigh says he despises. The 2002 *All or Nothing* was an entirely nihilistic representation of working-class life on a London housing estate. Leigh is said to create his movies through extended improvisation with his actors and I have to say that this shows. Many of the performances in the movies he has directed can only be described as examples of "coarse acting" at its coarsest. Cinemagoers beg to differ, so Leigh will continue to prosper.

SAM MENDES (b. 1965)

Mendes directed *American Beauty* in 1999, a movie that won several Oscars and was a box-office success. For me, it was a shallow movie, glib, superficial and pretentious. *Road to Perdition* (2002) had the misfortune to have Tom Hanks cast as a hitman, but

BELOW Mike Leigh directed this grim tale, Naked. *Katrin Cartlidge and Lesley Sharp share their troubles over a glass of beer.*

that is not the only reason the film sinks almost without trace. Mendes goes for "style", drowning routine Mafia material in a sea of self-conscious and arty visual effects. However, Mendes is undoubtedly going to be a major player in the movie world if that is what he wants to do with his directing career.

LYNNE RAMSAY (b. 1969)

With *Ratcatcher* and *Morvern Callar*, Lynne Ramsay has raised expectations that a major new directing talent is emerging. In the male-dominated world of movie-making and directing, it is encouraging to see female directors such as Ramsay making a breakthrough into mainstream film-making. She seems a distinctive voice and is prepared to take some risks.

OTHER NOTABLES

Other significant British directors include: Thorold Dickinson (1903–84), who directed *Queen of Spades* (1949) and *Secret People* (1952); Anthony Asquith (1902–68), who made *The Way to the Stars* (1945), *The Winslow Boy* (1948), *The Browning Version* (1950), *The Importance of Being Earnest* (1951) and *Orders to Kill* (1958); Tony Richardson (1928–91), director of the "new" British school of the 60s, who made *The Entertainer* (1960), *A Taste of Honey* (1961), *The Loneliness of the Long-Distance Runner* (1963), *Tom Jones* (1963), *The Loved One* (1965), *The Charge of the Light Brigade* (1968) and *The Border* (1982); John Schlesinger (b. 1926), who came to prominence with his documentary about Waterloo Station, *Terminus* (1961), and then went on to direct *A Kind of Loving* (1962), *Billy Liar* (1963), *Darling* (1965), *Far from the Madding Crowd* (1967), *Midnight Cowboy* (1969), *Sunday Bloody Sunday* (1971), *The Day of the Locust* (1975), *Marathon Man* (1976), *Yanks* (1979), *Honky Tonk Freeway* (1981) and *An Englishman Abroad* (1983).

FRENCH DIRECTORS

MARCEL CARNÉ (1909–96)

Carné was the most important French director of the immediate pre-World War II and Occupation years, directing a number of poetic and atmospheric melodramas that somehow made statements about France and its situation. *Drôle de Drame* (1937), *Le Quai des Brumes* (1938) and *Le Jour Se Lève* (1939) are three classics of the French cinema. Who can forget Jean Gabin as the decent working-class man holding out against the massed forces of law and order in *Le Jour Se Lève*? Gabin also starred in *Le Quai des Brumes* with Michel Simon and a very young Michèle Morgan. It is a melancholy film, somehow capturing the unease and sadness of an immediate pre-war France. *Les Enfants du Paradis* is a parable about the Occupation made right under German noses in 1944; it has Jean-Louis Barrault as a milksop mime artist, Pierre Brasseur as an exhibitionistic actor and sundry 19th-century nasties (who stood in for the Nazis), all quarrelling over Arletty, who represented France. Carné's post-war movies were not of the same standard, almost certainly because, apart from *Les Portes de la Nuit* (1946), he was no longer collaborating with screenwriter Jacques Prévert, who had written the screenplays for his most memorable movies.

JEAN RENOIR (1894–1979)

Jean was the son of the painter, Auguste Renoir; he had a long and distinguished career in the French cinema right from the silent years through to the late 1960s. His best-known films include *La Chienne,*

Boudu Sauvé des Eaux, Le Crime de Monsieur Lange, Les Bas-fonds, Une Partie de Compagne and two classics, *La Grande Illusion* and *La Règle du Jeu*. During the war and the post-war years, he made films in Hollywood which included *The Southerner, The Diary of a Chambermaid* and *The Woman on the Beach*. Later movies were *The River, The Golden Coach* and *Picnic on the Grass*. Like Carné, Renoir peaked around the

ABOVE *Marcel Carné's major directing achievement is* Les Enfants du Paradis, *made during the German occupation of Paris.*

late 1930s and he will be remembered for *La Grande Illusion* and *La Règle du Jeu*. There is a likeable humanism to the movies he made and they were mostly intelligently directed and written. Perhaps his movies are too literary for the purist.

67

JEAN-LUC GODARD (b. 1930)

When Godard made *À Bout de Souffle* (*Breathless*) in 1960, he became the doyen of the "New Wave" of French directors. His innovative techniques – jump cuts, hand-held cameras, a semi-documentary approach and a disregard for "normal" narrative – helped him to "genius director" status. Subsequent films also gained a great deal of attention: *Une Femme est une Femme, Vivre Sa Vie, Le Petit Soldat, Les Carabiniers, Bande à Part, Une Femme Mariée, Alphaville* and *Le Mépris*. Like most of the New Wave directors, Godard was besotted with the American cinema, especially *film noir* and "B" movies. However, around the mid-1960s he went down with a bad case of Mao-itis and his films have

> "FILM IS TRUTH 24 TIMES A SECOND."
> *JEAN-LUC GODARD*

never really recovered. In his attempts to interrupt classical story-telling in the cinema and hammer home political points, he has become a bore. He is quoted as saying, "My aesthetic is that of the sniper on the roof"; the trouble is that he is shooting himself in the foot.

BELOW *Les Carabiniers is a typical Godard movie of the 1960s. Dispensing with conventional narrative, it makes polemical points by inviting the audience to distance itself emotionally from the characters' actions.*

FRANÇOIS TRUFFAUT (1932–84)

If Godard was the Marxist conscience of the French New Wave, Truffaut was its soft centre. A rather self-conscious charm oozed from his films and this sometimes edges over into preciousness and sentimentality. However, his best films had an edge to them that belied his innately gentle nature: *Les Quatre Cent Coups, Shoot the Pianist, Jules et Jim, Fahrenheit 451, L'Enfant Sauvage, Anne and Muriel, La Nuit Américaine, Le Dernier Métro* and *Vivement Dimanche*. Truffaut also made a memorable appearance in Spielberg's

ABOVE *Jean-Luc Godard explored femininity and the reality of women's lives in a number of movies, including* Vivre Sa Vie *(1962), which starred Anna Karina.*

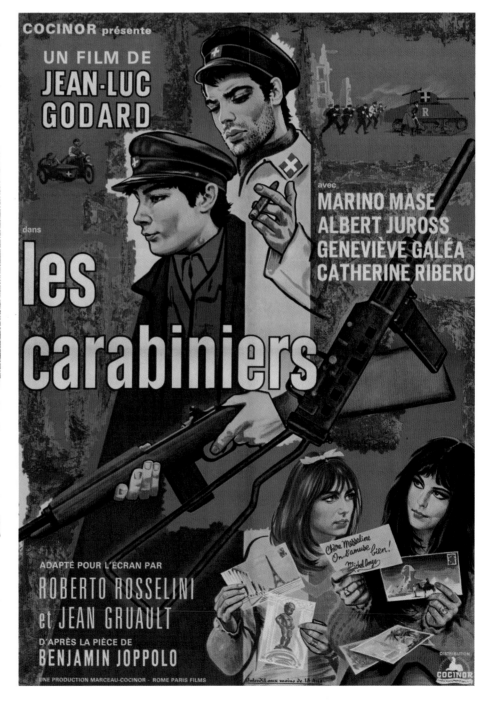

Close Encounters of the Third Kind as the only scientist who was sympathetic to the ordinary people who tried to make direct contact with the aliens.

LOUIS MALLE (1932–95)

One of the French New Wave in the 1950s, Malle survived as a major director into the 90s. His first film, *L'Ascenseur pour l'Echafaud*, was a Hitchcockian thriller with an improvised jazz score by Miles Davis. *Les Amants* caused a furore in the late 50s because it showed a wealthy bourgeois French wife and mother (Jeanne Moreau) abandoning husband and children for a lover who has introduced her to sensual pleasures. Most of his other films also explored controversial territory. *Le Feu Follet* was a brooding, pessimistic study of the last day in the life of a self-destructive writer, while *Viva Maria* was, by contrast, a rather mindless romp starring Moreau and

ABOVE *Francois Truffaut directed Oskar Werner and Julie Christie in* Fahrenheit 451 *(1966), a bleak glimpse of a bookless future. It would have been more interesting if Jean-Luc Godard had directed it.*

Brigitte Bardot. *Le Souffle au Coeur* explored the theme of incestuous feelings between mother and son, while *Pretty Baby*, his first American film, dealt with child prostitution. Both of his best films – *Lacombe Lucien* and *Au Revoir les Enfants* – dealt with aspects of the French Occupation. *Atlantic City*, with Burt Lancaster, was another American film – an interesting treatment on the theme of regeneration. *My Dinner with André* was about two men talking in a restaurant about life and regeneration (again). *Damage* (1992) and *Uncle Vanya on 42nd Street* (1994) were his last movies. Malle was a curious mixture of deeply-felt emotion and a shallow chicness.

ABOVE *One of Claude Chabrol's most effective psychological thrillers is* Le Boucher (1969), *about a serial killer in a small French town.*

CLAUDE CHABROL (b. 1930)

Most of the New Wave directors revered Hitchcock as "the master" and none more so than Chabrol, many of whose films are very Hitchcockian and full of Catholic obsessions about transference of guilt and punishment. After his early successes with *Le Beau Serge* and *Les Cousins*, Chabrol directed *Les Biches, La Femme Infidèle, Le Boucher,*

Violette Nozière, L'Enfer, Blood Relatives, Cop au Vin and *Inspector Lavardin.* The quality of his films varies enormously (he managed to make *Madame Bovary* (1991) extremely tedious), but his forte is murder within a French bourgeois setting, with or without adulterous connotations.

JACQUES TATI (1908–82)

Tati carried the tradition of silent-screen comedy into sound movies. His best films, *Jour de Fête* (1949), *Monsieur Hulot's Holiday* (1952), *Mon Oncle* (1958) and *Traffic* (1961), are practically wordless. He avoids the pathos of Chaplin and Keaton and his movies are the better for that. Tati's movies divide audiences: there are those who think he is a comic genius both as director and actor; others can watch his movies without laughing.

LEFT *Jacques Tati starred in and directed some of the most popular French comedies ever made: they included* Jour de Fête, Monsieur Hulot's Holiday, Mon Oncle *and* Traffic.

RIGHT *Patrice Leconte, the French director of* The Hairdresser's Husband *and* L'Homme du Train, *on location.*

BERTRAND TAVERNIER (b. 1941)

A classic French film director, Tavernier's films have frequently had Philippe Noiret as their star: *The Watchmaker of St Paul's, Coup de Torchon, A Sunday in the Country, Round Midnight, Life and Nothing But, These Foolish Things* and *Laissez-Passer.* Tavernier is in the radical tradition of French cinema and he seldom makes a movie that is less than interesting.

PATRICE LECONTE (b. 1947)

Monsieur Hire (1989) and *The Hairdresser's Husband* (1990) established Leconte as the director of quirky, "small" movies that take a healthy

interest in sexual foibles. *Ridicule* (1996) presented a larger canvas to Leconte and he scored with his representation of intrigues at the French court. The 2002 *L'Homme Du Train* concentrated once more on relationships, this time between a loner criminal and a seemingly respectable retired schoolteacher. Leconte makes intimate movies about outsiders and obsessives.

CLAUDE BERRI (b. 1934)

Berri had directed numerous feature films before he had a huge success with *Jean de Florette* (1986) and the sequel *Manon des Sources* from the same year. He followed that with *Uranus* (1990), a laudable attempt to deal with the running sore of the German Occupation years in France. *Germinal* (1993) was adapted from the Zola novel and starred Gérard Depardieu.

MATHIEU KASSOVITZ (b. 1967)

Kassovitz is an actor turned director, and he made one of the best French movies of the 1990s, *La Haine*, which focused on three young men from a Parisian housing estate determined to get their revenge on a violent, sadistic and racist police force.

ABOVE Jour de Fête (*1949*) *was Jacques Tati's first major international success. He played a village postman who has dreams of speeding up his delivery with American-type methods.*

71

ITALIAN DIRECTORS

VITTORIO DE SICA (1902–74)

De Sica was best known to the general public as a comedy actor, but he was also one of the leading directors of the post-war Italian Neo-realist school who influenced directors in the rest of Europe and in Hollywood. His most famous film is *Bicycle Thieves* (1948); set amidst the poverty of post-war Italy, it concerns the theft of a bicycle from a working-class man who needs it desperately to carry out his treasured job as a bill-poster. The film may be sentimental in parts, but it would take a heart of stone not to be touched by the scene where the bill-poster's young son defends his beleaguered father when an angry crowd turns on him after he is forced to steal another man's bicycle to make up for the loss of his own. *Shoeshine* (1946) and *Umberto D* (1952) were two other Neo-realist classics, but of the later films he directed, only *Two Women* (1960) with Sophia Loren and the 1972 *The Garden of the Finzi-Continis*

BELOW *By the time Vittoria De Sica made* Gold of Naples (1954), *he had abandoned Neo-realism and used glamorous stars such as Silvana Mangano and Sophia Loren.*

made much of an impact. Neo-realism aimed to present a naturalistic picture of the lives of ordinary people using actual locations and avoiding the sentimentality and narrative structures of the commercial cinema. Frequently, amateur actors were used rather than professionals.

ROBERTO ROSSELLINI (1906–77)

Rossellini was the other leading director of the Neo-realists, but he became famous for other reasons – his affair with, and subsequent marriage to, Ingrid Bergman. A documentary style, the use of a mixture of amateur and professional actors, a refusal to glamorize, a radical social viewpoint – these are the characteristics of Rossellini's films such as *Open City, Paisà, Stromboli, Europa '51* and *Louis XIV Seizes Power*. The fashion for Neo-realism passed relatively quickly, and Rossellini never found a niche in the commercial cinema.

ABOVE *Here Federico Fellini megaphones his instructions to the cast and crew on one of the elaborate sets of his 1987 film,* Intervista.

LUCHINO VISCONTI (1906–76)

Visconti's early films, such as *Ossessione* (1942) and *La Terra Trema* (1948), were heavily influenced by Neo-realism, but he soon abandoned that for an operatic, bravura style in movies such as *Senso* (1954), *Rocco and his Brothers* (1960), *The Leopard* (1963), *The Damned* (1969) and *Death in Venice* (1971). A former art director, Visconti seemed at times to indulge his taste for opulent sets and costumes at the expense of his films' thematic content. He also directed operas, and this shows in the over-emotionalism that mars some of his movies.

FEDERICO FELLINI (1920–93)

Fellini's early films were clearly influenced by Neo-realism: *I Vitelloni* (1953), *La Strada* (1954) and *Il Bidone* (1955). In these movies Fellini was

OPPOSITE *Fellini's 1960 movie* La Dolce Vita *satirized Roman high society. It starred Mastroianni as a jaundiced journalist and Anita Ekberg as a film star whose character was based closely on herself.*

UN FILM PONTI - DE LAURENTIIS prodotto da DINO DE LAURENTIIS e CARLO PONTI produttore esecutivo MARCELLO GIROSI

SILVANA MANGANO *in* L'ORO DI NAPOLI *un film di* VITTORIO DE SICA *con*

SOPHIA LOREN EDUARDO DE FILIPPO PAOLO STOPPA ERNO CRISA

soggetto tratto dal libro omonimo di GIUSEPPE MAROTTA edizioni bompiani · con la eccezionale partecipazione di TOTO' · riduzione cinematografica di CESARE ZAVATTINI

Angelo
Rizzoli
présente
stelt voor

**JULIETTA MASINA
SANDRA MILO
VALENTINA CORTESE
SYLVA KOSCINA**

un film de
een film van
FELLINI

JULIETTE
des   der
ESPRITS✴GEESTEN

Distr. FRANCORIZ

Affiches "WIK,. TEL. 43,88,92 - Bruxelles 18

LEFT *Fellini directed his wife Giulietta Masina in the* 1965 Juliet of the Spirits, *a movie you either love or loathe.*

clearly drawing on autobiographical material and using backgrounds and a way of life he knew intimately. However, once he became an international name and the fashion for Neo-realism passed, he discarded Neo-realism to make highly personal and exhibitionistic movies, including

films such as *La Dolce Vita, Boccaccio 70, 8½* (which was an extended reflection on himself as a director), *Juliet of the Spirits* (which people either hate or love), *Satyricon, Fellini's Roma, Amarcord* and *Ginger and Fred. 8½* is a brilliant movie in many ways, but it also marked a dead-end for the

director. Thereafter, he was parodying himself and being self-consciously "Fellini-esque". Fellini's world is a world of dreams and fantasies; he is consumed with memories of his childhood and his relationship with Catholicism. At his best he was skilful at depicting the uncertainties of

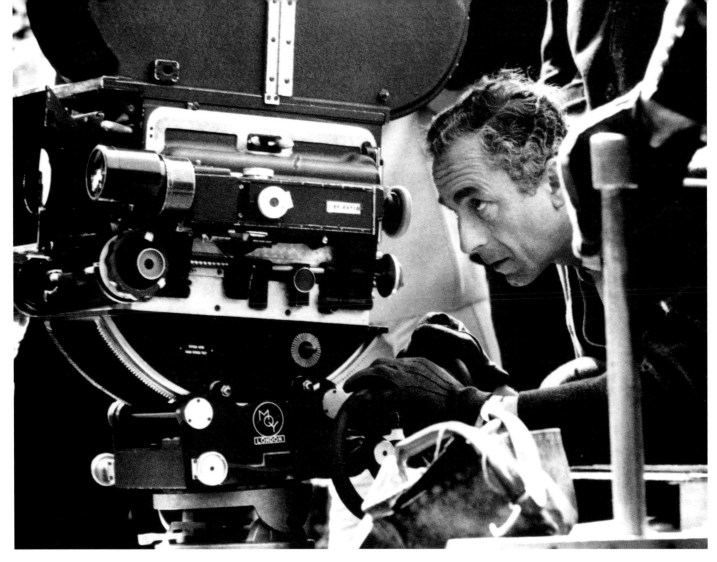

ABOVE *Michelangelo Antonioni lines up a shot from behind the camera. The composition of the image within the frame was extremely important to this director.*

human relationships, at his worst he was showily indulgent and modish. Feminists, on the whole, dislike his movies because he treats women as objects while pretending to worship them. After 8½, he scarcely made a decent film; perhaps he was right in depicting the director in the movie (clearly intended to be a self-portrait) as having run out of ideas.

MICHELANGELO ANTONIONI (b. 1912)

Antonioni came to international prominence with *L'Avventura* (1960), then went on to make *La Notte* and *L'Eclisse*. The 1966 *Blowup* was a

commercial success for him, and this led MGM to give him the money to make *Zabriskie Point*, which failed at the box office. He made *The Passenger* with Jack Nicholson in 1975, his last important movie. Later movies, *The Oberwald Mystery*, *Identification of a Woman* and *Beyond the Clouds*, are fairly unengaging attempts to expand the boundaries of film beyond narrative

coherence and continuity. Antonioni is an intellectual whose films explore bourgeois aridity and questions of identity. The pace of his films is slow and the dialogue is sparse. He creates images that encapsulate the thematic content of the film. For directing *L'Avventura* alone, he will always have an honoured place in film history.

75

RIGHT *Antonioni directed David Hemmings and Vanessa Redgrave in the 1966* Blowup, *a bleak picture of "swinging London".*

BERNARDO BERTOLUCCI (b. 1940)

Bertolucci has left-wing views that inform most of his early films. One of his best is *The Conformist* with Jean-Louis Trintignant as a fascist, and a study of fascism also makes both parts of *1900* interesting social documents. He made the controversial *Last Tango in Paris* with Marlon Brando and Maria Schneider in 1972, and *La Luna* with Jill Clayburgh in 1979. He had a surprising success with *The Last Emperor* which is not, however, one of his better films. *The Sheltering Sky* was a worthy attempt to translate Paul Bowles's novel to the screen, but his later films such as *Little Buddha* and especially *Stealing Beauty* mark a steady deterioration in his powers as a director. He seems to have been seduced by the more superficial aspects of the movie world in his later works.

GIUSEPPE TORNATORE (b. 1956)

Tornatore had a major worldwide success with the 1988 *Cinema Paradiso*, a success which he has been unable to replicate in subsequent movies. Later movies include *Especially on Sundays*, *A Pure Formality*, *The Star Maker* and *The Legend of the Pianist on the Ocean*.

ROBERTO BENIGNI (b. 1952)

Benigni was better known as an actor before he wrote and directed *Johnny Stecchino* (1991), which proved an enormous box-office success in Italy but is virtually unknown outside of it. However, with *Life is Beautiful* (1998) he achieved worldwide fame and success. This is a movie that definitely divides audiences: there are those who see it a warmly humanistic tribute to the human spirit in the face of the nightmare of Nazi concentration camps and those who see it as a trivializing, exploitative and crassly

ABOVE *The frank sexuality of Bertolucci's* Last Tango in Paris *caused much controversy when the film was released in 1972. It starred Marlon Brando and Maria Schneider.*

sentimental picture of the Holocaust. Benigni's best-known movies as an actor (apart from *Life is Beautiful*) are *Down by Law* (1986) and *Night on Earth* (1991), both directed by Jim Jarmusch, and the abysmal *Son of the Pink Panther* (1993).

ABOVE *Bertolucci directed John Malkovich and Debra Winger in his adaptation of the Paul Bowles novel* The Sheltering Sky.

ABOVE *Pier Paolo Pasolini (1922–75) was a controversial Italian film director. He directed* The Arabian Nights *in 1974.*

GERMAN DIRECTORS

FRITZ LANG (1890–1976)

Lang will always be remembered for having directed *Metropolis* (1927), a dark picture of a technologically advanced but oppressive society. His two *Dr Mabuse* movies also enhanced his reputation, but his leftist leanings did not endear him to Hitler's henchmen, and he left Germany in the early 1930s to work in Hollywood, where he made the noteworthy *Fury* in 1936. In the 1940s he directed *The Woman in the Window* and *Ministry of Fear*, while in the 1950s he made *Rancho Notorious*, *The Big Heat* and *Beyond a Reasonable Doubt*. He played himself in Jean-Luc Godard's 1963 *Le Mépris* (*Contempt*), a cynical view of Hollywood values.

LENI RIEFENSTAHL (b. 1902)

Riefenstahl will always be remembered for two movies: *Triumph of the Will* (1934), which filmed one of the Nazis' Nuremberg Rallies, and *The Olympiad* (1938). Undoubtedly an extremely talented director, Riefenstahl allowed herself to be used

ABOVE *A young Leni Riefenstahl, the director of* Triumph of the Will, *adorns the cover of a fan magazine in the 1930s.*

RIGHT *Fritz Lang's most famous movie is* Metropolis, *an outstanding example of German expressionism of the 1920s, evoking a bleak picture of the future, which in some ways forecast Nazi horrors.*

by the Nazi propaganda machine, for which she has never been forgiven by her own people. Her two movie "masterpieces" raise important questions about how we evaluate film: is the power of, say, *Triumph of the Will* to be denied because it was an instrument of a vile regime? Can we stand back from the content and intention behind a piece of film and admire the artistry that created it?

RAINER WERNER FASSBINDER (1946–82)

Fassbinder was a fashionable director of the 1970s, but it remains to be seen whether the films he made stand the test of time. Personally, I could not bear to sit through *The Bitter Tears of Petra Von Kant* again, but Fassbinder undoubtedly has his supporters. His best-known films are *Effi Briest*, *Fear Eats the Soul*, *Despair*, *The Marriage of Maria Braun* and his TV mini-series *Berlin Alexanderplatz*. The last two are the most accessible of his works.

WERNER HERZOG (b. 1942)

Herzog is an obsessive film-maker and he often makes films that are about obsessives, such as the Klaus Kinski protagonist in *Fitzcarraldo*, who is determined to bring grand opera to the jungles of South America. His first major success was *Aguirre: The Wrath of God* (1973), but before that he had made *Even Dwarfs Started Small* and *Fata Morgana*. *The Enigma of Kasper Hauser* attracted a good deal of attention, as did his version of the legend of Dracula, *Nosferatu the Vampyre*, which reflected Murnau's silent original. Apart from *Fitzcarraldo*, the 1980s did

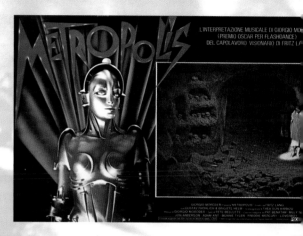

not bring him much success. He is quoted as saying that he is not out to win prizes, which he considers to be suitable only for dogs and horses.

WIM WENDERS (b. 1945)

Wenders makes odd, often slow-paced movies that frequently pay some kind of oblique homage to Hollywood, but are described as pretentious by his detractors. *Kings of the Road* and *The American Friend*, for example, are recognizably reworkings of the road movie and thriller genres. In the latter, he gives a part to the cult American director, Nicholas Ray; then, in *Lightning over Water*, the subject is Ray himself during the last few months of his life. Francis Coppola employed Wenders to direct *Hammett* at Coppola's Zoetrope Studio – a convoluted treatment of *film noir* themes that involved a representation of Dashiel Hammett himself. But there were great difficulties during the making of the film, and it is not clear how much of the final movie was directed by Wenders. *The Goalkeeper's Fear of the Penalty*, one of Wenders' first films, at least has a novel title. *Alice in the Cities* attracted attention, while *Paris, Texas* achieved minor box-office success and made a star of Harry Dean Stanton. He co-directed the 1995 *Beyond the Clouds* with Michaelangelo Antonioni and in 1999 he had a success with *Buena Vista Social Club*.

AUSTRALIAN DIRECTORS

PETER WEIR (b. 1944)

Weir's first big success was *Picnic at Hanging Rock* (1975), one of the first films of the 1970s to signal the revival in Australian cinema. It is an

ABOVE The Year of Living Dangerously *(1982), which starred Mel Gibson and Sigourney Weaver, was an international success for Australian director Peter Weir.*

evocative, "arty" and resonant film that raises more issues than it can adequately deal with, but it is still a real achievement. Weir followed this up with *The Last Wave* (1977), which again had mystical and religious elements and tried to explore Australian guilt about the Aborigines. *Gallipoli* (1981) to a certain extent dealt with the theme of what it is to be an Australian. Weir's first big-budget movie was one of the key films of the 1980s: *The Year of Living Dangerously* (1982) with Mel Gibson and Sigourney Weaver, and Linda Hunt memorably cast as a male dwarf. It is about the conflict between the drive to succeed and the need to commit yourself to loving another person. After that success he directed Harrison Ford in *Witness* (1985) and

The Mosquito Coast (1986). Both of these films, and others he has directed, deal in part with culture clash, and have a charismatic figure representing some kind of life force at the centre of the narrative. This is certainly true of the Robin Williams character in *Dead Poets Society* (1989), which was another big success. However, his 1990 film *Green Card*, with that other life force Gérard Depardieu, may be thought of as somewhat disappointing from a director who has made such unusual movies to date. However, with the 1993 *Fearless* and the 1998 *The Truman Show*, Weir returned to form.

JANE CAMPION (b. 1955)

Campion is a New Zealander by birth, but has worked mostly in the Australian film industry. Her sensitive direction of *An Angel at my Table* (1990) marked her down as a director worth watching and she followed that up with *The Piano* (1993), which starred Holly Hunter (she won the

ABOVE *Holly Hunter plays a mute Scottish emigrant to New Zealand in Jane Campion's* The Piano. *Campion also wrote the script.*

Best Actress Oscar) and became an international hit. *The Portrait of a Lady* (1996) starred Nicole Kidman and was an adaptation of the Henry James novel; it was unfairly savaged by the critics and it seems Campion's career has still to recover from that failure.

BAZ LUHRMANN (b. 1962)

Luhrmann's first big success was with *Strictly Ballroom* (1992) and he followed that up with his movie of *Romeo and Juliet* (1996), which starred Leonardo DiCaprio and made Shakespeare accessible to teenage

ABOVE *Baz Luhrmann's first big success was with* Strictly Ballroom, *a satire on ballroom dancing competitions and their participants.*

audiences. However, it was with *Moulin Rouge* (2001) that Luhrmann really hit the big time. This reworking of the movie musical divided audiences and critics: you either love or hate it. Undoubtedly Luhrmann is a talented director, but whether he can graduate from cinematic pyrotechnics and high camp frolics to more challenging material remains to be seen. Perhaps style is all to Luhrmann.

FIVE INTERNATIONAL DIRECTORS

INGMAR BERGMAN (b. 1918)

Bergman is a Swedish writer-director who first came to international prominence with his medieval allegory, *The Seventh Seal* (1957). This success led to the release outside Sweden of earlier films such as *Summer with Monika, Sawdust and Tinsel* and *Smiles of a Summer Night*. *Wild Strawberries* was another major film in 1957. Bergman's films tend to the austere and gloomy, notably in *The Virgin Spring, Through a Glass Darkly* and *The Silence*. Bergman is wrestling with his doubts about the existence of God; if God does exist, he seems to say, why are evil deeds and such cruelty allowed to happen?

Women are very often the central protagonists in his movies, for example in *Persona, Cries and Whispers* and *Autumn Sonata*. The impossibility

LEFT *Ingmar Bergman's best film – in the estimation of many critics – is* Wild Strawberries *(1957), a moving account of the last day in the life of an elderly academic.*

Bergman's characteristic blend of austere Calvinism and fear of punishment for sins that have been committed.

Working with a distinguished repertory company of actors drawn from Stockholm's Royal Academy Theatre, Bergman drew fine performances from actors such as Max Von Sydow, Gunnar Björnstrand, Liv Ullmann, Harriet Anderson, Ingrid Thulin and Erland Josephson. Bergman is the "art house" director par excellence, but his movies are both

"entertaining" and involving with an emotional intensity that is disturbing at times. Bergman must rank as one of the most talented directors ever to have worked in the medium. He is also an extremely creative stage director.

Bergman usually writes his own screenplays, imposing his personal vision on the subject matter. As he has created considerable independence for himself, he of all directors can surely be seen as an auteur.

AKIRA KUROSAWA (1910–98)

The Japanese director built up an international following with *Rashomon* (1950) and *Seven Samurai* (1954), the latter remade in Hollywood as

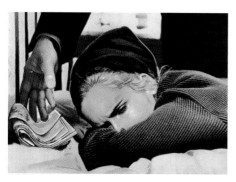

ABOVE *Ingmar Bergman made several movies with Liv Ullmann, including the dark, violent film* The Shame *(1968).*

of man–woman relationships and bourgeois marriage is a recurring theme. However, *Fanny and Alexander* revealed a warmer, more humanistic side to his artistic personality when he used affectionate memories of his Stockholm childhood to paint an evocative picture of extended family life. Mixed in with this, however, is

ABOVE *The 1972* Cries and Whispers, *directed by Ingmar Bergman, starred Erland Josephson and Liv Ullmann.*

ABOVE *Akira Kurosawa's* Rashomon (1950) *won the Golden Lion at the 1951 Venice Film Festival. The picture was remade by director Martin Ritt in 1964 as* The Outrage.

The Magnificent Seven. Later films such as *Throne of Blood* and *The Hidden Fortress* reinforced his reputation for action movies within the samurai tradition; he was often likened to John Ford. His later films were highly praised but seem too leisurely and indulgent for some tastes, as if he had become too conscious of his artistic status, as in, for example, *The Shadow Warrior* and *Ran.* Apart from his samurai epics, he directed modern-day pictures, including the impressive *Living* and *The Lower Depths.*

ANDREI TARKOVSKY (1932–86)

Some people would rather watch paint dry than sit through one of this late Russian director's films again; others see Tarkovsky as a genius of the modern cinema. He died in 1986 at the age of 54, having directed a handful of long, slow-paced arty

RIGHT *Andrei Tarkovsky's movie* Andrei Rublev (1966) *is about a medieval painter, but can be interpreted as being about the role of the artist in a repressive regime such as the Soviet Union under communism.*

movies that elevated him to major auteur status in many people's minds. In constant bother with the pre-glasnost Soviet authorities, Tarkovsky first came to prominence with *Andrei Rublev* (1966), then directed an obscure movie about space, *Solaris* (1972), that won the jury prize at the Cannes Film Festival. *Mirror* and *Nostalgia* were more overtly

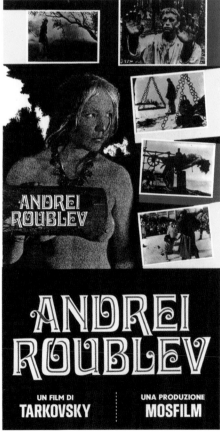

ABOVE *The 1965* Repulsion *explored classic Polanski territory: repressed sexuality and the havoc such repression causes.*

personal and political statements. It is tragic that Tarkovsky died before the present thaw in the Soviet Union happened; it would have been interesting to see what kind of movies he would have made in his homeland in the new circumstances.

ROMAN POLANSKI (b. 1933)

Polanski first came to international prominence when he directed *Knife in the Water* (1962). Thereafter, he made all of his films outside his native Poland. His films are full of violence, sexual quirks and the occult. *Repulsion* and *Cul-de-Sac* are odd, claustrophobic studies of repression. He had a major Hollywood success with *Rosemary's Baby*, which dealt with devil-worship. Tragically, Polanski's own life became inextricably linked with the macabre and the occult when his wife Sharon Tate was one of the victims of ritual murder at the hands of the Charles Manson "family".

Polanski's version of *Macbeth* emphasized witchery and violence, while *Chinatown* was a brilliant reworking of *film noir* themes. Polanski has also had his out-and-out

commercial flops, including *What?* and *Pirates*. *Tess* was a surprisingly subdued version of the Thomas Hardy novel, *The Tenant* explored themes of gender and identity, and *Frantic* was only a partially successful thriller starring Harrison Ford. Along the way Polanski picked up a charge of statutory rape in America for allegedly sleeping with a minor, which means he must work abroad unless he is prepared to stand trial in America. In the 1990s he directed *Bitter Moon*, *Death and the Maiden* and *The Ninth Gate*, then won a Best Director Oscar for *The Pianist* (2002).

SATYAJIT RAY (1921–92)

Ray's *Apu* trilogy in the 1950s put Indian cinema firmly on the international film map. *Pather Panchali*, *Aparajito* and *The World of Apu* are brilliant representations of Indian life. What makes Ray so accessible to western audiences is his command of film technique and his control of the narrative and acting in his films. Other distinguished films he made

include *The Music Room, Company Limited, Distant Thunder, The Middleman, The Chess Players* and *Days and Nights in the Forest*. Ray could be described as rather a "literary" director in that his films are often adaptations of novels, strong on plot and character, but he also had a genuine instinct for what can hold an audience in the cinema. He is probably the only Indian movie director to achieve lasting international fame; certainly the *Apu* trilogy is a fine achievement.

ABOVE *Satyajit Ray's movies often examined the underlying corruption in Indian society.* The Middleman *was one of his best films.*

BELOW *Spanish director Pedro Almodóvar directs Joaquin Cortes and Marisa Paredes in* The Flower of My Secret *(1995), which explores the breakdown of a woman writer. Almodóvar's movies inhabit borderline territory between art movies and exploitative commercial fare. He won a Best Original Screenplay Oscar for* Talk to Her *(2002), which he wrote and directed.*

81

THE STARS

MOVIE STARS are America's version of royalty. Becoming a movie star elevates a human being to an unnatural level of existence, on which he or she is accorded attention, adulation and vast sums of money. But stars are basically commodities, and like all commodities, they have their sell-by dates. "You're only as big as your last picture" is a common saying in the movie industry, and many actors have discovered this to their cost. Nevertheless, while the aura lasts, movie stars can command incredible fees and followings. In this section of the book, we look at the phenomenon of stardom in the cinema.

LEFT *Gone with the Wind is arguably the most successful movie ever made in box-office terms. It made Vivien Leigh a major star and enhanced Clark Gable's status in Hollywood.*

INTRODUCTION

When the movies began to emerge as a popular mass entertainment, there were no movie stars as we know them. Gradually, however, the hucksters who ran Hollywood saw the percentage in creating these luminaries of the silver screen to lure the paying public into the cinemas. They realized they could sell a picture on the strength of the star appearing in it: they would do a "Chaplin", "Pickford" or "Fairbanks" movie and then repeat the formula again and again. Soon Hollywood success depended partly on the pulling power of these personalities who were catapulted to world fame, despite the lack of talent many of them displayed.

ABOVE *Movie stars such as Bette Davis and Errol Flynn (seen here in* The Private Lives of Elizabeth and Essex) *had an aura created for them by the full-time publicity departments of the studio they worked for.*

Some observers of the mass media see something sinister in how stars are used in movies. Herbert Marcuse, the German-American philosopher, wrote the following about how star images were used in Hollywood: "They are no longer images of another way of life but rather freaks or types of the same life, serving as an affirmation rather than a negation of the established order." In other words, stars have an ideological function; they make life more palatable for us by ironing out

LEFT *Marilyn Monroe was photographed in every possible pose and from every angle in the attempt to create for her an aura of ultimate glamour.*

the contradictions and worries that inevitably work their way into even the sunniest of movies. For example, if a "good joe" star such as James Stewart is shown to be poor but happy with his lot and the American Way of Life, then it is more likely that we will be seduced into feeling the same way.

There is no doubt that stars convey meaning of one kind or another. They signify something "extra" in a movie, especially if they have created a star persona from numerous films. John Wayne signified a kind of macho integrity, promising straight-shooting and straight-talking. Henry Fonda carried an aura of incorruptibility with him into almost all of his movies; he was the personable, archetypal "liberal" star. Monroe encapsulated for many an innocent joy in sex, and for others a child-like vulnerability. All the major stars had their dominant persona, arousing the audience's expectations. Sometimes a star would be cast against "type", so occasionally Gregory Peck or even Fonda would play a villain, but even that is an

example of how star personas can be used, because casting "against type" is still dependent upon our expectations as an audience of what these stars signify and how we react to them.

During the heyday of the Hollywood studio system, there was an elaborate grooming process for potential stars. They generally had to be glamorous, above reproach, and recognizable American types. If the moguls considered that they were wanting in some area, then the remodelling process could be severe. Rita Hayworth, for example, had to have her hairline raised by an

ABOVE *This "candid" shot of stars David Niven and Ginger Rogers was released to the press by Universal-International to publicize a movie called* Magnificent Doll (1946). *Here the stars are meant to be earnestly discussing script matters.*

ABOVE *Photo opportunities were seized on avidly by the publicists. Here Janet Leigh and Carleton Carpenter pose for the camera with Forgan, a sedated lion.*

inch through electrolysis (a very painful exercise) because Harry Cohn, Columbia's boss, thought she would look better that way. Names were the first thing to go if an actor's real moniker did not fit: Marion Michael Morrison became John Wayne, Doris von Kappelhoff became Doris Day,

and Britain's Diana Fluck became Diana Dors. The fan magazines and gossip writers would be handed publicity material to boost the public's awareness of up-and-coming stars and, once they were established, their reputations would be protected and continually polished.

Under old Hollywood, the stars were constrained by seven-year contracts with options every six months to be picked up or dropped by the employing studio. This contract tied the stars to their employers; the option clauses were used to make them toe the line and force them to make the movies the studios wanted them to make. Bette Davis and Olivia de Havilland took on their studios in the courts in an attempt to break the feudal hold the moguls had over them. They helped break up the old studio system, and the stars were in time largely released from the tyranny of the long-term contract. Burt Lancaster and Kirk Douglas were two early examples of producer-stars who took a financial risk in their own films and formed companies to make independent productions, which they then sold to the studios to market and distribute.

Soon the major stars became enterprises in themselves – millions of dollars for a movie budget could be raised on one star name. Agents became enormously important because the really powerful ones could promise a package of several stars and probably a top director, a successful screenwriter and a commercial vehicle for them all to participate in. Contemporary stars such as George Clooney or Julia Roberts are as much businessmen and women as actors.

ABOVE *The importance of the black audience in the United States led to the creation of African-American stars such as Dorothy Dandridge and Harry Belafonte.*

ABOVE *Stars acquired off-screen reputations that were used by the producers to publicize their movies. The Rat Pack's aura – with Frank Sinatra, Dean Martin, Sammy Davis Jr and Peter Lawford as the main men – helped to sell Ocean's Eleven (1960).*

ABOVE *Stars in the old days had to be glamorous above all else. Here Stewart Granger and Elizabeth Taylor do their best to match up.*

THE SCREEN GODDESSES

There have been many contenders for the status of screen goddess. To qualify, the star must have become immensely popular with millions of people, have signified something transcendental to her fans, have conquered the medium of film through her beauty, charisma and talent, and have acquired a cult status either before or after her death. Every movie fan would have a different short-list, so I offer these first four stars very tentatively as contenders for the title.

MARY PICKFORD (1893–1979)

Pickford was known as "America's Sweetheart" during the heyday of silent movies. Her forte was a child-like demureness allied to an all-American steeliness, for beneath her girlish locks was the mind of an astute businesswoman who knew her own market-worth in the industry that made her world-famous. Sam

Goldwyn stated that it took longer to frame one of Pickford's contracts than it did to shoot her movies. With Charlie Chaplin, D.W. Griffith and Douglas Fairbanks, to whom she was married, she was one of the co-founders of United Artists in 1919.

Pickford earned mega-bucks even by today's standards, Paramount paying her $675,000 a year at one time. A succession of "childwoman" parts in movies such as *The Little Princess, Rebecca of Sunnybrook Farm, Pollyanna* and *Tess of the Storm Country* gave her immense clout with her bosses. Other movies she made included *Little Lord Fauntleroy, Dorothy Vernon of Haddon Hall, Little Annie Rooney* and *My Best Girl*. By the time sound arrived in Hollywood she was in her mid-30s; she could no longer play ingenues and she was so identified with the silents that there was clearly no future for her. However, she stayed active in the business through United Artists and lived on until 1979. Pickford lived out the American Dream, reaching dizzying heights of popular and financial success. Unlike many other Hollywood luminaries, however, she was a survivor. "Rebecca of Sunnybrook Farm" was no pushover.

GRETA GARBO (1905–90)

Garbo was born Greta Gustafsson in Stockholm in 1905. Her early Swedish films show her as an unremarkable young woman, more tomboyish than alluring. But her early silent movies in America – *The Torrent, The Temptress* and *Flesh and the Devil* –

ABOVE *MGM believed in "classy" product. Their idea of this was to adapt Tolstoy's* Anna Karenina *in the 1927 picture* Love *and cast glamorous stars Greta Garbo and John Gilbert. Garbo and Gilbert enjoyed their off-screen affair but Garbo ended it in 1929.*

established her as a woman men would die for, or at least commit adultery with.

In the talkies she went for a more realistic image with *Anna Christie* and *Susan Lenox (Her Fall and Rise)*, then resorted to ethereal parts such as *Queen Christina* and *Camille*. She lost her heart to John Barrymore in *Grand Hotel* and to Fredric March in *Anna Karenina*, but no male co-star was really good enough for her, according to her admirers. Her fans adored her mixture of spirituality and sensuality. She also had an androgynous quality that meant she had a wider appeal than more overtly heterosexual stars. William Daniels was her favourite cameraman and he made sure, as she

ABOVE *Mary Pickford starred in the sentimental drama* Secrets *(1933). Dubbed "America's Sweetheart", she married Douglas Fairbanks.*

ABOVE *Garbo was presented as the ultimate symbol of female beauty and mystery in romantic melodramas such as* Camille, *which co-starred Robert Taylor. Garbo played the doomed courtesan Marguerite Gautier.*

ABOVE *Garbo made* A Woman of Affairs *with former silent-screen star John Gilbert in 1929. Despite Garbo's support, Gilbert's career vanished with the coming of sound because he had a high-pitched voice.*

herself did, that the lighting and the poses she struck were always kind to her.

But could she act? The jury is still out on that one. Sometimes she is very bad indeed (witness her part as the ballerina in *Grand Hotel*) but to Garbo fanatics, questions about her acting skills are totally irrelevant. They worship her as a transcendent symbol of beauty and of the human spirit, as an embodiment of love – albeit a bisexual love.

The hard fact was that Garbo was always much more popular in Europe than in the USA, so when America entered World War II and the European markets for US films were cut off, the studios were none too keen to make more films with her, especially as her last, *Two-Faced Woman*, had been a flop. Her famous "I want to be alone" retirement line may be misleading; her screen career was almost certainly in serious decline by then. However, that is doubtless sacrilege to the many millions of fans who, despite her death in 1990, will go on worshipping at her shrine.

MARLENE DIETRICH (1901–92)

Dietrich was another screen goddess with an androgynous appeal. Like Garbo, she was European-born – in Berlin in 1901. Her first big hit was in the German movie *The Blue Angel*. Director Josef Von Sternberg also directed her first American film, *Morocco* (1930), in which she starred with Gary Cooper. Von Sternberg was a key figure in Dietrich's Hollywood career, directing her in *Dishonored, Shanghai Express, Blonde Venus, The Scarlet Empress* and *The Devil is a Woman*. In all these movies Dietrich played the vamp, the imperious mistress for

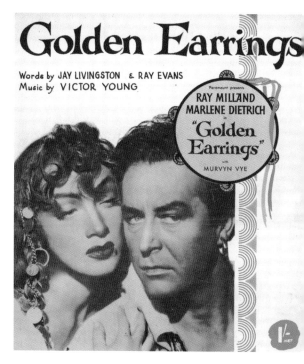

ABOVE *Marlene Dietrich was meant to be exotic and mysterious, so in* Golden Earrings *she played a romantic gypsy.*

whom men ruined themselves. Von Sternberg's wife certainly thought Dietrich played that part in real life because she served a writ on Dietrich accusing her of alienating her husband's affections.

After Von Sternberg's professional relationship with Dietrich ended, her career was never quite the same. Indeed, she was labelled "box-office poison" for a time, before movies such as *Destry Rides Again, Rancho Notorious* and *Witness for the Prosecution* partly revived her film career. Finally, in the 1950s, and in her own 50s, she embarked on an international cabaret career which brought her new fans and fame.

For those who adored Dietrich, there was no one like her. For those who found her eminently resistible, it was puzzling why she won herself such cult status. Dietrich was never an acting talent; what she had was a certain bisexual appeal, an icy beauty, an exotic style and a ravenous ego that saw to it that she was shown on the silver screen in as flattering a light as possible.

87

MARILYN MONROE
(1926–62)

More words have been written about Monroe than any other movie star. A mixture of fantasy, fact, legend and downright fabrication make up the Monroe legend; indeed, "Marilyn Monroe" is now an industry even 40 years after her death. Fans of "Norma Jean" collect everything associated with her, writers never tire of writing about her and her movies are still very popular. Along with James Dean, she is the Hollywood star who has provoked and continues to provoke the most intense cult worship.

Born in Los Angeles in 1926, Norma Jean Mortenson had a paranoid schizophrenic mother, no father, various unbalanced relatives and several foster homes. These childhood experiences must have contributed hugely to her later instabilities and her search for that solid parent figure, particularly the male parent, that led her into disastrous relationships and marriages with older men. The hardships she endured undoubtedly also gave her the drive to succeed, to get herself out of this morass of abuse and poverty.

To do this, Monroe was forced to exploit her looks: her (dyed) blonde hair, her appealing face and her voluptuous body. Evidence has piled up that her early film career was greatly helped by various elderly gentlemen in the movie business. Monroe is quoted as saying she spent a lot of time on her knees in her early starlet days. Her first significant role was in *The Asphalt Jungle*, directed by John Huston, in which she played

elderly Louis Calhern's mistress. She looked beautiful and she was also rather touching in this small part.

Undoubtedly Monroe had a quality when she was on screen. She could play dumb blonde parts with an instinctive grasp of comedy, as in *How to Marry a Millionaire, Gentlemen Prefer Blondes, The Seven Year Itch* and *Some Like it Hot*. Male viewers were attracted by her sexuality but felt unchallenged by her "little girl" voice and general helplessness; men were allowed to be attracted to her and be protective as well. Because she played powerless young women, this angered the more feminist of cinema-goers, who dismissed her as a middle-aged man's fantasy object, but many women liked her because of her vulnerability.

Marriages to James Dougherty, baseball star Joe DiMaggio and playwright Arthur Miller all failed. Attracted to the mixture of power and sex that John Kennedy exuded, Monroe had an affair with the president, who seemingly asked brother Bobby to take care of her when she started to get "troublesome". Bobby himself had an affair with her and then the scenario becomes

ABOVE *Marilyn Monroe had a big hit with* Some Like it Hot *(1959), but the way she was represented in that Billy Wilder comedy undoubtedly contributed to the tensions that arose during filming.*

blurred. Whether Monroe's death through an overdose of barbiturates was an accident, suicide or murder has not yet been finally established. Certainly, what we do know about the end of her life exposes the seamier side of Hollywood's connections with power politics.

Monroe is often written about as a victim figure, and undoubtedly she was treated shabbily at times. But she was a determined woman, driven by her need to make up for childhood deprivations of material and emotional security. Finally, she never achieved that security because she was never allowed, in the years of her fame, to be herself. The men who became involved with her went to bed with Marilyn Monroe but made sure they never woke up with Norma Jean Mortenson. Perhaps what fans worship about Monroe is the ordinary Norma Jean they sense under the glamorous Marilyn exterior.

LEFT *Many people's idea of a contemporary, glamorous star is Julia Roberts, here with Patrick Bergin in* Sleeping with the Enemy *(1991).*

JULIA ROBERTS (b. 1967)

Roberts is many people's idea of a glamorous leading lady. Certainly, she is currently a top box-office star. For some of us, this is a very puzzling phenomenon. Whereas her many fans see her as a beautiful and talented star, others wonder exactly why this actress with such limited talents and average looks has reached such a position in the cinema hierarchy. She first came to prominence in the appalling *Pretty Woman* (1990), a piece of Hollywood fluff that was decidedly unappealing. *Sleeping with the Enemy* and *Flatliners* did her career no harm, while the lachrymose *Dying Young* positively enhanced it. *My Best Friend's Wedding* and *Notting Hill* were the type of light and forgettable comedies that endear her to her adoring audience. Amazingly, her role in *Erin Brockovich* won her the Best Actress Oscar, which says more about the judgement of the members of the Academy than her acting abilities.

NICOLE KIDMAN (b. 1967)

Born in Hawaii and raised in Australia, Kidman has acquired major star status within a relatively short time. *Dead Calm* (1989) was the first movie she was really noticed in, and then *Flirting* and *Far and Away* consolidated her status. The 1995 *To Die For*, in which she played an ambitious television weather girl, showed she was more than just a glamorous leading lady, and the underrated *The Portrait of a Lady* proved she could tackle serious roles. She fared better in Kubrick's *Eyes Wide Shut* than her husband at the time, Tom Cruise, and she followed this up with a major success in *Moulin Rouge*. *The Others* was a small-scale thriller which found an audience, then she won her first Oscar for her portrayal of Virginia Woolf in *The Hours*. In between movies, she returns to the theatre and takes on more demanding roles than the cinema can give her. The test for Kidman as a movie star is whether she can jump over the age barrier that Hollywood erects to frustrate actresses.

ABOVE *Nicole Kidman showed she was more than a glamorous movie star in films such as* To Die For *(1995) and* The Hours *(2002), for which she won the Best Actress Oscar.*

THE ROMANTIC HEROES

Romantic heroes or male heart-throbs – call them what you will – there have been numerous major stars who were famous for their combination of good looks, devil-may-care screen personas and their on-screen womanizing. Here is a short list of seven.

RUDOLPH VALENTINO (1895–1926)

Valentino was the screen's first "Great Lover", a title that caused him problems both with other men and his wives. He danced a tango in *The Four Horsemen of the Apocalypse* (1921) and set female pulses racing. His preposterous role in *The Sheik*, a desert chieftain with propensities towards rape, found an ecstatic audience. Marital difficulties with actress Jean Acker and designer Natasha Rambova

and problems with Paramount put a great deal of pressure on the superstar, as did press insinuations of bisexuality. He died of a ruptured appendix in 1926 at the age of 31. The scenes of extravagant mourning at his funeral have passed into Hollywood legend. The Valentino phenomenon is evidence of the power of the screen image over a mass audience hungry for erotic fantasy.

CLARK GABLE (1901–60)

Gable was known as "The King of Hollywood". He was certainly the most popular male star of the late 1930s and 40s. His most famous role was Rhett Butler in *Gone with the Wind*. He was popular with men because he was an uncomplicated action hero and did not make a big deal about his success with the ladies. Women liked him for his sexuality, his ready charm and his easy-going persona. He won an Oscar for *It Happened One Night* but was never perceived as a great screen

ABOVE *Ronald Colman was an English actor who played romantic heroes initially in the silents, then very successfully in the sound era. Sidney Carton in the 1935 version of Dickens's* A Tale of Two Cities *was one of Colman's most famous roles.*

ABOVE *Rudolph Valentino was one of the biggest stars of the silent era. His sudden death at a young age set off a worldwide surge of grief, and several women reportedly committed suicide because of their sense of loss. His appeal has certainly dated.*

ABOVE *Clark Gable did not get on well with Vivien Leigh, his co-star in* Gone with the Wind. *He married his third wife, Carole Lombard, in the midst of filming this picture in 1939.*

actor, although he was praised for his performance in his final film with Marilyn Monroe, *The Misfits*. He was married to Carole Lombard for a few years before she died in an air crash in 1942. In 1961, 12 days after filming ended on *The Misfits*, Gable died of a heart attack, probably brought on by the action scenes he had insisted on doing himself in the movie. Perhaps it was a case of Gable's screen image catching up with the man.

ERROL FLYNN (1909–59)

The greatest of the swashbuckling stars, Flynn was as famous for his off-screen antics as his celluloid heroics. Determinedly self-destructive, Flynn drank his health and wealth away and died in 1959 at the age of 50. At his peak in the 1930s and early 40s, he was very big at the box office in movies such as *Captain Blood, The Charge of the Light Brigade, The Sea Hawk, They Died with Their Boots On*

and *The Private Lives of Elizabeth and Essex*. By the 1950s his alcoholism had ruined his outstanding good looks and he was reduced to starring with Anna Neagle in film versions of *Lilacs in the Spring* and *King's Rhapsody*. He played a drunk in *The Sun Also Rises* and *Too Much Too Soon* (as John Barrymore), but the end was near. His body finally gave out in a Vancouver hotel when he died of a heart attack. Since his death, bizarre rumours have linked him with Nazi espionage and the IRA. Flynn, even in death, is seldom far from a headline.

ROBERT REDFORD (b. 1937)

Redford is unlike Valentino, Gable and Flynn in that he is not predominantly an action hero. However, he has become a symbol of male beauty whether he likes it or not. His roles in *Butch Cassidy and the Sundance Kid, The Candidate, The Way We Were, The Sting, All the President's Men*

ABOVE *Robert Redford as Bob Woodward of Woodward and Bernstein, the investigative reporters who broke the Watergate story, in Alan J. Pakula's* All the President's Men.

and *The Natural* have made him a major star, albeit not in the tradition of Gable. Redford has no great range as an actor. He tends to play the honest guy trying to make his way in the world in as honourable a manner as he can. In the process, however, he always looks impossibly handsome in the tradition of Hollywood romantic heroes. However, he is much more than a handsome leading man, as his direction of *Ordinary People, A River Runs Through It, Quiz Show* and *The Horse Whisperer* clearly shows. Other notable movies he has acted in include *Jeremiah Johnson* (1972), *The Great Gatsby* (1974), *Three Days of the Condor* (1975), *Brubaker* (1980), *Out of Africa* (1985), *Up Close and Personal* (1996) and *Spy Game* (2001).

"THEY THROW THAT WORD 'STAR' AT YOU LOOSELY AND THEY TAKE IT AWAY EQUALLY LOOSELY. YOU TAKE THE RESPONSIBILITY FOR THEIR LOUSY MOVIE, THAT'S WHAT THAT MEANS." ROBERT REDFORD

GEORGE CLOONEY (b. 1961)

Clooney graduated to the cinema from the television series *ER* and is now a major box-office star. He began to be really noticed when he made *From Dusk Till Dawn*, *One Fine Day* and *Batman and Robin*. He can play action heroes as in *Three Kings* and *The Perfect Storm*, but his performances are usually leavened with a good measure of humour and self-deprecation. He

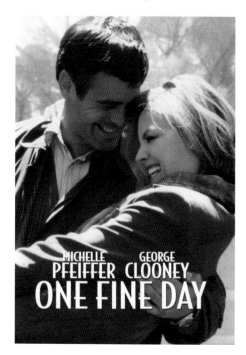

ABOVE *George Clooney starred with Michelle Pfeiffer in the light-hearted romantic comedy* One Fine Day *(1996).*

showed his talent for comedy in the Coen Brothers' *O Brother, Where Art Thou?*, which was a very welcome change of style for him. However, the routine remake of *Ocean's Eleven* reminded us how mainstream Hollywood he is. He is likely to have real lasting power as a major star.

TOM CRUISE (b. 1962)

After appearing in "youth pics" such as *Taps*, *All the Right Moves* and *The Outsiders*, Cruise hit the big time with *Top Gun*, a mindless piece of macho nonsense. Cruise exudes a kind of rather smug, locker-room masculinity, but this seems to appeal to a large proportion of the female cinema

audience. *The Color of Money*, *Cocktail*, *Rain Man* and *Born on the Fourth of July* further enhanced his career. The *Mission Impossible* movies made him a fortune but only added to the list of no-brainers he has appeared in. He tried something more ambitious with Stanley Kubrick's final movie, *Eyes Wide Shut*, in which he appeared with his then-wife, Nicole Kidman, but failed to convince in a disappointing film. Whether the public will ultimately tire of his cocky college jock persona is difficult to say. Now in his 40s, it is perhaps time for Cruise to grow up as an actor.

BEN AFFLECK (b. 1972)

The fact is that Affleck has attained major box-office status in recent years, so he must appeal to a lot of people. He exudes a kind of smugness on screen, however, that is un-appealing to some. He had a hit with the amusing *Chasing Amy* and followed that up with *Good Will Hunting*, which he co-wrote with his friend, Matt Damon. His career has survived a succession of

ABOVE *Tom Cruise played agent Ethan Hunt in the first of the* Mission Impossible *movies that he starred in. Here he comes to grips with the bad guy, played by Jean Reno.*

awful movies, the worst of which was *Pearl Harbor* (2001), a truly authentic turkey that reached ludicrous levels of badness. Affleck's name never seems to be far from the gossip columns and he is one of those Hollywood actors who seem to settle for being more Hollywood than actor.

BELOW *An icon for teenagers, here Leonardo DiCaprio woos Kate Winslet in* Titanic.

93

THE SENSITIVE ANTI-HEROES

In the 1950s there appeared a new kind of male star: the intuitive, almost feminized hero. Usually anti-authoritarian in stance, these stars grew out of the naturalistic, "Method" school of acting and the commercial need to give Hollywood's dominant audience in the 1950s – young people of between 16 and 25 – stars they could identify with.

MONTGOMERY CLIFT
(1920–66)

Clift was the first of the sensitive, emotional actors to make it as a major star. His mumbling, hesitant style suited his roles in *A Place in the Sun, The Heiress, I Confess, From Here to Eternity, The Young Lions, Suddenly Last Summer* and *The Misfits*. His spectacular good looks did not harm his career either,

but a serious car smash in 1957 altered his appearance and probably eventually shortened his life. Insecure in his private life and uncertain about his sexual identity, he resorted to drink and drugs and died prematurely at the age of 46. Clift influenced other young stars of the 1950s and was undoubtedly, in his own way, a powerful screen presence.

JAMES DEAN (1931–55)

An enormous worldwide cult has grown around James Dean which, almost 50 years after his death at the age of 24, shows no sign of dying out. Like Monroe, he is still big business. People who have never seen his films buy posters and other memorabilia of him because he represents youth, rebellion and charisma.

In real life, Dean rebelled against the straitjacket that Hollywood tried to put him into; he would not conform to the image-makers' idea of what a Hollywood star should be, and in this he was just like his great hero, Marlon Brando. Dean's style is similar to Brando's except it is even more mannered, boyish and self-conscious. But he had tremendous screen presence, and an ability to dominate the screen space and force the audience to look at him.

All actors are narcissistic, but Dean seemed to have narcissism to excess. The need to display himself and his emotions on screen was

BELOW *Method actor Montgomery Clift starred with Eve Marie Saint in the Civil War epic* Raintree County *(1957).*

LEFT *"You're tearing me apart!" screams Dean at his father. Sal Mineo played another teenager with extreme angst in the 1955* Rebel Without a Cause.

BELOW *James Dean in a convincing role as Jet Rink with co-star Elizabeth Taylor, and squaring up to Rock Hudson in* Giant *(1956), the last movie Dean completed before his death in a car accident.*

overwhelming, whatever he might have said about remaining a private person. But he did acknowledge that acting was about an actor's inner fantasies: "My neuroticism manifests itself in the dramatic. Why do most actors act? To express the fantasies in which they have involved themselves." Dean's talent lay in his power to involve mass audiences in those inner fantasies.

He had made only three major films by the time of his death: *East of Eden* and *Rebel Without a Cause* (both 1955) and *Giant* (1956). In *East of Eden* he played Cal Trask, the moody, disaffected son of Adam Trask, played by Raymond Massey.

Elia Kazan directed the movie and has written about how Dean's improvisatory style irritated Massey, who was of the old school of actors, believing in knowing your lines and your moves. In one famous scene in the movie, Dean throws his arms around Massey's neck, imploring him to say that he (his father) loves him. This had not been rehearsed and completely threw Massey, although the scene as it was shot remains in the film. Kazan admits that he used the antagonism between Dean and Massey to generate on-screen tension – in fact, he surreptitiously encouraged it between the two stars. *Rebel Without a Cause* had Dean as a

disturbed high-school teenager on the verge of becoming a fully developed teenage delinquent – largely because of the lack of love and stability in his home life. Although Natalie Wood and Sal Mineo form a kind of substitute family, Dean completely dominates. Nicholas Ray, the director, privileged him by allowing him to steal scenes and placing him in the dominating space on the screen. Dean in this persona, and in his playing of Cal Trask, seemed to encapsulate a rebellious attitude among America's youth that was to boil over into the mass protests of the 1960s.

Giant was his last film (only *East of Eden* had been released by the time of his death). In it he co-starred with Rock Hudson and Elizabeth Taylor, playing another outsider part: Jet Rink, the penniless orphan who becomes an oil millionaire. His hesitant style suited the young Jet Rink, but when he had to age in the latter parts of the movie, his lack of technique showed through and his acting is almost amateurish.

On September 30, 1955, Dean was killed while driving his Porsche along a Californian highway. He died a death that fed the legend of the rebel who lived for kicks, speed and fighting adult hypocrisy and conformity. The myths grew around him: was he homosexual or bisexual? Was his death an accident or was he murdered by proxy by Rock Hudson, a one-time lover? Truth never mixes well with legend, so it is unlikely we will ever know the real James Dean. The only Dean that really counts is the one who appeared in those three films, but the cultists want much more than that from this icon of the cinema. The Dean legend represents something meaningful to millions of people, and shows no sign of disappearing from our culture.

95

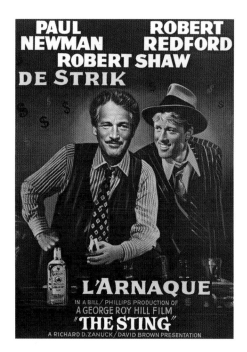

ABOVE *Paul Newman and Robert Redford teamed up very successfully as conmen in* The Sting *(1970), which was a box-office hit.*

PAUL NEWMAN (b. 1925)

At the beginning of his career Paul Newman was accused of copying Brando, but he went on to become a superstar in his own right. His first success was playing an inarticulate boxer in *Somebody Up There Likes Me*, and he followed that by playing Billy the Kid in Arthur Penn's *The Left-Handed Gun*, a western that aimed to demythologize cowboy legends. Newman's sensitive style suited his roles in *Cat on a Hot Tin Roof* and *The Hustler*, but was less successful in comedies such as *Lady L* and *The Secret War of Harry Frigg*.

Of the new breed of actor, Newman was always more macho than the rest, notably in *Hud, Hombre* and *Cool Hand Luke*. He had great success in the 1970s with *Butch Cassidy and the Sundance Kid* and *The Sting*. He also turned to directing, including directing his wife Joanne Woodward in *Rachel Rachel*.

His pursuits in real life include liberal politics, and these liberal sentiments are reflected in some of his movies: *WUSA, Absence of Malice* and *The Verdict*. He has accepted the aging process gracefully and played roles accordingly: in *Harry and Son, The Color of Money, Blaze, The Hudsucker Proxy, Nobody's Fool* and *Road to Perdition*. He is quoted as being sick of morons coming up to him and asking him to remove his dark glasses so they can see his steely blue eyes. He has always fought against being stereotyped as a romantic leading man.

DUSTIN HOFFMAN (b. 1937)

Hoffmann became a star with his role as an unsure young man eaten up by Mrs Robinson in *The Graduate* (1967). Other notable parts have been in *Midnight Cowboy, Little Big Man, Kramer vs Kramer, Tootsie* and *Rain Man*. Hoffman obviously prides himself on the range of roles he has attempted; he has also appeared in overtly violent movies (*Straw Dogs, Papillon* and *Marathon Man*), but he basically always plays the decent individual with doubts and inadequacies struggling against a cruel and indifferent world. He returns to the stage from time to time and appeared in the film version of David Mamet's play *American Buffalo*. In the late 1980s and 90s he made some poor films such as *Family Business, Outbreak* and *Sphere*. He has a reputation for being "difficult", but that probably arises

ABOVE *Dustin Hoffmann had a major success playing the character of Ratso in John Schlesinger's movie about New York low life,* Midnight Cowboy *(1969).*

from his obsession with getting things right on screen. During the making of *Marathon Man* he so exasperated Laurence Olivier with his detailed Method-style preparation for a scene that Olivier finally declared, "Why don't you just try acting?"

BELOW *Sean Penn and Michael J. Fox starred in the Vietnam movie* Casualties of War, *directed by Brian De Palma.*

ABOVE *Matt Damon has proved himself an actor of some depth in movies such as* Good Will Hunting *and* The Talented Mr Ripley.

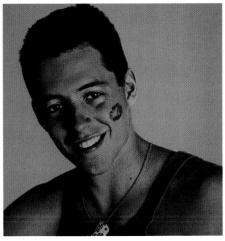

ABOVE *Matthew Broderick as he appeared in* Biloxi Blues. *Broderick plays contemporary good guys and has a likeable screen presence.*

ABOVE *Johnny Depp as the legendary worst director of all time, Ed Wood, in the 1994 movie of the same name directed by Tim Burton.*

JOHN CUSACK (b. 1966)

Cusack seems to care more than most Hollywood actors about the roles he is willing to take on. As a rule he avoids macho, violent roles and prefers playing ambivalent parts such as his characters in *The Grifters, Grosse Pointe Blank, The Thin Red Line, Being John Malkovich* and *Pushing Tin*. He scored another success in *High Fidelity* (2000). He is definitely one of the more intelligent of the younger breed of Hollywood actors.

SEAN PENN (b. 1960)

Penn was one of the group of young Hollywood actors who graduated in the early 1980s from movies such as *Taps, Fast Times at Ridgemont High, Bad Boys* and *Racing with the Moon* to more adult roles. He occasionally plays the heavy as in De Palma's *Casualties of War*, or self-destructive hedonists as in *Carlito's Way*. He was memorable in *Dead Man Walking* and *Hurly Burly*, and played against type as a jazz guitarist in *Sweet and Lowdown*. He has directed three movies: *The Indian Runner, The Crossing Guard* and *The Pledge*. His public pronouncements often come over as arrogant and dismissive, but the man has talent – although playing a mentally deficient father in *My Name is Sam* constituted a major error in judgement and taste on his part.

MATT DAMON (b. 1970)

Damon is a talented actor of intelligence and versatility. He came to the fore with *Good Will Hunting*, for which he wrote the screenplay. He then appeared in *Saving Private Ryan* and memorably in *The Talented Mr Ripley*, a remake of the classic French thriller, *Plein Soleil*. It is apt that Redford choose Damon to star in *The Legend of Bagger Vance*, the movie about golf that Redford directed in 2000; Damon does not have the young Redford's matinée idol looks, but he has something of the same screen presence about him. Unlike many of his Hollywood contemporaries, Damon seems willing to take on unglamorous roles, and his career should continue to prosper.

MATTHEW BRODERICK (b. 1962)

Broderick came to the fore with the 1986 hit *Ferris Bueller's Day Off*. He followed that up with *Biloxi Blues* and *Glory*. He starred opposite Brando in *The Freshman* and Jim Carrey in *The Cable Guy*. His niche part is the decent guy facing life's problems with a puzzled but honourable attitude.

BRAD PITT (b. 1963)

Fans of the television series *Dallas* will probably remember Pitt appearing in a few episodes of the soap, but it was with his small part in *Thelma and Louise* that he really came to prominence. Redford chose him to play the self-destructive brother in *A River Runs Through It*, then he played a psychotic killer in *Kalifornia*. Appearing in Tarantino's *True Romance* helped to consolidate his growing cult status and then *Legends of the Fall, Seven, Twelve Monkeys* and *Sleepers* all proved beneficial to his career. He was major box-office, but that did not prevent the failure of *Meet Joe Black* and *Seven Years in Tibet*. *Fight Club* and *Snatch* provided two more macho roles.

BELOW *Brad Pitt has shown he can act in Redford's* A River Runs Through It *and* Legends of the Fall.

97

THE COMEDY STARS

LEFT *Charlie Chaplin in his classic "Chaplin" persona in* The Gold Rush *(1925): the bowler hat, the cane and the baggy trousers.*

was a cinematic phenomenon, and however opinions diverge about his worth as a performer and director, his fame illustrates how cinema is a worldwide form of communication that crosses barriers of language and culture.

W.C. FIELDS (1879–1946)

Fields played misogynistic braggarts and cheats, who viewed the world cynically and through a whisky bottle. He communicated his dislike for women and children in his "act", which almost certainly owed a great deal to the real-life Fields. His comic appearance with that bulbous, whisky-red nose meant that he could never play for pathos although,

ABOVE *Charlie Chaplin starred with his then-wife Paulette Goddard in* The Great Dictator *(1940), a satire on Hitler. Chaplin's left-wing political views eventually brought him into hot water with the US authorities, and his American passport was withdrawn in the 1950s.*

CHARLIE CHAPLIN (1889–1977)

The little man with the baggy pants and bowler hat became one of the icons of the cinema. However, opinions divide over Chaplin, and I find myself having to admit that I find his movies unfunny. They are also spoiled by a gross sentimentality. But there is no denying Chaplin's fame and popularity. Early movies such as *The Tramp*, *The Pawnshop* and *Easy Street* established him as a major star and *The Kid*, *The Gold Rush*, *The Circus* and *City Lights* are perceived as masterpieces by Chaplin fans. In the 1930s *Modern Times* and *The Great Dictator* showed Chaplin's brand of sentimental liberal politicizing, and it was this aspect of his work that gave ammunition to reactionaries in America who demanded that his passport be withdrawn until he could prove his "moral worth".

Monsieur Verdoux (1947), perhaps Chaplin's best film, was followed by *Limelight* (1952), *A King in New York* (1957) and *A Countess from Hong Kong* (1967). Finally, Hollywood "forgave" Chaplin and awarded him a special Oscar in 1972. "Charlie Chaplin"

ABOVE *W.C. Fields played the Great McGonigle in* The Old Fashioned Way *(1934).*

unlike Chaplin, he was temperamentally unwilling to milk tears anyway. His biggest successes were *The Old Fashioned Way, It's a Gift, David Copperfield* (as Mr Micawber), *Poppy, You Can't Cheat an Honest Man, My Little Chickadee, The Bank Dick* and *Never Give a Sucker an Even Break.* His alcoholism caught up with him on Christmas Day, 1946.

RIGHT *W.C. Fields was the ultimate cynical funny man in* Never Give a Sucker an Even Break.

LEFT *Laurel and Hardy are for many fans the greatest of the movie clowns. Indeed, their fans are among the most loyal of all in the movie world, despite the fact that the duo ceased making movies almost half a century ago.*

GROUCHO MARX (1890–1977)

The only one of the Marx Brothers really to count, it was Groucho who gave the brothers class and wit in movies such as *Animal Crackers, Monkey Business, Horse Feathers, Duck Soup, A Night at the Opera, A Day at the Races* and *Room Service.* His best partner in comedy was the mountainous matron, Margaret Dumont, whom Groucho systematically insulted. Irretrievably sexist, Groucho still managed to be funny and sharp. His trademarks were a painted-on moustache, heavy eyebrows, steel-rimmed spectacles, a cigar and a mad, crouching walk. He was a verbal and physical clown whose humour depended on elaborate wordplay and puns. Perhaps it was this aspect of his clowning that gained him intellectual fans, including T.S. Eliot, with whom he conducted a long correspondence: "Marry me and I'll never look at another horse!"

BOB HOPE (1903–2003)

At the peak of his career Bob Hope was among the biggest box-office stars, especially in the series of *Road* movies he made with Bing Crosby.

Paramount made a mint out of these (which included *Road to Singapore, Road to Zanzibar, Road to Morocco, Road to Utopia*). Other Hope hits were *The Cat and the Canary, The Ghost Breakers, My Favorite Blonde, Monsieur Beaucaire, The Paleface* and *The Lemon Drop Kid.*

His screen persona was based on a cowardly and rather narcissistic nincompoop, always falling for Crosby's streetwise ruses and seldom getting the girl.

As his films deteriorated in the late 1950s and 60s, he turned more and more to television. He also became extremely reactionary in his politics and was associated with jingoistic tours of Vietnam. But Hope was also something of a national institution and the resident White House clown.

ABOVE *Bob Hope was one of the biggest stars of the 1940s and 50s. Here he plays his usual coward in the spoof western* Alias Jesse James (1959).

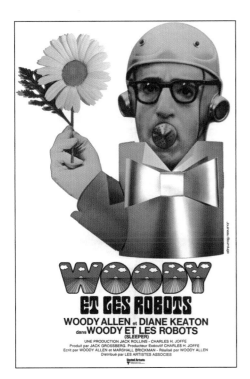

ABOVE Sleeper (1973) is Woody Allen's spoof sci-fi movie. Allen is still churning out a movie a year, but they now have a more tired feel to them.

WOODY ALLEN (b. 1935)

Allen could have appeared in the section on directors because he has directed and written most of his most important films. However, he is best known in the public mind as a performer in worldly New York comedies such as *Play It Again, Sam, Annie Hall, Manhattan, Stardust Memories, Broadway Danny Rose, The Purple Rose of Cairo* and *Radio Days*. In the 1990s he directed *Husbands and Wives, Manhattan Murder Mystery, Bullets Over Broadway, Mighty Aphrodite, Everyone Says I Love You, Deconstructing Harry, Celebrity* and *Sweet and Lowdown*. Allen keeps making movies but even his most ardent fans must detect a falling away in quality. This was confirmed by the feeble *Small Time Crooks* (2000).

For his humour he leans heavily on his Jewish background and his show-business career. His obsessions are death, sex, potency, his looks and his Jewishness. Allen started in stand-up comedy and those origins are reflected in the one-liners that pepper his scripts. There is a knowing, self-conscious quality to the writing that flatters the audience who congratulate themselves on picking up the Freudian or cultural references. He has also directed "serious" movies such as *Interiors* and *September*, which are very much influenced by his cinematic hero, Swedish director Ingmar Bergman.

Woody Allen divides people like few other performers: if you are an Allen fan, you tend to be a devotee who becomes boring after a while recounting favourite bits from the movies; if you're not, you can't see what all the fuss is about. His view of life? "I don't believe in an after-life, but I'm bringing along a change of underwear."

STEVE MARTIN (b. 1945)

Graduating from stand-up comedy and television's *Saturday Night Live*, Martin did not take long to establish himself as one of Hollywood's top comic actors. *The Jerk* (1979) featured one of his comic personas, the hopeless naive adrift in a knowing world. *Dead Men Don't Wear Plaid* was a clever parody of detective *film noir* and

ABOVE Dean Martin and Jerry Lewis formed a highly successful comedy team in the 1940s and 50s before an acrimonious split. Thereafter Lewis's career spiralled downwards, whilst Martin's zoomed upwards.

BELOW The Secret Life of Walter Mitty is one of Danny Kaye's most enduringly popular movies. Kaye was a great favourite on screen for many years – an inspired clown who too often fell back on pathos in his later years.

ABOVE *Steve Martin had a huge success with* The Man with Two Brains *(1983), a story about a world-famous surgeon who invented screw-top, zip-lock brain surgery.*

Roxanne a reworking of *Cyrano de Bergerac.* He starred with Michael Caine in *Dirty Rotten Scoundrels* as a con man. But not all of Martin's choices of work have been wise: why remake the 1950 *Father of the Bride* with himself in the Spencer Tracy role and then follow it up with a feeble sequel? Martin is, however, an actor who can play "serious", as he showed in *Grand Canyon* and *The Spanish Prisoner.* *Bowfinger* marked a return to comic form, but a remake of the Jack Lemmon movie *The Out-of-Towners* smacked of desperation.

JIM CARREY (b. 1962)

A Canadian, Carrey is "funny in his bones", but too often the movies he makes fail to exploit his undoubted talents. He made his breakthrough with *Ace Ventura: Pet Detective* (1994), and followed that with *The Mask* and the gross-out comedy *Dumb and Dumber.* His humour is too often scatological and tends to the juvenile, which is a pity because he is a genuinely funny guy. He made a second *Ace Ventura* movie, *When Nature Calls* and then tried a change of style

and pace in *The Cable Guy*, in which he played a sinister television installer who gradually impacts big time on a customer's life. In that movie and perhaps also in *Liar, Liar* and *The Truman Show*, Carrey is more than hinting at the latent aggression that many comedians have towards their potential audiences. He received high praise for his performance in *The Truman Show* and it would not be surprising if he attempted more straight roles in the future, as he is basically a very competent actor as well as a natural clown.

MIKE MYERS (b. 1963)

Myers, like Jim Carrey, is a Canadian (perhaps you need a well-developed sense of humour to live in Canada). He too emerged from the US television show *Saturday Night Live*, in which he and Dana Carvey created *Wayne's World*, a very knowing spoof of teen rock programmes. They transferred that show to the big screen in 1992 and it was a gigantic hit. On the back of that success, he made *So I Married an Axe Murderer* and then inevitably *Wayne's World 2*. However, Myers really hit the big time with the first *Austin Powers* movie in 1997. This spoof of James Bond and other 1960s culture icons was a surprise megahit. The first movie was very knowing and relatively amusing, but the later sequels were feeble in comparison.

ABOVE *Jim Carrey's career took off with the* Ace Ventura *movies. He has since proved himself a competent actor in movies such as* The Truman Show *(1998).*

In Hollywood, the danger is that you can sometimes be too successful so that you go on churning out what has made you hugely popular in the first place – and that usually spells artistic death. If Myers wants to exploit his comic talents – and he is a funny man – then he will have to leave *Austin Powers* behind him and try to expand his comic range.

BELOW *Mike Myers reached new heights with the* Austin Powers *movies. A talented man, Myers has to beware of pandering to easy laughs and the lowest common denominator.*

THE GLAMOUR QUEENS

In the heyday of Hollywood, female stars usually had to conform to a stereotyped image of female beauty as defined by men. Hopefully, the pressure on contemporary actresses to present a manufactured glamour image is now less intense – witness stars such as Kathleen Turner and Glenn Close. In the days of old Hollywood, however, there were many contenders for the role of glamour queen or sex object.

JEAN HARLOW (1911–37)

Harlow is one of the prime candidates for the dubious honour of being the all-time Hollywood victim. She died at the age of 26, after a short but highly successful career playing blondes-on-the-make. Harlow was one of Howard Hughes's "starlets" – in other words, one of his mistresses whose careers he boosted. She had little acting talent but came over on the screen as a brash, vulgar but determined young woman.

   She co-starred with Cagney in *The Public Enemy*, then she became the *Platinum Blonde*. MGM bought up her contract and with them she made *Red Dust*, *Dinner at Eight*, *Reckless* and *Saratoga*. Her marriage to Paul Bern, MGM executive, landed her in scandal: Bern, shortly after their marriage, either shot himself because he was impotent or was murdered by a former woman friend. Harlow's frenetic existence came to an end in 1937 when she died of uremic poisoning. Known as the "blonde bombshell", Harlow discovered the hard way – as many other female stars of her type did – that notoriety and stardom have their own price tag. She is sometimes likened to Monroe, but she seldom revealed the vulnerability that was a Monroe trademark. No doubt in real life Harlow had her vulnerable side, but her public image never allowed her to reveal that side of herself. She was hard-boiled right up until her premature end.

ABOVE *Jean Harlow in a typically would-be glamorous pose. The actress was the USA's pre-eminent sex symbol in the mid-1930s.*

104

MAE WEST (1892–1980)

Of all the manufactured female sex objects, Mae West was the most self-conscious and processed. Both a sex symbol and a parody of a sex object, West appealed to a wide spectrum of audience. Her forte was the unsubtle double entendre such as "Is that a gun in your pocket or are you just glad to see me?" Lines like that made West notorious and helped give ammunition to the Legion of Decency and other vigilante censorship groups to clamp down on Hollywood licentiousness. She looked like a man in drag, presenting a grossly stereotypical image of what passed for female sexuality. But she knew what she was doing and was no dumb blonde, writing her own scripts and proving herself to be an expert self-publicist and businesswoman. Her films include *She Done Him Wrong* (1933), *I'm No Angel* (1933), *Belle of*

ABOVE *"Why don't you come up sometime 'n' see me? I'm home every evening." Mae West was, for many, like a male drag queen and had as much sex appeal as a cabbage, but for some time she was portrayed as a sex*

the Nineties (1934), *Klondike Annie* (1936) and *My Little Chickadee* (1940). She made a late and disastrous appearance in the dire *Myra Breckinridge* (1970), and died at the age of 88 in 1980.

RITA HAYWORTH (1918–87)

Hayworth could be seen as another victim of the Hollywood system. When she said that the years that she was married to Orson Welles were the happiest of her life, Welles replied that, if that was her idea of happiness, what must the rest of her life have been like? But in the 1940s Hayworth became the glamour queen, enduring painful transformations of her appearance to reach the standard of Hollywood glamour that her studio bosses demanded.

Her best films were *Cover Girl*, *Gilda* and *The Lady from Shanghai*, the latter directed by husband Orson Welles who dyed her hair blonde and made her portray a duplicitous femme fatale. In 1949 Hayworth married Prince Aly Khan, a Muslim leader-cum-playboy, but they were divorced in 1953. In the 1950s her most notable films were *Miss Sadie Thompson*, *Salome*, *Pal Joey* and *Separate Tables*. Alzheimer's Disease came to her at the early age of 62; for the last few years of her life she had to be cared for like a baby.

RIGHT *Lana Turner was an actress of extremely limited talent who survived scandal – including being involved in the stabbing of her lover – to be an enduring top star. She starred with top male star Clark Gable in the 1941* Honky Tonk.

LEFT *Rita Hayworth was a manufactured screen beauty who underwent excruciating treatment to fashion her to studio boss Harry Cohn's ideal of female beauty.*

LANA TURNER (1920–95)

Turner was another totally manufactured Hollywood glamour object. Rarely was she ever anything other than wooden in her roles, but she did achieve some credibility as an actress in *The Bad and the Beautiful* and *Imitation of Life*. Earlier films included *Ziegfeld Girl*, *Dr Jekyll and Mr Hyde*, *The Postman Always Rings Twice* and *The Three Musketeers*. Even the legend of her so-called discovery at Schwab's Drugstore on Sunset Boulevard has been exposed as a manufactured myth dreamed up by some cynical agent.

Her early film career prospered with her label as the "Sweater Girl" and she acquired husbands at a rate of knots: seven in all, including Artie Shaw the bandleader, and Lex Barker, one of many screen Tarzans. In 1958 she was involved in a steamy scandal when her 14-year-old daughter

ABOVE *Hedy Lamarr was a very beautiful Austrian-born actress who was defined as a star by her stunning looks.*

RIGHT *Jane Russell adorns the front cover of a French fan magazine. This was important exposure for the top female stars.*

stabbed to death her lover, a Mafia hood. Her career survived and even thrived on the notoriety. But parts eventually ran out for an aging glamour queen with few acting resources to fall back on in her old age.

JANE RUSSELL (b. 1921)

"Discovered" by Howard Hughes, Russell survived the furore surrounding her debut in *The Outlaw* to show, in some movies, that she was more than a male fantasy

object. Her best films were *Macao* and *Gentlemen Prefer Blondes*. In later life Russell found God, perhaps as a response to the crudeness with which

> "I HAVE DECIDED THAT WHILE I AM A STAR, I WILL BE EVERY INCH AND EVERY MOMENT THE STAR. EVERYONE FROM THE STUDIO GATEMAN TO THE HIGHEST EXECUTIVE WILL KNOW IT."
> GLORIA SWANSON

Hollywood marketed her shape in movies such as *Double Dynamite*, *The French Line* and *Underwater!*

AVA GARDNER (1922–90)

Carrying the burden of the tag of the "world's most beautiful woman" could not have been easy, but Gardner appeared to be quite a tough cookie until her later years, when the ravages of alcohol and burning the candle at both ends finally took their toll with her premature death at the age of 67 in 1990. Along the way she survived marriages to Artie Shaw, Mickey Rooney and Frank Sinatra. Gardner was never a great actress, but

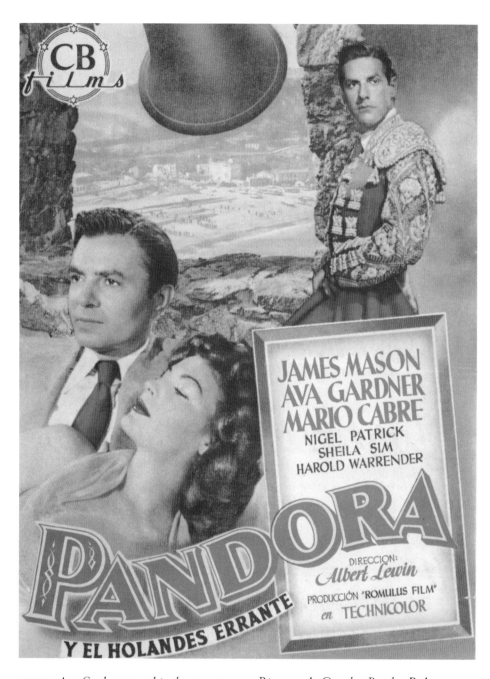

JAMES MASON
AVA GARDNER
MARIO CABRE
NIGEL PATRICK
SHEILA SIM
HAROLD WARRENDER

PANDORA
Y EL HOLANDES ERRANTE

DIRECCIÓN:
Albert Lewin

PRODUCCIÓN "ROMULUS FILM"
en TECHNICOLOR

ABOVE *Ava Gardner starred in the strange, portentous melodrama* Pandora and the Flying Dutchman *(1951) with British co-star James Mason.*

she had a certain screen quality of warmth mixed with resilience that went beyond mere beauty. After serving her time in a succession of minor movies, she finally made the big time with the role as Kitty in *The Killers* playing opposite Burt Lancaster. In the 1950s, major film followed major film: *Show Boat, Pandora and the Flying Dutchman, The Snows of Kilimanjaro, Mogambo, The Barefoot Contessa, Bhowani Junction, The Sun Also*

Rises and *On the Beach*. Roles were harder to come by in the 1960s and 70s, but she did continue to work right into the 80s. Gardner was undoubtedly a product of the Hollywood glamour machine and, as such, she was never allowed to show whether she was a more capable actress than her limited roles suggested.

ELIZABETH TAYLOR (b. 1932)

At the height of her career Taylor was the highest-paid star of them all. Born in England of American parents, she joined MGM as a child star and appeared in *Lassie Come Home* and

National Velvet during World War II. Graduating to adult parts, she was dubbed the screen's most beautiful woman and starred in *A Place in the Sun* (1951), *Giant* (1956), *Cat on a Hot Tin Roof* (1958) and *Butterfield 8* (1960). The ponderous epic *Cleopatra* (1963) almost bankrupted 20th Century Fox, partly because of the long delays caused by her ill health. During the shooting of the movie, she began an affair with Richard Burton, whom she subsequently married (twice). Taylor and Burton became the most famous Hollywood show-business couple since Fairbanks and Pickford, earning huge salaries for appearing in some worthless movies (although exceptions included *Who's Afraid of Virginia Woolf?* and *The Taming of the Shrew*), and indulging in conspicuous consumption that merely added to their rather tawdry public image.

BELOW *Grace Kelly was famous as the ice-cool, upper-class blonde. Hitchcock used her in three movies:* Rear Window, Dial M for Murder *and* To Catch a Thief.

After her relationship with Burton finally ended, Taylor's career nose-dived, and recent years have seen her more in the news for her fight against alcoholism, her recovery from a brain tumour and her Aids charity work than for her acting career. But whatever estimation might be made of her abilities, it cannot be denied that she is nothing if not resilient.

SHARON STONE (b. 1958)

Stone shot to notoriety when she appeared in *Basic Instinct* (1992). A former model, she has perhaps suffered from the expectation that all she has to offer is Hollywood glamour. However, she has shown that she can act in movies such as *Casino* (for which she was nominated for an Oscar) and *Last Dance* (in which she played a murderer on Death Row). As she gets older, however, she will find it difficult to get roles because of the totally unfair Hollywood practice of assigning erstwhile glamour ladies to oblivion.

BELOW *Sharon Stone is in the tradition of Hollywood glamour stars, but she has tried to break free from that mould in movies such as* Sliver, *in which she played a victim and* Last Dance, *in which she played a murderer.*

ABOVE *A young Elizabeth Taylor poses for the MGM camera. Female stars such as Taylor had thousands of glamorous publicity shots released to the print media.*

THE GOOD JOES

The good joe stars are the "Mr Reliables", the archetypal quietly-spoken heroes who don't make a lot of fuss but who are around to sort everything out when a situation turns nasty.

GARY COOPER (1901–61)

Cooper's screen persona is the straight-down-the-line, on-the-level, slow-talking, slow-burning but

interpreted by many as an anti-McCarthy movie, but if it was, Cooper was unaware of it because he was one of the stars who publicly testified to the Congress investigating committee about alleged Communist infiltration into Hollywood: "From what I hear about Communism, I don't like it because it isn't on the level." But you don't have to be a genius to be a movie star, and there is no doubting Cooper's enduring popularity as a major star. Other notable movies in which he starred include *Meet John Doe, Ball of Fire, Pride of the Yankees, For Whom the Bell Tolls, The Fountainhead* (in which he rather uncharacteristically played a Frank Lloyd Wright-type architect), and *Vera Cruz*. But the enduring memory of "Coop" will be on those empty, lonely streets of the western town in

High Noon, abandoned by all including Grace Kelly playing his wife. However, to the strains of the song "Do not forsake me, oh my darling" on the Tex Ritter soundtrack, Kelly returns to help her husband shoot down the baddies. They don't make 'em like that any more!

JAMES STEWART (1908–97)

Stewart was another slow-speaking, drawling star who played his share of "honest joe" parts, notably in Frank Capra's *Mr Smith Goes to Washington* and *It's a Wonderful Life*. Hitchcock and Anthony Mann were two other directors who played important roles in Stewart's career. Hitchcock used Stewart in *Rope, Rear Window, The Man Who Knew Too Much* and *Vertigo*, while Mann made eight westerns with Stewart, including *Winchester 73* and *The Man from Laramie*. Both these directors gave Stewart the opportunity to play more complex characters than he usually did. John Ford also used Stewart when he needed an actor who could

ABOVE *Gary Cooper was a natural choice to play American heroes. In the 1942* Pride of the Yankees *Cooper appeared as baseball star Lou Gehrig opposite Teresa Wright.*

handsome American good guy. *Mr Deeds Goes to Town*, a Frank Capra-directed fable about how a good joe can melt even Washington's hard heart, typified the Cooper role – an incorruptible, unworldly Mr Average who defeats the crooks in the end by sheer integrity. Cooper was also used in westerns and adventures, such as *The Plainsman, Beau Geste, The Westerner* and *Unconquered*. He was a natural choice for the eponymous World War I hero in *Sergeant York* and won an Oscar for his most famous role as the isolated marshal in *High Noon*,

ABOVE *Hitchcock cast good joe James Stewart as an obsessive voyeur working out his own repressed desire while solving a murder case in* Rear Window *(1954).*

communicate integrity: *Two Rode Together* and *The Man Who Shot Liberty Valance*. Other major movies for Stewart were *The Philadelphia Story, Harvey, Anatomy of a Murder* and *Shenandoah*. He played real-life American heroes in *The Stratton Story, The Glenn Miller Story* and *The Spirit of St Louis* (about the aviator, Charles A. Lindbergh).

HENRY FONDA (1905–82)

Fonda seemed to be first choice for playing presidents, presidential candidates or senators: *Young Mr Lincoln, Advise and Consent, The Best Man* and *Fail-Safe*. He often played the soft-spoken hero who represents American justice and free speech. In *The Grapes of Wrath, The Ox Bow Incident* and *12 Angry Men* he defended the downtrodden, and through his presence signified that the American Way of Life was basically fair and just. He played American heroes such as Frank James, Alexander Graham Bell and Wyatt Earp. Only rarely did he not play the good guy, notably in *Once Upon a Time in the West*. He was rather irascible in his last movie, *On*

Golden Pond, a role perhaps closer to his real-life persona. He gave up Hollywood between 1948 and 1955 and returned to the stage, until the good guy part in *Mister Roberts* drew

ABOVE *Henry Fonda found his quintessential role in Sidney Lumet's 1957 movie* 12 Angry Men. *Fonda plays a man in a cream suit who alone on a jury holds out against a verdict of guilty against a Hispanic youth.*

ABOVE *Spencer Tracy played a no-nonsense priest in* Boys Town *(1938), co-starring with a young Mickey Rooney. The picture was a glutinous mixture of worthiness and sentimentality.*

him back to the screen. While shooting that film, he reputedly had a fist fight with director John Ford. As the actor himself once said, "I'm not really Henry Fonda. Nobody could have that much integrity."

SPENCER TRACY (1900–67)

Solidity was Tracy's trademark – he could always be relied on and trusted. Tracy had a strong screen presence, although his range was limited and he sometimes allowed himself to edge over into sentimentality – for example, in his roles as a priest in *Boys Town, San Francisco* and *Men of Boys Town*. His limitations as an actor were exposed when he played *Dr Jekyll and Mr Hyde*, but he scored in comedies with Katharine Hepburn: *Woman of the Year, State of the Union, Adam's Rib* and *Pat and Mike*. His power was used profitably in *Fury, Northwest Passage* and *The Last Hurrah*. His liberal politics were reflected in some of the movies he made: *Keeper of the Flame* (about American fascism), *Bad Day at Black Rock* (anti-racism), *Inherit the Wind* (anti-religious fundamentalism), *Judgment at Nuremberg* (as a judge of war crimes) and *Guess Who's Coming to Dinner* (as a father coming to terms with his daughter's marrying Sidney Poitier). Tracy was separated for a

long time from his wife and family and had a long relationship with Katharine Hepburn. But the demon drink proved to be his enemy and contributed to his death in 1967.

GREGORY PECK (1916–2003)

Opinions vary about Peck's acting abilities, and in some parts such as Captain Ahab in *Moby Dick* and Scott Fitzgerald in *Beloved Infidel* he was clearly out of his depth. He was at his best in solid, caring roles: as Atticus, the southern lawyer in *To Kill a Mockingbird*, he won an Oscar, and he had other good-guy roles in *The Keys of the Kingdom, The Yearling, Gentleman's Agreement, The Man in the Grey Flannel Suit, The Big Country* and *On the Beach*. He tried to break the heroic pattern by playing villains in *Duel in the Sun*

LEFT Gregory Peck starred in the war yarn adapted from an Alistair MacLean book, The Guns of Navarone. *As a good-guy actor, he is saved from shooting a female traitor by another woman doing the dirty work. Good guys just don't do that kind of thing!*

ABOVE Charlton Heston had a late success in his career with this sci-fi thriller The Omega Man. *When civilization is threatened big time, send for Heston! His latter years have been spent as a spokesman for the National Rifle Association in the USA.*

and *The Boys from Brazil*, and also had his share of romantic lead parts, notably in *Spellbound, David and Bathsheba, The Snows of Kilimanjaro, Roman Holiday* and *Arabesque*. Man-of-action roles have included *The Gunfighter, Captain Horatio Hornblower, Twelve O'Clock High, Pork Chop Hill* and *The Guns of Navarone*. Peck became a pillar of the Hollywood establishment, representing the more liberal side of filmland's politics.

CHARLTON HESTON (b. 1924)

Heston is mainly associated with roles in epics, but basically he played good guys whether he was Moses, Ben-Hur or El Cid. However, Heston took himself very seriously as an actor (witness his autobiography *An Actor's Life*). His career really took off when

111

ABOVE *Sidney Poitier was one of the first of a new generation of black American stars. He rarely strayed from his good-guy screen persona.*

he played Moses in De Mille's *The Ten Commandments* and this was followed by *Ben-Hur, El Cid* and *The Agony and the Ecstasy* (as Michelangelo). Other epic parts included *The War Lord, Khartoum* (as General Gordon) and *55 Days at Peking*. His westerns have included *The Big Country, Major Dundee* and *Will Penny*. Sci-fi roles in *Planet of the Apes, Soylent Green* and *The Omega Man* gave his career a boost, but Shakespearian roles in *Julius Caesar* and *Antony and Cleopatra* failed to make the critics enthuse. In his later years he returned to the stage and dabbled in directing, and even appeared in the television series *The Colbys* for a season. His politics moved from the Democratic Left to becoming a spokesman for the National Rifle Association, defending the right of Americans to own guns and shoot people in defence of their property. In *Bowling for Columbine* (2002) Michael Moore made good use of Heston's confused and simple-minded patriotism to attack those attitudes.

KEVIN COSTNER (b. 1955)

Costner is seen as resembling Stewart and Fonda in his quiet but authoritative style. His first big success was as Eliot Ness in *The Untouchables* (1987) and this was followed by his role as the duplicitous spy in *No Way Out. Field of Dreams* was a Capraesque exercise in nostalgia and down-home American values, but *Revenge* involved Costner in a macho tale of betrayal and bloodletting.

However, it was *Dances with Wolves* (1990) that put the seal of major stardom on Costner's career. Directing this "liberal" reappraisal of the myth of the American frontier and the white man's interaction with Native Americans brought Costner a Best Director Oscar. *Robin Hood, Prince of Thieves* (1991) was also a major box-office success for him and seemed to indicate that he would be a major star for a long time to come. However, his career seemed to falter in the 1990s. *Waterworld* (1995) was a hugely expensive turkey, as was *The Postman* (1997). He clearly likes to portray sportsmen on screen, as *Bull Durham, Tin Cup* and *For Love of the Game* indicate. *13 Days*, about the Cuba crisis, was a change of pace for him, in some ways recalling his role in *JFK* (1991), which Oliver Stone directed.

TOM HANKS (b. 1956)

Hanks is Hollywood's current top "good guy" actor. He can play comedy roles and heavy dramatic parts. The actor he most resembles from old Hollywood is perhaps James Stewart.

His first major success was *Big* (1988) and then he survived *The Bonfire of the Vanities* in which he was woefully miscast. His next big hit was the romantic comedy *Sleepless in Seattle*, which he followed with *Philadelphia*, in which he played a gay man dying of Aids. It is a testimony to changing social attitudes that Hanks could take on this role without harming his career. *Forrest Gump* unaccountably was another major hit for him, as was *Apollo 13* in which he played a good-guy astronaut. He turned writer-director in *That Thing You Do* and then

RIGHT *Tom Hanks is in the mould of James Stewart and Henry Fonda. He had a huge success with the romantic comedy* Sleepless in Seattle *(1993), co-starring Meg Ryan.*

led the cast in Spielberg's *Saving Private Ryan*, an ultimate good-guy role. Other hits for him were the *Toy Story* series, *The Green Mile* and *Cast Away*, but for many critics he was miscast in *Road to Perdition* (2002). Hanks is a talented actor; he deserves credit for some unusual roles but needs to guard against wanting to be liked all of the time.

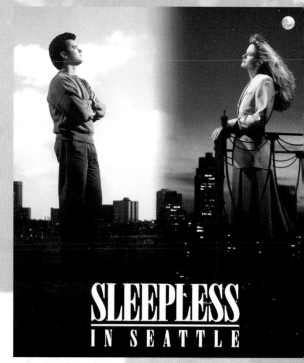

SLEEPLESS IN SEATTLE

BELOW *Kevin Costner starred in and directed* Dances with Wolves *(1990), which won seven Oscars, including Best Picture, Best Director, Best Adapted Screenplay and Best Cinematography.*

113

THE HEAVIES, VILLAINS AND DOWNRIGHT CADS

Baddies come in all shapes and sizes. Sometimes a heavy is not quite a villain – however, a villain is always a villain, whereas a cad may be a villain but he's charming with it. The actors awarded honoured status in this section represent all three categories.

BELA LUGOSI (1882–1956)

Of Hungarian origin, Lugosi was the screen's most famous Dracula in *Dracula* (1931), *Mark of the Vampire* and *The Return of the Vampire*, and also played the monster in *Frankenstein Meets the Wolf Man*. He was typecast in horror movies such as *Murders in the Rue Morgue*, *White Zombie*, *The Raven* and *The Ghost of Frankenstein*. In the

latter part of his career he appeared in spoof versions of the Frankenstein and Dracula legends: *Abbott and Costello Meet Frankenstein*, *Bela Lugosi Meets a Broadway Gorilla* and *Mother Riley Meets the Vampire*. He was played by Martin Landau in the 1994 movie *Ed Wood*, which documented the last months of Lugosi's life, by which time he was penniless, living in an anonymous LA suburb and hopelessly addicted to hard drugs.

BORIS KARLOFF (1887–1969)

Karloff in real life was an Englishman of the old school, a pillar of the 1930s British colony in Hollywood who liked to show the natives how to dress for dinner and how to play cricket.

ABOVE *Three very heavy heavies: Bela Lugosi, Akim Tamiroff and Basil Rathbone, who starred in the 1956 The Black Sleep. Lugosi was the screen's most famous Dracula; Tamiroff was terrific in Welles's Touch of Evil; and Rathbone was a familiar public-school bad guy in Hollywood movies, crossing many a sword with Errol Flynn.*

On screen he was the monster in the 1931 *Frankenstein* and was involved in *The Old Dark House*, *The Mask of Fu Manchu*, *The Mummy*, *The Bride of Frankenstein* and *The Raven*. In the mid-1940s he made three more notable movies: *The Body Snatcher*, *Isle of the Dead* and *Bedlam*. In the 60s he appeared in three Roger Corman spoofs of the horror genre: *The Raven*,

The Terror and *Comedy of Terrors*. In 1968 he made one of his last films and one of his best, *Targets*, which was Peter Bogdanovich's first movie. Karloff was refreshingly modest about his achievements: "You could heave a brick out of the window and hit 10 actors who could play my parts. I just happened to be on the right corner at the right time."

EDWARD G. ROBINSON (1893–1973)

It is probably doing Robinson a disservice to include him in this section, but it is as a movie baddie that he will largely be remembered. The 1931 *Little Caesar* made him a star, and a succession of gangster roles in the 1930s created Robinson's tough-guy screen persona. He was a memorable insurance claims investigator in *Double Indemnity* and, in the 1940s, was more often the good guy in movies such as *The Woman in the Window*, *Scarlet Street* and *The Stranger*. He returned to

playing villains in *Key Largo*, *Black Tuesday*, *The Ten Commandments* (as Dathan), *Seven Thieves* and *Two Weeks in Another Town*. His small stature and menacing looks meant he would never be cast as a hero, but he brought real quality to many of his roles.

ABOVE *Edward G. Robinson was one of the best actors of his generation. In* All My Sons *(1948), adapted from the Arthur Miller play, he was an aeroplane parts manufacturer with a guilty secret. Robinson was a very cultured man in real life, despite the fact that he played so many criminal thugs on screen.*

GEORGE SANDERS (1906–72)

Sanders was the archetypal British cad – smooth, urbane and as trustworthy as a car salesman in Mayfair. He was the cad in *Rebecca*, but then had a saintly spell in *The Saint* and *The Falcon* series. He was the Gauguin figure in *The Moon and Sixpence*, another rotter in *Summer Storm*, *The Picture of Dorian Gray*, *Hangover Square*, *Forever Amber* and, memorably, in *All About Eve* for which he won the Best Supporting Actor Oscar. However, Sanders was never really committed to his profession and used to disparage his work. Perhaps it was not surprising that he took his own life in 1972, writing in his suicide note that he was bored and that he was glad to be leaving "this sweet cesspool that was the world". A cad to the last.

LEFT *George Sanders on the cover of* Picturegoer *in 1946, looking every inch the cad he played in many movies.*

115

LEFT *Sydney Greenstreet made his film debut in* The Maltese Falcon *(1941). Here he discusses the whereabouts of the black bird with Sam Spade (Humphrey Bogart).*

SYDNEY GREENSTREET (1879–1954)

One of the screen's great fat men, Greenstreet's film debut could hardly have been more auspicious: he played the villainous Kasper Guttman in *The Maltese Falcon* (1941). He came up against Bogart again in *Casablanca* and *Passage to Marseilles* and was another heavy in *The Mask of Dimitrios*. None of his later roles brought him similar success, and when he died aged 75 in 1954, he had packed all of his film career into nine years.

CHARLES LAUGHTON (1899–1962)

Laughton certainly played a variety of roles but he was always at his most watchable when he played an over-the-top villain such as Nero in *The Sign of the Cross* (1932), the incestuous Mr Barrett in *The Barretts of Wimpole Street* (1934), Captain Bligh in *Mutiny on the Bounty* (1935), the unrelenting policeman in *Les Misérables* (1935) and the newspaper proprietor in *The Big Clock* (1948). He also played Quasimodo in *The Hunchback of Notre Dame*, a weak but finally courageous schoolteacher in *This Land is Mine* and a wily Roman senator in *Spartacus*. He is remembered as well for his direction

of *The Night of the Hunter*. Married to Elsa Lanchester for years, he was nonetheless seemingly tortured by his homosexuality. For some, Laughton was the epitome of the ham actor; for others a performer of real genius.

PETER LORRE (1904–64)

A Hungarian by birth, Lorre was a star in German movies before moving to Britain and Hollywood. He starred as the child murderer in Fritz Lang's *M* (1930) and was in Hitchcock's *The Man Who Knew Too Much* (1934) and *The Secret Agent* (1936). After starring in a series of eight *Mr Moto* movies playing the Japanese detective, Lorre had a memorable role in *The Maltese Falcon* and a small but significant part in *Casablanca*. His oddball manner and sinister looks were used to effect in *The Mask of Dimitrios* (1944) and *Arsenic and Old Lace* in the same year. He was inevitably used in horror flicks, and one of the best he made was *The Beast with Five Fingers* (1946). The latter part of his career

was filled with parts that parodied his screen persona; he appeared in two Jerry Lewis movies, *The Sad Sack* (1958) and *The Patsy* (1964). Lorre was undoubtedly a better actor than Hollywood allowed him to be, but no self-respecting impersonator does not have Lorre in his repertoire.

VINCENT PRICE (1911–93)

Price was another over-the-top actor who only achieved real fame late in his career in horror films. He was unpleasant in *Laura* (1944) and *The Three Musketeers* (1948) and then appeared in *House of Wax* (1953). *The Bat* and *The Fall of the House of Usher* further enhanced his Grand Guignol screen persona, and these exercises in camp excess were followed by *The Pit and the Pendulum*, *The Raven*, *The Tomb of Ligeia*, *The Abominable Dr Phibes*, *Theatre of Blood* and *Journey into Fear*, as well as numerous others. He brought a quality of high camp to his roles and his performances teetered on the edge of absurdity.

BELOW *Peter Lorre was a familiar criminal in many movies. Here he is being arrested in* Casablanca *while Rick, played by Humphrey Bogart, doesn't lift a finger to save him.*

ROD STEIGER (1925–2002)

"You shoulda looked after me a little, Charlie", complains Brando to Steiger in the famous taxi cab scene in *On the Waterfront*. Steiger's naturalistic acting style, and his tendency to ham, made him one of the best of the 1950s villains in movies such as *Oklahoma!*, *The Harder They Fall* and *Al Capone*. He clearly loved playing Mr Joyboy in *The Loved One* and outacted everyone else in *Doctor Zhivago* as the repellent Komarovsky. He won an Oscar for his bigoted policeman in *In the Heat of the Night* and was a psychopathic killer in *No Way to Treat a Lady*. He played Napoleon in *Waterloo* and Lucky Luciano in the 1973 movie of the same name. His career had its troughs and he certainly made far too many bad movies, but he allowed his talent to shine through in a handful of worthwhile films: *On the Waterfront*, *The Big Knife* (playing a Harry Cohn-type Hollywood producer and eating the scenery in the process), *The Pawnbroker* and *In the Heat of the Night*. A ham or a genius: the jury is divided.

BELOW After making a career for himself playing smooth, rather camp bad guys, Vincent Price made a second career in horror movies, such as this three-tale epic Twice Told Tales *(1963).*

LEE MARVIN (1924–87)

Marvin made his reputation playing psychopathic villains and, even when he was nominally the hero, he always managed to bring an ambiguous quality to his roles. He threw hot coffee in Gloria Grahame's face in *The Big Heat* and was Brando's adversary in *The Wild One*. He was one of the villains in *Bad Day at Black Rock* and Liberty Valance in *The Man Who Shot Liberty Valance*. He won an Oscar for his role as the drunken gunfighter in *Cat Ballou*. Around this time he began to play tough guys with some kind of integrity, as in *The Professionals*, *Point Blank*, *The Dirty Dozen*, *Prime Cut* and

LEFT Rod Steiger could not be accused of not getting his teeth into a part. In The Big Knife *(1955) he played a Harry Cohn-type mogul being very nasty indeed to Jack Palance and Shelley Winters.*

BELOW Lee Marvin had become a the bigger star when Bad Day at Black Rock *was re-released in the late 1950s so, despite his supporting role in the picture, his name was billed above those of the principal actors Spencer Tracy and Robert Ryan.*

Emperor of the North. Off-screen he had a reputation for being a drinker and a wild man; latterly, he seemingly settled down, but perhaps too late to reverse his declining health. He died in 1987 at the age of 62.

117

THE QUEENS OF MELODRAMA

The principal characteristic of melodrama – and screen melodrama in particular – is excess. These five queens of melodrama were adept at unleashing extremes of emotion on the screen. In Hollywood's heyday the performances of actresses such as Bette Davis and Joan Crawford gave the so-called "women's picture" a good name.

BETTE DAVIS (1908–89)

Bette Davis's talents as an actress are debatable, but as a movie star she was undoubtedly effective. Highly mannered if not affected, Davis had her own style – love her or loathe her. Too often, perhaps, she was playing "Bette Davis" or even a parody of that persona, but in some movie roles she was highly successful. For me Barbara Stanwyck was a much better actress than Davis, but there is no doubt that Davis in her heyday was much the more important star.

ABOVE *One of the characteristics of the melodrama/women's picture was that the leading lady had to be sacrificial. In* The Old Maid *(1939) Davis made the sacrifice and was noble; Miriam Hopkins was dislikeable.*

Davis was mostly very effective in "wicked women" roles such as in *The Little Foxes, The Letter, Mr Skeffington, A Stolen Life* and *Whatever Happened to Baby Jane?* She was noble in *Dark Victory, The Old Maid, The Corn is Green* and *Old Acquaintance*. She suffered for love in *Now Voyager* and *Deception*. Her later Grand Guignol roles included *Hush... Hush, Sweet Charlotte* and *The Nanny*.

At the height of her career in the late 1930s and 40s Davis was one of Hollywood's biggest box-office stars. She took on her studio, Warners, over the seven-year contract system and, although she lost the court case, she ultimately helped to free movie actors from that form of bonded slavery. Always independent and forceful, she acquired a reputation for being difficult, which may have contributed to the fact that her career in the 1950s suddenly went into decline, so much so that she had to put an advertisement in *The Hollywood Reporter* announcing that she needed work. Her most famous role

> "WHEN I SAW MY FIRST FILM TEST, I RAN FROM THE PROJECTION ROOM SCREAMING."
> BETTE DAVIS

LEFT *One of the Bette Davis's biggest movies was* Now Voyager *(1942). Remember Paul Henreid and his two cigarettes: "We have the stars, let's not reach for the moon." Oh, sacrifice again!*

may be Margo Channing in *All About Eve*, a movie in which she utters the immortal line, "Fasten your seatbelts, it's going to be a bumpy night." Most impersonators of stars can do a passable Bette Davis: that throaty New England voice with its cutting edge, those large eyes and the exaggerated inhaling of a cigarette. Her style was the opposite of naturalistic acting – with Davis, there was always a performance going on.

JOAN CRAWFORD (1904–77)

Another great "sufferer" was Crawford, but only in the latter part of her long film career. Christened Lucille Le Sueur, Crawford was cast as a "flapper" in her early film parts, and some misguided studio executives thought she could dance. In the 1930s and early 40s she made eight mostly forgettable films with Clark Gable. Her archetypal roles were as the ambitious stenographer in *Grand Hotel* and as Sadie Thompson in *Rain*. Whereas Davis was mostly playing society ladies, Crawford played shop girls and typists. When MGM dropped her in the 1940s she signed a new contract with Warners and came into her own as Davis's chief rival in the melodrama stakes. Movies such as *Mildred Pierce, Humoresque, Possessed, Daisy Kenyon, Sudden Fear, Torch Song* and *Autumn Leaves* had her suffering at the hands of her husbands, lovers, children and society in general. Her screen persona lent itself more to "victim" roles than Davis's, but

ABOVE *Joan Crawford worked very hard at being Joan Crawford. Here she adorns the cover of a 1941 issue of* Picturegoer.

Crawford, with a limited range of acting ability, still managed to project a powerful screen image.

Off-screen, Crawford built up a reputation for her ruthless pursuit of success and cleanliness. As her screen career wilted, she married a PepsiCola executive and the soft drink manufacturer had to defend itself from the attentions of the widow when her executive husband died. Her adopted daughter wrote a damning account of her as a mother in *Mommie Dearest*, which was later filmed with Faye Dunaway as Crawford. Crawford and Davis co-starred in *Whatever Happened to Baby Jane?*, in one scene of which Davis pushes Crawford, crippled in a wheelchair, down a staircase. It was a case of Hollywood feeding off its own legends again. Crawford symbolized that desperate hunger for Hollywood success that characterizes many stars.

"THE PUBLIC LIKES PROVOCATIVE FEMININE PERSONALITIES BUT IT ALSO LIKES TO KNOW THAT, UNDERNEATH IT ALL, THE ACTRESSES ARE LADIES."
JOAN CRAWFORD

INGRID BERGMAN (1915–82)

A Swedish actress, Bergman made her first Hollywood film *Intermezzo* with Leslie Howard in 1939, and became Hollywood's top female star in the 1940s. *Casablanca* opposite Bogart cast her again as a woman destined to end up suffering for love, as did *For Whom the Bell Tolls*, *Spellbound* and *Notorious*, the latter two directed by Alfred Hitchcock. She also suffered in *Dr Jekyll and Mr Hyde*, *Gaslight*, *Joan of Arc* and *Under Capricorn*. Then she had a real-life affair with Italian director Roberto Rossellini, who was married at the time, as was Bergman. She had Rossellini's child (Roberto Guisto Giuseppe) and scandalized hypocritical Hollywood. She made a series of films with Rossellini (*Stromboli*, *Europa '51*, *We the Women*) before returning to a contrite Hollywood who rewarded her with an Oscar for her role in *Anastasia*. She had further successes with *Indiscreet* and *The Inn of the Sixth Happiness* but her great days at the box office were over. Late in her career she made *Autumn Sonata* (1978), directed by

BELOW *Ingrid Bergman featured on another* Picturegoer *cover from 1941. Bergman broke the mould of Hollywood beauties with a more natural and less manufactured look.*

ABOVE *Gene Tierney (1920–91) communicated a kind of edgy, neurotic quality on the screen and she suffered from psychological problems off-screen as well. Some of her best films include* Laura *(1944),* Dragonwyck *(1946),* The Razor's Edge *(1946) and* Whirlpool *(1949).*

Ingmar Bergman, and she revealed what she might have achieved if her Hollywood roles had been more consistently worthwhile. Bergman had a beauty that escaped Hollywood stereotyping and a quality of "goodness" that illuminated her roles.

BARBARA STANWYCK (1907–90)

Stanwyck was more working class in origin and manner than Davis or Crawford. She also employed an iciness in her screen portrayals that the other two could not match. Her greatest role was in *Double Indemnity* as Phyllis Dietrichson, the femme fatale who snares insurance salesman Walter Neff, played by normally "good guy" actor, Fred MacMurray, in

her murderous plans. Stanwyck and MacMurray deserve to be as famous for those roles as Bogart and Bergman are for *Casablanca*.

Other archetypal Stanwyck roles were in *Stella Dallas* (as a sacrificial mother), *The Lady Eve, Ball of Fire, The Strange Love of Martha Ivers, The Two Mrs Carrolls* and *Sorry, Wrong Number*. She lost Fred MacMurray to Joan Bennett in Douglas Sirk's *There's Always Tomorrow* and must have known her screen career was on the wane when she starred with Elvis Presley in *Roustabout*. However, her television series *The Big Valley* was a success in the 1960s and she later co-starred with Richard Chamberlain in *The Thorn Birds*. A very underrated actress, Stanwyck had tremendous power on screen and this despite her quite ordinary looks. She was married to Robert Taylor, considered by some to be a glamour boy, for a number of years. She was known as a Hollywood professional who never threw a tantrum and just got on with her job.

BELOW *Barbara Stanwyck was in many people's opinions the best actress of her generation. Here she is in the 1937 version of the creaky melodrama* Stella Dallas. *She had a tremendous talent for suddenly upping the emotional stakes and reaching a state of hysterical emotion in a matter of seconds.*

FAYE DUNAWAY (b. 1941)

Dunaway is a contemporary star with something of the Davis–Crawford "over-the-top" style. Indeed, she played Joan Crawford in an unintentionally hilarious "biopic" of the old-time star, *Mommie Dearest* (1981). She came to stardom in *Bonnie and Clyde* and followed this up by playing opposite Steve McQueen in the ultra-smooth *The Thomas Crown Affair*. After that, her career seemed to mark time until she made *Chinatown*, *Three Days of the Condor*, *Network* and *Mommie Dearest*. Dunaway has always played the star off-screen as well, which is in itself a throwback to the old days of Hollywood. She has found it hard to sustain her box-office appeal, however, and satisfactory roles have been few and far between in the 1990s and early 2000s, but she resurfaced briefly in the weak remake of *The Thomas Crown Affair* (1999) and in a small part in *The Rules of Attraction* (2002).

ABOVE *Ronald Reagan's first wife, Jane Wyman (b. 1914) won an Oscar for playing a deaf mute in* Johnny Belinda *(1948), then Douglas Sirk used her in two of his best melodramas,* Magnificent Obsession *(1954) and* All That Heaven Allows *(1955).*

BELOW *Faye Dunaway can be likened to the old Hollywood melodrama queens if only for her tendency to go over the top. Here she shoots it out alongside Warren Beatty in* Bonnie and Clyde. *As an older actress in Hollywood, she has found roles hard to come by.*

THE GREAT MUSICAL STARS

FRED ASTAIRE (1899–1987)

Nominated by most people as the greatest dancer in movies, Astaire danced with Ginger Rogers in a series of highly successful musicals in the 1930s: *The Gay Divorcee*, *Roberta*, *Top Hat*, *Follow the Fleet*, *Swing Time*, *Shall We Dance?*, *A Damsel in Distress*, *Carefree* and *The Story of Vernon and Irene Castle*. Astaire was the effortless top-hat-and-tails dancer who made love to his leading ladies through his dancing, but he had a curiously sexless quality. Some fans prefer the movies he made in the latter part of his career: *Easter Parade*, *The Band Wagon*, *Daddy Long Legs*, *Funny Face* and *Silk Stockings*. Astaire was a perfectionist and a great worrier about his dance routines, which he usually worked out for himself with the help of choreographer Hermes Pan. His singing voice was also very pleasant and he could interpret a standard by Gershwin or Berlin like few others. A modest man, he could never really understand why people made such a fuss over his movies. "I just dance," he once said. Most people are glad he did. After his first screen test, some conventional studio functionary reported, "Can't act. Can't sing. Slightly bald. Can dance a little."

BETTY GRABLE (1916–73)

Grable was living proof of Hollywood's power to fragment the female body and make big bucks out of it: her legs were supposedly insured for millions of dollars with Lloyd's of London. A musical star of only average singing and dancing abilities, she was tailored to be the wartime pin-up of the American forces. Basically, she was a glamorized version of the American girl-next-door. Overt sexuality was absent in her movies; she was sold on the basis of peaches-and-cream, kid-sister appeal. This star persona proved very successful at the box office in a series of anodyne musicals such as *Million Dollar Legs*, *Down Argentine Way*, *Tin Pan Alley*, *Moon over Miami*, *Footlight Serenade*,

122

MON FILM

15 frs

Fred ASTAIRE et Ginger ROGERS dans

ENTRONS dans la DANSE

Nº 235. — 21 Février 1951.

Film METRO-GOLDWYN-MAYER

LEFT *Fred Astaire and Ginger Rogers are the most famous dancing couple in movie history. The Barkleys of Broadway (1949) was the last movie they made together.*

Springtime in the Rockies, Coney Island, Sweet Rosie O'Grady and Pin-Up Girl. Her career lasted well into the 1950s with musicals such as Mother Wore Tights, The Beautiful Blonde from Bashful Bend, My Blue Heaven and the nonmusical How to Marry a Millionaire. When these movies are seen today, you ask yourself what all the fuss was about, but then, 40 years from now, they'll be asking the same question about Madonna. The answer will be the same: publicity and money.

BELOW *Jeanette MacDonald and Nelson Eddy were a very popular singing team in the 1930s and 40s: here they are seen in* Bitter Sweet *(1940).*

ABOVE *Betty Grable became the GI pin-up during World War II. Here she is seen with Reginald Gardiner in Lubitsch's* That Lady in Ermine *(1948).*

GENE KELLY (1912–96)

Kelly was dogged all his movie career by comparisons with Astaire. The fact is that he was very different: Kelly was overtly masculine, athletic and sensual, whereas Astaire was graceful and largely sexless. However, it could be claimed for Kelly that he has been the single most important influence on the movie musical as a star, choreographer and director.

Kelly became a star on Broadway playing Pal Joey, then he went to MGM and made For Me and My Gal with Judy Garland. Cover Girl, with his choreography for his alter-ego dance, marked a breakthrough for Kelly and he went on to star in and co-direct with Stanley Donen On the Town, Singin' in the Rain and It's Always Fair Weather. In between he was directed by Vincente Minnelli in The Pirate, An American in Paris and Brigadoon. The "Singin' in the Rain" number in the movie of that name has become one of the most famous sequences of all time. Kelly's Irish-American charm and his grin that "could melt stone" endeared him to audiences, until the musical bubble burst and he was set free by

ABOVE Gene Kelly chose Leslie Caron to play opposite him in An American in Paris *(1951). This Vincente Minnelli-directed movie won the Best Film Oscar, and the same year Gene Kelly won a Special Oscar for his contribution to screen musicals. Especially in his role as choreographer, Kelly remains the single most important influence on the American film musical.*

MGM. His career went into reverse until he was given the chance to direct Hello Dolly! in 1969. In his latter years, he appeared in three That's Entertainment movies that were compilations of the best numbers from the great MGM musicals.

JUDY GARLAND (1922–69)

Garland is another icon of the movie musical. A child prodigy, she was overworked by her studio, MGM, in a series of musicals with Mickey Rooney. She was also Dorothy in The Wizard of Oz. Graduating from teen musicals, she made Meet Me in St Louis in which she was directed by Vincente Minnelli, who shortly afterwards married her. Their marriage produced Liza Minnelli. Garland starred with

Gene Kelly in three movies: For Me and My Gal, The Pirate and Summer Stock. She made Easter Parade with Astaire, by which time she was in serious trouble with the studio and herself. Addicted to pills of various kinds, she blamed MGM for exploiting her and not using her talent intelligently, but when she failed to turn up for the shooting of Annie Get Your Gun, MGM sacked her. Her comeback film was the classic A Star is Born, in which she co-starred with James Mason. Her film appearances after that were few and far between. She resumed her concert career, but stories of her drinking and broken marriages dogged her, and she finally died in 1969. Around Garland arose a legend of the kind that only show business could create, and her fans are among the most loyal of all, even 30-odd years after her death.

OPPOSITE Doris Day made a series of highly popular musicals in the 1940s and 50s, including April in Paris *(1952),* Calamity Jane *(1953),* Young at Heart *(1955) and* The Pajama Game *(1957). Then she became a star in gender-war comedies.*

126

BING CROSBY (1903–77)

The "Old Groaner" got by on a voice that was pleasant and a personality that smacked of good humour and easy-going ways. Off-screen he was a tyrannical father and mean with a buck. He always knew that he was a very lucky man, and he was certainly fortunate to team up with Bob Hope in the series of *Road* movies they made. He also co-starred with Astaire in *Holiday Inn* and *Blue Skies*. Crosby used that Irish charm of his in two schmaltzy movies about priests, *Going My Way* and *The Bells of St Mary's*. He also tried his hand at straight acting in *The Country Girl* and the remake of *Stagecoach*, in which he played the drunken doctor part. One of his best musicals was *High Society* with Sinatra.

ABOVE *Bing Crosby and Frank Sinatra starred together in* High Society, *the hugely enjoyable musical remake of the equally popular* The Philadelphia Story, *which starred Gary Grant in the Crosby role.*

FRANK SINATRA (1915–98)

Sinatra's movies range from musicals to westerns to straight dramas. Indeed, he won an Oscar for Best Supporting Actor in *From Here to Eternity*. But "The Voice" naturally started out in musicals, all of which were entirely forgettable until *Anchors Aweigh*, *Take Me Out to the Ball Game* and *On the Town* gave him some kind of screen respectability. However, a series of terrible films made him box-office poison for a while until he begged to play Maggio in *From Here to Eternity*. From then on, he could choose his roles. Among the musicals were *Young at Heart*, *Guys and Dolls* and *High Society*. Sinatra became the most famous entertainer in the world, partly because of his dubious off-screen Mafia acquaintances, but too many of his movies were utterly worthless, particularly the "home movies" he made with his gang, the Rat Pack, in the 1960s: *Ocean's Eleven*, *Sergeants Three*, *Four For Texas* and *Robin and the Seven Hoods*.

When he took the trouble and deigned to do more than one complacent take of a scene, he could turn in creditable performances: for example, in *From Here to Eternity*, *The Man with the Golden Arm* and *The Manchurian Candidate*.

BARBRA STREISAND (b. 1942)

Streisand had a great success as Fanny Brice in *Funny Girl* after having made her name in the stage version on Broadway and in London. She then had two flops in a row with *Hello Dolly!* (in which she was miscast) and *On a Clear Day You Can See Forever*, which, despite Vincente Minnelli's direction and having Yves Montand as her co-star, failed to find a large enough audience. However, her screen career recovered with *What's Up, Doc?* in which she revealed her innate comic talent, and *The Way We Were* playing a radical who fought for Roosevelt's New Deal and against McCarthyite tactics in Hollywood during the 1950s. She made the sequel to *Funny Girl, Funny Lady*, in 1975 and yet another remake of *A Star is Born* in 1976. This was a huge box-office success, but by this time she wanted to control her career and managed to co-write, co-produce and direct *Yentl* in 1983. She also later directed and

ABOVE *Barbra Streisand made her name in the stage version of* Funny Girl *before starring in the 1968 movie version.*

ABOVE *Streisand starred in the 1969 film version of the stage musical* Hello, Dolly! *Gene Kelly directed and Walter Matthau co-starred in the movie.*

starred in *The Prince of Tides* and *The Mirror Has Two Faces*. She has a reputation for egomania, but it is difficult to know how accurate this charge is or how much it is the reaction of chauvinists to a powerful woman making her way in the male-dominated movie industry. Now she appears to have disappeared from the big screen and has made her last world tour as a singer. However, she frequently makes appearances in Washington when the Democrats are in power, and she retains a vast army of devoted and even hysterical fans, who will always see her as a diva of the pop world. Mostly, people either love her or loathe her, but perhaps the adulation she has received from her millions of fans has had a negative effect on some of her choices of material and her performances. First and foremost, Streisand is a singer.

127

THE NEW WOMEN

KATHARINE HEPBURN (1907–2003)
Katharine Hepburn largely played emancipated, strong-minded women, albeit often with a quavering voice and trembling lip. Early Hollywood successes with *Morning Glory* and *Little Women* (both 1933) were followed by less commercially successful movies such as *Alice Adams*, *Sylvia Scarlett* and *Mary of Scotland*. She emanated an almost androgynous quality in some of these movies. Labelled "box-office poison" by distributors, she hit back in comedies such as *Bringing Up Baby* and *The Philadelphia Story*. In these classic pictures she was shown at her best: intelligent, witty, possessing a great sense of comic timing and with an individual charm of her own. *Woman of the Year* paired her with Spencer Tracy, with whom she had a long relationship and made several notable movies, including *Keeper of the Flame*, *Adam's Rib*, *Pat and Mike* and *Guess Who's Coming to Dinner*. The gruff and alcoholic Tracy may not have

ABOVE *Katharine Hepburn and James Stewart starred in* The Philadelphia Story *(1940), which was later remade as a musical* High Society *(1956). Grace Kelly took over the Hepburn role in the latter.*

appeared to be the perfect mate for Hepburn, but their relationship somehow worked off-screen as well as on-screen. She played spinsters in *The African Queen* (directed by John Huston), *Summer Madness* (directed by David Lean) and *The Rainmaker*. Never an actress who could be accused of underplaying, opinions divide over her performances in movies such as *Suddenly Last Summer*, *The Lion in Winter* and *The Madwoman of Chaillot*. By this time she was into her quivering upper lip stage. However, she starred with Ralph Richardson in *Long Day's Journey into Night* (1962), directed by Sidney Lumet, and with John Wayne in *Rooster Cogburn* (1975). Her last major role was opposite Henry and Jane Fonda in *On Golden Pond* (1981).

LEFT *John Huston directed Hepburn and Bogart in* The African Queen. *Clint Eastwood's 1990 movie* White Hunter, Black Heart *dealt with events that happened during the shooting of that film.*

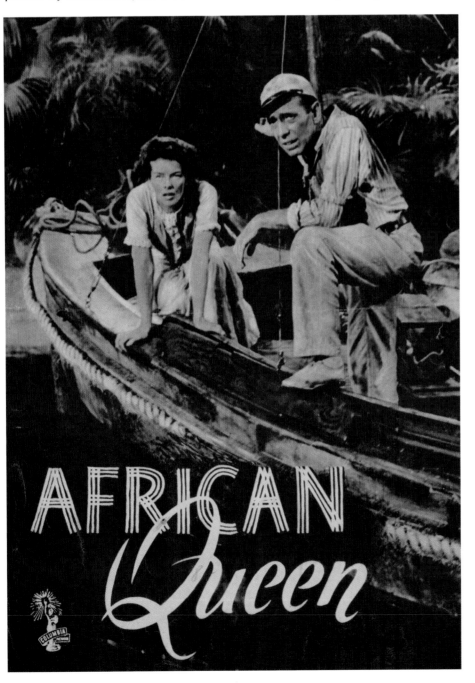

LEFT *Jane Fonda in her unreconstructed pre-feminist phase as* Barbarella *(1968), an adaptation of Jean-Claude Forest's comic strip. Soon after, Fonda left these glamour-girl roles behind her and went on to become the conscience of the nation in movies such as* A Doll's House *(1973),* Julia *(1977) and* The China Syndrome *(1979).*

were reconciled. She had a popular success in *Nine to Five* but has also played in some flops – *Rollover* and *Agnes of God*, for example. She co-starred with Jeff Bridges in *The Morning After* and with De Niro in *Stanley and Iris*. Her liberal politics made her hated by many Americans during the Vietnam War, but she has been better known in latter years for the exploitation of her own image in promoting her health and beauty business. Married and divorced from media mogul Ted Turner, Fonda has recently announced her conversion to a born-again type of Christianity.

BELOW *Jane Fonda with her then-husband in the late 1960s, French director Roger Vadim.*

Her upper-class New England manner was best suited to her early roles in which she symbolized a new kind of female star who depended hardly at all on physical allure.

JANE FONDA (b. 1937)

Fonda has had to work hard to be taken seriously in serious roles, partly because of her glamorous appearance and partly because her early film career landed her with decidedly unliberated parts such as those in *Cat Ballou* and *Barbarella* (with her then-husband Roger Vadim directing). Her

first real success was in *Klute* for which she won an Oscar and this was followed by more overtly feminist roles in *A Doll's House*, *Julia* and *The China Syndrome*. In 1981 she appeared with her father, Henry, in *On Golden Pond*, playing a daughter having difficulties with her father, which apparently she had always had in real life with Henry until they

MERYL STREEP (b. 1949)

Streep's quest for variety in her roles has led to her being identified with parts demanding that she perfects yet another accent of one kind or another. She was British in *The French Lieutenant's Woman* and *Plenty*, Polish in *Sophie's Choice*, Danish in *Out of Africa* and Australian in *A Cry in the Dark*.

Streep first came to prominence as De Niro's lover in *The Deer Hunter* and they appeared together again in *Falling in Love*. She played unsympathetic women in *Manhattan* and *Kramer vs. Kramer*, whilst in *Silkwood* she played the tough, working-class rebel Karen Silkwood who was bumped off for exposing secrets of the American nuclear industry. She has had her bad reviews, notably for *Ironweed* and *She-Devil*. She was miscast in *Postcards from the Edge*, and made some turkeys such as *House of the Spirits*, before she starred with Clint Eastwood in *The Bridges of Madison County*. After that came *Before and After, Marvin's Room, One True Thing,*

ABOVE *Meryl Streep played a wronged wife to Jack Nicholson's husband in the 1986 comedy* Heartburn.

Dancing at Lughnasa and *Music of the Heart*. Streep prepares meticulously for her roles, and she may have an element of clinical overkill that prevents her from achieving real presence on screen.

JESSICA LANGE (b. 1949)

Lange's acting talents were hardly used in the 1976 remake of *King Kong*, for which she was taken from near obscurity to play the female lead. The film was not a success, but she fared better in *All That Jazz, The Postman Always Rings Twice* and *Frances* (playing 1930s star Frances Farmer). Lange

ABOVE *Jessica Lange and Jack Nicholson play the murdering lovers in Bob Rafelson's version of* The Postman Always Rings Twice *(1981).*

chooses her roles with care and makes movies that "say something". Even *Tootsie*, the comedy in which she starred opposite Dustin Hoffman, reflected something about men-women relationships, whilst *Country*, *Sweet Dreams*, *Crimes of the Heart* and *The Music Box* all attempt to reflect aspects of contemporary society. Her sincere approach has clearly worked, winning her the Best Actress Oscar in 1994 for *Blue Sky*. She has also made some poor movies, including *Rob Roy*. She returns to the stage from time to time, taking on major roles in Tennessee Williams and Eugene O'Neill plays. She is an intelligent, creative actor.

SIGOURNEY WEAVER (b. 1949)

Weaver achieved star status in her role as Ripley in *Alien* and again played the feminist hero in the sequel, *Aliens*. She starred opposite Mel Gibson in *The Year of Living Dangerously* and had a great success in *Ghostbusters*. She played the baddie in *Working Girl* and the goodie in *Gorillas in the Mist*. She made two more Alien movies, was in the dud *1492*, and was very effective as the icy wife in *The Ice Storm*. However, good roles have been drying up for Weaver, which is a pity because she shows an intelligence and strength on screen – a major star.

ABOVE *Sigourney Weaver appeared as Lieutenant Ripley in all of the* Alien *movies, including* Alien Resurrection *(1997).*

KATHLEEN TURNER (b. 1954)

Turner combines a "new woman" persona with the allure of the old-time Hollywood beauty queens. She made her first big impression in *Body Heat* playing a spider woman who frames William Hurt, in a virtual remake of *Double Indemnity*. Then she went against image and starred as the overweight romantic novelist in *Romancing the Stone*. In *Prizzi's Honor* she played a rather unconvincing hit-woman, whilst in the Ken Russell-directed *Crimes of Passion*, she was a career woman turned prostitute. She reluctantly made *Jewel of the Nile*, the sequel to *Romancing*, and then appeared in the title role in *Peggy Sue Got Married*. She actually lost screen husband William Hurt in *The Accidental Tourist* to Geena Davis, which seemed almost unbelievable, and managed to more or less destroy her fictional husband in *The War of the Roses*. Another strong part came along when she played the title role as private detective in *V.I. Warshawski*. She had some success with *Serial Mom*, but she has had health problems, and screen appearances have been few throughout the 1990s and 2000s. She has, however, returned to the stage, notably playing the Anne Bancroft part, Mrs Robinson, in the stage version of *The Graduate*.

131

She taught him everything she knew – about passion and murder.

BODY HEAT
x

LEFT *Kathleen Turner made a big impact in* Body Heat *(1981) playing opposite William Hurt in a contemporary noir thriller directed by a young Lawrence Kasdan.*

LEFT *Debra Winger co-starred with Theresa Russell in the 1987* Black Widow.

DEBRA WINGER (b. 1955)

A spiky, off-the-wall image has been created for Winger in movies such as *An Officer and a Gentleman* and *Terms of Endearment*. She is usually allowed to be unglamorous in her roles, although the dowdy young woman at some point in the screenplay usually turns into the beautiful princess, as in *Officer* and *Black Widow*. Playing Shirley MacLaine's daughter in *Terms of Endearment* did not seem to harm her career, although the bombing at the box office of *Legal Eagles* in which she co-starred with Robert Redford, dented her record of being associated with hit films. She was effective in *The Sheltering Sky* and *Shadowlands*, for which she was nominated for an Oscar.

SUSAN SARANDON (b. 1946)

Two films in the late 1970s for the French director, Louis Malle – *Pretty Baby* and *Atlantic City* – helped to establish Sarandon as a sensitive and powerful actress. She did not have a major success after that until *The Witches of Eastwick*, which she followed up with portrayals of sadder but wiser "older women" in *White Palace* and *Thelma and Louise*. Her usual persona is the tough, worldly-wise, attractive working woman. Her 1996 Oscar for her portrayal of a nun in *Dead Man Walking* confirmed her status as one of the most effective current female stars. Off-screen, she is one of Hollywood's most active political activists, supporting liberal and anti-war causes, thereby attracting conservative opposition.

BELOW *Susan Sarandon, Michelle Pfeiffer and Cher played three witches in the 1987* The Witches of Eastwick.

JODIE FOSTER (b. 1962)

Foster came to prominence as a "child star" in two Martin Scorsese movies, *Alice Doesn't Live Here Anymore* and *Taxi Driver*. After a Disney film, *Freaky Friday*, and a teen angst pic, *Foxes*, she made her mark again in *The Hotel New Hampshire* before she won an Oscar for her role in *The Accused*, in which she played a rape victim. It was *The Silence of the Lambs* in which she gained the status of major star (and the 1992 Best Actress Oscar); she played Clarice Starling, an FBI agent who tracks down a serial killer with the help of Hannibal Lecter. She made a noted transition into an actor/director role, directing *Little Man Tate* and *Home for the Holidays*. As an actress, she had successes with *Sommersby*, *Maverick*, *Contact* and *Panic Room*.

DIANE KEATON (b. 1946)

A rather more "whiny" and "kookie" version of Hollywood's new women, Keaton was associated with Woody Allen in the earlier part of her screen career. She played the title role in *Annie Hall*, for example, and also appeared in *Love and Death*, *Interiors* and

133

ABOVE *Jodie Foster played an FBI agent in* The Silence of the Lambs.

Manhattan. She took on "tougher" roles in movies that were not directed by Allen: the *Godfather* movies, in which she played the wife of Michael Corleone, *Looking for Mr Goodbar*, *Reds*, *Shoot the Moon*, *The Little Drummer Girl* and *Crimes of the Heart*. She starred with Allen again in *Manhattan Murder Mystery* and also made *The First Wives' Club* and *Marvin's Room*.

LEFT *Diane Keaton played Louise Bryant, the radical journalist in* Reds *(1981), which also featured Jack Nicholson in a cameo role as playwright Eugene O'Neill. The movie was directed by and co-starred Warren Beatty.*

"IF YOU REALLY DON'T LIKE PUBLICITY YOU DON'T DECIDE TO BECOME AN ACTRESS. IT GOES WITH THE TERRITORY."
DIANE KEATON

POST-FEMINIST HEROINES

A new kind of post-feminist leading lady emerged in Hollywood in the 1990s. These stars are not on the barricades for female liberation, but are generally cast in roles that represent them as powerful and independent while also seeming to want what Hollywood has always said women want: a long-term relationship with a man, family, security.....plus ça change....

KIM BASINGER (b. 1953)

Basinger is often likened to oldtime Hollywood stars such as Rita Hayworth or Veronica Lake, but she is certainly a better actress than either of those. After being the bad girl in *The Natural* (1984) and appearing in the soft-porn *9½ Weeks* with Mickey Rourke, she was in *No Mercy* and *Batman*. *Final Analysis* cast her as a neurotic vamp again, but it was with *L.A. Confidential* (1997) that she finally won respect as an actress – and an Oscar. Having been seen as a glamour girl who can act some, whether she will win further powerful roles as she approaches 50 remains to be seen. (Meryl Streep seems to have cornered this market.)

MICHELLE PFEIFFER (b. 1957)

Pfeiffer first made an impact in *Scarface* (1983) with Al Pacino; she proved herself much more than just a pretty face. She had meaty roles in *The Witches of Eastwick* and *Married to the Mob*, then followed those with *Dangerous Liaisons*, *The Fabulous Baker Boys* (for which she was nominated for an Oscar), *The Russia House* (playing a Russian woman), *Frankie and Johnny* and *Batman Returns* as Catwoman. She has worked with some top directors such as Scorsese on *The Age of Innocence* and Mike Nichols on *Wolf*. She has also made some stinkers such as *Dangerous Minds* and some mediocre movies that have made little impact: *What Lies Beneath*, for example. A spirited woman, Pfeiffer has often complained about the roles Hollywood actresses are usually offered.

ANNETTE BENING (b. 1958)

Bening made some impact in *Valmont* (1989), but it was with *The Grifters* (1990) that she broke through to stardom. She acted opposite De Niro in the movie about McCarthyite persecution in 1950s Hollywood, *Guilty By Suspicion*. After starring with Harrison Ford in *Regarding Henry*, she worked with her future husband

ABOVE *Michelle Pfeiffer showed she could carry a tune as well as act in* The Fabulous Baker Boys, *seen here with co-star Jeff Bridges.*

Warren Beatty in *Bugsy*. She was in *The President* with Michael Douglas, *Mars Attacks!* with Jack Nicholson and *The Siege* with Denzel Washington. She was nominated for an Oscar for her comic role in *American Beauty*. Her star status is well established and she should continue to win good roles because she is one of the more intelligent of Hollywood actors.

ABOVE *Kim Basinger co-starred with Richard Gere in* Final Analysis, *a psychological thriller in the* film noir *tradition.*

ABOVE *Annette Bening made a big impression as a petty criminal in* The Grifters, *starring with Anjelica Huston and John Cusack.*

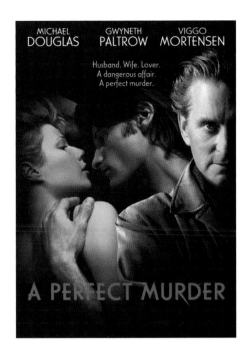

In A Perfect Murder *(1998), a remake of Hitchcock's* Dial M for Murder, *Gwyneth Paltrow played the Grace Kelly role, Michael Douglas took on the Ray Milland role and Viggo Mortensen played the Bob Cummings part.*

then she won a Best Actress Oscar for *Shakespeare in Love*. She took something of a back seat to the two male leads in *The Talented Mr Ripley*, but had a decent role in *Possession* (2002). Paltrow is rather wan for some tastes, but has an appeal that should last.

MEG RYAN (b. 1961)

Ryan survived some turkeys in her early years in Hollywood (*Rich and Famous, Amityville-3D*), but then hit the big time with *When Harry Met Sally...* (1989) starring with Billy Crystal. Her young-woman-next-door star persona was further exploited in another romantic comedy – *Sleepless in Seattle* (1993) with Tom Hanks. Hollywood decided that romantic comedies were her thing so she was cast in *When a Man Loves a Woman* and *French Kiss*, which flopped. The 1996 *Courage Under Fire* marked a change of pace for her, but *Addicted to Love* and *You've Got Mail* were attempts to resurrect the Ryan of *Sally* and *Seattle*.

ABOVE *Meg Ryan starred with Kevin Kline in the Lawrence Kasdan romantic comedy* French Kiss. *Kline played a somewhat unconvincing screen Frenchman.*

HALLE BERRY (b. 1968)

A former beauty queen, Berry was in Spike Lee's *Jungle Fever* (1991), in *Bulworth* (1998) with Warren Beatty, and played Dorothy Dandridge in a television movie. She became the first black actress to win the Best Actress Oscar for her role in *Monster's Ball* (2001). She also starred in the James Bond movie *Die Another Day* (2002).

GWYNETH PALTROW (b. 1973)

After appearing in two superior Hollywood movies, *Mrs Parker and the Vicious Circle* (1994) and *Jefferson in Paris* (1995), this daughter of actress Blythe Danner and director Bruce Paltrow played the title role in *Emma* and was henceforth able to demand star status. The romantic comedy *Sliding Doors* reinforced the Paltrow persona: a rather bemused modern young woman searching for lasting love. She found rather less than that in *A Perfect Murder*, a remake of Hitchcock's *Dial M for Murder*, and

PENELOPE CRUZ (b. 1974)

Spanish-born Cruz starred in two Spanish movies *Jamon, Jamon* (1992) and Almodóvar's *All About My Mother* (1999) which brought her to the attention of Hollywood. There she quickly made *The Hi-Lo Country, All the Pretty Horses, Blow, Woman on Top, Captain Corelli's Mandolin* and *Vanilla Sky*. She seems to have established herself in Hollywood and is much in demand.

LEFT *Before she won her Oscar for* Monster's Ball *(2001), Halle Berry had to serve her time by playing second fiddle to tough guys Kurt Russell and Steven Seagal in* Executive Decision *(1996).*

THE STREETWISE STARS

There is a group of stars whose screen persona is hard to categorize because of the range of parts they take on. The following male stars emerged from the 1960s onwards, and all have varying degrees of "street wisdom". They represent characteristics of the time, and their roles usually involve them in moral dilemmas of a specifically contemporary nature.

WARREN BEATTY (b. 1937)

Beatty first came to prominence playing an angst-ridden teenager in Elia Kazan's *Splendor in the Grass* (1961). His "pretty boy" image was enhanced when he played a gigolo to middle-aged Vivien Leigh in *The Roman Spring of Mrs Stone*. His first huge success was as Clyde Barrow in *Bonnie and Clyde* in 1967, which he also co-produced. Beatty's looks and off-screen reputation for womanizing meant he had to fight to get roles that stretched him as an actor. *The Parallax View* and *Shampoo*, which he also co-wrote, both attempted to comment on contemporary American society, but it was *Reds* in 1981, which he starred in, produced, co-wrote and directed, that finally freed him from the charge of being "lightweight". In *Reds* he played a left-wing American journalist, John Reed, who was also a Communist. Hollywood, anticipating a thaw in the relations between the superpowers, gave Beatty an Oscar for his direction. Beatty had to survive the 40-million-dollar flop that was *Ishtar* (1987), but *Dick Tracy* (1990) and *Bugsy* (1991) brought him some popular success. From time to time Beatty has been active in American politics on the left of the Democrat Party and it has even been whispered that he might run for high office at some point. *Bulworth* (1998), which he starred in, co-wrote and directed, was a satirical comment on the image-driven platitudinous and profoundly dishonest nature of mainstream American politics. Beatty married Annette Bening after they met on the set of *Bugsy* and he has lived down his womanizing reputation.

ABOVE *Warren Beatty has fought hard to establish his credibility as an actor and a radical film-maker in the face of massive publicity about his private life.*

GENE HACKMAN (b. 1930)

Hackman's first important movie was *Bonnie and Clyde* (1967), and he also gave a fine performance in the underrated *I Never Sang for My Father.* However, it was with *The French Connection* (1971) that he achieved real stardom in a performance for which he won the Best Actor Oscar. Coppola's *The Conversation* was another high point in the actor's blossoming career. Thereafter, his career levelled off and he took too many routine roles in some poorish movies – *No Way Out, Mississippi Burning, Unforgiven* and *Absolute Power* were perhaps the best of them. Hollywood seems to have found it hard to find rewarding parts for Hackman, but he shone as the roguish lawyer father in *The Royal Tenenbaums* (2001).

ABOVE *Gene Hackman made an immense impact in his memorable role as tough detective Popeye Doyle on the trail of drug barons in* The French Connection *(1971).*

JACK NICHOLSON (b. 1937)

If "streetwise" describes Nicholson's screen persona in his earlier films, the adjective "demonic" would certainly have to be added in relation to his later films. Nicholson had small parts in some of Roger Corman's horror films of the early 1960s and then had a huge success as the alienated and drug-addicted lawyer in *Easy Rider*. In *Five Easy Pieces*, *Carnal Knowledge* and *The King of Marvin Gardens* Nicholson played loners imbued with self-dislike, alienated from their roots and out of touch with their feelings. A succession of "streetwise" roles followed in *The Last Detail*, *Chinatown*, *Tommy*, *One Flew Over the Cuckoo's Nest*, *The Missouri Breaks* and *The Last Tycoon*. His demonic side first appeared in *The Shining*, was reprised in part in *Terms of Endearment* and replayed in full for *The Witches of Eastwick*. He played a homeless bum in *Ironweed*, stole *Batman* as an over-the-top comic villain, reprised his *Chinatown* role in *The Two Jakes* (he also directed the movie), took the title role of *Hoffa*, has twice acted under Sean Penn's direction in *The Crossing Guard* and *The Pledge*, and won an Oscar for his comedy role in *As Good As It Gets* (1997). Yet, his best performances were in the early 1970s when he seemed to symbolize the restless alienation and cynicism of Nixon's America.

137

ABOVE *Jack Nicholson as the streetwise but ultimately bemused private eye in Roman Polanski's homage to film noir,* Chinatown. *When Nicholson is good on screen, he is very, very good. When he is bad...*

LEFT *Tony Curtis as Sydney Falco in* Sweet Smell of Success. *Burt Lancaster as the corrupt columnist J.J. Hunsecker says to Falco, "You're a cookie full of arsenic", and he sees to it that the streetwise press agent gets his comeuppance.*

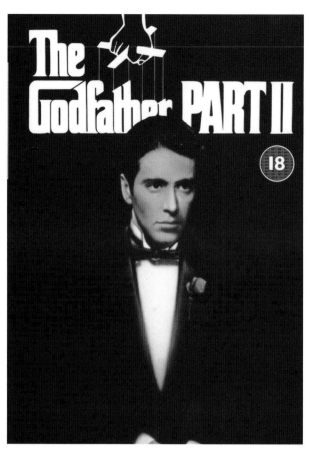

AL PACINO (b. 1940)

Of New York-Sicilian descent, Pacino became a major star after *The Godfather* and *The Godfather Part II*, playing Michael Corleone. He has balanced powerful roles as a Mafia chieftain with a penchant for outsider parts, such as in *Scarecrow* and *Dog Day Afternoon*. He has played a lawyer defending no hopers in *And Justice for All* and a cop who blows the whistle on police corruption in *Serpico*. His aura of suppressed violence was used in *Cruising* and *Scarface*, while a softer, more humane face was revealed in *Bobby Deerfield* and *Author! Author!* He won an Oscar for his role in *Scent of a Woman* (1992), but he was far better in *Glengarry Glen Ross* in the same year. Among the big movies he made in the 1990s, *Carlito's Way*, *City Hall*, *Donnie Brasco*, *The Insider* and *Heat* stand out.

MICHAEL DOUGLAS (b. 1944)

Son of Kirk Douglas, Michael first came to prominence in the television cop series *The Streets of San Francisco*. Being second-generation Hollywood

LEFT *Al Pacino first made an impression in* The Godfather (1972) *and then followed that up with an impressive performance in the 1974 sequel* The Godfather Part II.

probably gave him an early insight into the movie business and he followed in his father's footsteps by becoming a major star, but he also became a producer. He co-produced *One Flew Over the Cuckoo's Nest* and then achieved success as an actor in *Coma*, *The China Syndrome*, *Romancing the Stone* and *A Chorus Line*. In 1987 he really hit the jackpot with two major hits, *Fatal Attraction*, where he played an errant husband who pays heavily for his adultery with Glenn Close, and *Wall Street*, in which he played a very rich but unscrupulous dealer in junk bonds. In *The War of the Roses* he was again in the midst of marital trouble. In the 1990s *Basic Instinct*, *Falling Down*, *Disclosure*, *The American President*, *The Game* and *A Perfect Murder* were a string of hits for Douglas. A change of pace and style for his worn-down academic role in *Wonder Boys* did his reputation no harm and *Traffic* further enhanced it. He married Welsh star Catherine Zeta-Jones in 2000.

JEFF BRIDGES (b. 1949)

Son of Lloyd Bridges, Jeff's first major film was *The Last Picture Show*, directed by Peter Bogdanovich. He often plays charming rogues as in *Bad Company*, *Thunderbolt and Lightfoot* and *Stay Hungry*. That charm can also be used to suggest hidden pathological intent as in *Jagged Edge* and *The Morning After*. *The Fabulous Baker Boys* was a hit for Bridges and his brother Beau. *Fearless* and *The Big Lebowski* were two of the better movies Bridges made in the 1990s.

ABOVE *Michael Douglas found himself in trouble with the female sex again in the highly successful but dubious* Basic Instinct (1992).

RIGHT The Fabulous Baker Boys (1989) *featured real-life brothers Jeff and Beau Bridges as a piano-playing night-club act, with Michelle Pfeiffer as their glamorous singer.*

RICHARD GERE (b. 1949)

Gere came to prominence with *Days of Heaven* and *Yanks*. His good looks and the impression of overt narcissism were used to good effect in *American Gigolo* and *An Officer and a Gentleman*, the latter confirming his star status. A series of failed films (*Breathless*, *The Cotton Club*, *King David* and *No Mercy*) did his career no good, but *Internal Affairs* and *Pretty Woman* were hits for him. *Final Analysis*, *Sommersby*, *Intersection* and *First Knight* were among the so-so movies Gere made in the 90s.

ABOVE *Richard Gere plays sensitive in* Sommersby (1993), *which was a Hollywood remake of the French movie,* The Return of Martin Guerre. *Gere too often comes over on screen as immensely self-satisfied and vain, but he still retains a legion of mainly female fans.*

ABOVE *Nicolas Cage in leopard-skin jacket as Sailor Ripley in David Lynch's* Wild at Heart *(1990).*

NICOLAS CAGE (b. 1964)

Nicolas Cage has gradually become a major star in Hollywood, his status confirmed by his 1995 Oscar for his portrayal of an alcoholic in *Leaving Las Vegas*. He is famous for his brooding intensity, apparent in films such as *Wild at Heart*, but he is equally successful in more sensitive roles such as the soft-hearted policeman in the gentle comedy *It Could Happen to You*. He has the credentials to succeed in Tinsel Town; his uncle is Francis Ford Coppola and he has been married to Patricia Arquette and Lisa Marie Presley. However, his talent and screen presence more than surpass his background and he remains one of the most impressive stars of his generation. Not all his choices of movies have been wise, however. *The Rock, Con Air* and *Face/Off* were all forgettable, but *Bringing Out the Dead* (1999) and *Adaptation* (2002) restored his reputation.

KEVIN SPACEY (b. 1959)

Spacey is one of the most talented actors to emerge from Hollywood since the early 1990s. He is, however, much more than a movie star, which he proves by returning to the stage from time to time to take on important dramatic roles, for example in *The Iceman Cometh*. He first made an impact on screen in *Glengarry Glen Ross*, then really made star status with his role in *The Usual Suspects* (1995). He followed this with his performance as the deranged serial

ABOVE *Kevin Spacey as the glacial Williamson with Jack Lemmon as the loser salesman Levene in the 1992 movie version of David Mamet's play* Glengarry Glen Ross.

killer in *Seven*, his corrupt detective in *L.A. Confidential* a couple of years later and a cold Hollywood wheeler-dealer in *Hurly-Burly*. He finally won an Oscar for his leading role in *American Beauty*. He has a tremendous presence on screen, but what he has to guard against is repeating too often the "Kevin Spacey" performance – that sardonic, cynical, coldly detached persona that he does so well.

DENZEL WASHINGTON (b. 1954)

Washington first made a real impression when he played South African activist Steve Biko in *Cry Freedom* (1987). He also triumphed in *Glory, Mo' Better Blues* (directed by

ABOVE *Denzel Washington is hired to trace a missing woman in the stylish homage to film noir,* Devil in a Blue Dress *(1995). The picture was directed by Carl Franklin.*

Spike Lee) and as Malcolm X in the 1992 Lee-directed movie of that name. He was an honourable private eye in *Devil in a Blue Dress* and an American soldier in *Courage Under Fire*. Washington can play tough and cynical, but mostly he is cast as the good guy, although ironically he won the Best Actor Oscar in 2002 for playing a corrupt cop in *Training Day*. He had given much better performances in much better movies, but Hollywood had decided it was time to award a black American actor the top male acting award and Denzel fitted the bill that year.

THE TOUGH GUYS

JAMES CAGNEY (1899–1986)

Cagney played a succession of gangster roles in movies such as *The Public Enemy* (1931), *Jimmy the Gent* (1934), *Angels with Dirty Faces* (1938) and *The Roaring Twenties* (1939). So convincing was he in these roles that much of his fan mail reputedly came from men in prison. Cagney could never have been accused of underplaying in these roles, but the lack of subtlety in his acting style did not seem to worry his legion of fans. In between these gangster pictures, he displayed his dancing skills in *Footlight Parade* (1933) and he even appeared bizarrely as Bottom in *A Midsummer Night's Dream* (1935). He was identified with rather mindless action flicks as well, including *The Crowd Roars* (1932), *The St Louis Kid* (1934), *Devil Dogs of the Air* (1935) and *Each Dawn I Die* (1939). However, Cagney continually chafed against type-casting and proved his point by winning an Oscar for his portrayal of Irish-American hoofer George M. Cohan in *Yankee Doodle Dandy* (1942). He was curiously unsuited to western roles and bombed in *The Oklahoma Kid* (1939) and *Tribute to a Bad Man* (1956). The last good gangster role he had was in Raoul Walsh's 1949 *White Heat*, in which he played a mother-fixated psychopath ("Top of the world, Ma!"). The 1950s were not particularly kind to Cagney: only *Mister Roberts* (1955), *Love Me or Leave Me* (1955) and *Man of a Thousand Faces* (1957) in which he

played Lon Chaney Senior, made any kind of impact. Thereafter, his career went into decline, although he made one last movie appearance in the 1981 *Ragtime*. Cagney was one of those actors who disdained the profession that brought them fame and wealth; but his power and cockiness on screen, where he dominated the frame in a succession of psychopathic roles, won him a huge following. Cagney snarling "You dirty rat!" is an essential part of any mimic's repertoire.

JOHN WAYNE (1907–79)

For some reason known as "The Duke", Wayne evoked strong responses among movie-goers and non-movie-goers alike. Fans loved him for his stature and presence on screen; detracters hated him for his over-emphatic macho image and his extreme right-wing views. No one could deny his box-office impact, however; after *Stagecoach* (1939) established him as a star, he became

ABOVE *George Raft (1895–1980) was one of Cagney and Bogart's great rivals for meaty gangster roles. The logic of this is debatable, though, because he was as wooden an actor as they come. Perhaps his real-life connections with the Mafia did him no harm.*

Hollywood's most bankable asset in a succession of movies, most of which were far from memorable. His best

RIGHT *John Wayne began to be taken seriously after starring in the 1939 John Ford western* Stagecoach. *After this movie, Wayne was a Grade A star.*

work was done for two directors: John Ford and Howard Hawks. Ford directed him in *Stagecoach*, *The Long Voyage Home*, *Three Godfathers*, *Fort Apache*, *She Wore a Yellow Ribbon*, *Rio Grande*, *The Quiet Man*, *The Searchers*, *The Man Who Shot Liberty Valance* and *Donovan's Reef*; Hawks directed him in *Red River*, *Rio Bravo* and *El Dorado*. Wayne won an Oscar for his role as Rooster Cogburn in *True Grit*, but it is the movies he made with Ford and Hawks that he will be remembered for.

Wayne's political views led him to support the persecution of liberals and lefties in Hollywood during the McCarthyite investigations. There was even talk of his standing as Goldwater's vice-presidential candidate in the 1964 election, but that might not now appear any more risible than the fact that America twice elected Ronald Reagan as president!

HUMPHREY BOGART (1899–1957)

Bogart, or "Bogey", has a cult status close to that of Monroe and Dean. He symbolized the tough guy with integrity, the kind of guy whom you'd want around if things turned ugly, but on whom you could also count to do the decent thing. These characteristics made him a natural for the part of Philip Marlowe in *The Big Sleep* and Sam Spade in *The Maltese Falcon*. His role as Rick in *Casablanca* also reflected the "Bogey" persona: tough, cynical, worldly but with a heart of gold under that veneer of nihilism. When Woody Allen is having difficulties with women in *Play It Again, Sam* he turns to Bogart (or an actor impersonating Bogey) for advice, which naturally leads to successs with the ladies.

The Bogart persona is a favourite with most professional and amateur impersonators. Dressed in a shabby raincoat, with the ever-present cigarette, the Bogey imitator usually does an abbreviated version of his

ABOVE *One of Humphrey Bogart's most memorable gangster roles was in the 1941 Raoul Walsh-directed* High Sierra, *adapted from a W.R. Burnett novel.*

speeches in the famous last scene of *Casablanca*: "It doesn't take a genius to figure that the problems of three little people don't amount to a hill of beans in this crazy world..." Bogart was married four times. His last marriage to Lauren Bacall, with whom he made *To Have and Have Not*, *The Big Sleep* and *Key Largo*, was by far the most successful relationship. Happiness with Bacall coincided with later film triumphs such as the Oscar he won for his role in *The African Queen* and his performance as Captain Queeg in *The Caine Mutiny*. However, cancer cut short his life in 1957, probably because of the accumulative effect of too much smoking and drinking. But the Bogart persona lives on.

RIGHT *Edward G. Robinson was an actor with a much wider range than tough guy roles allowed him to display. Here he appears as the kindly patriarch in* Our Vines Have Tender Grapes *(1945), co-starring Margaret O'Brien and Agnes Moorhead.*

142

ALAN LADD (1913–64)

Ladd became a star after *This Gun for Hire* (1942); his co-star was Veronica Lake, and he went on to make *The Glass Key* and *The Blue Dahlia* with her. Raymond Chandler wrote that Ladd was a small boy's idea of a tough guy, and certainly Ladd suffered from "sizist" jokes because of his diminutive stature. But at the peak of his career he was enormously popular – partly because of his brooding choirboy features, which suggested imminent violence. His best part was Shane in the western of the same name.

BELOW *In the 1954 western* Drum Beat *Alan Ladd plays the role of an Indian expert, Johnny MacKay, who tries to be understanding to Charles Bronson, an Apache chief called Captain Jack. The movie attempted to recapture the west authentically.*

RIGHT *In* The Blue Dahlia *(1946), Alan Ladd plays a returning GI suspected of murder. His death was a result of pills and booze. Whether this was intentional or accidental is not known.*

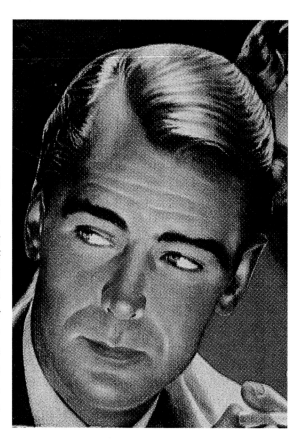

Despite this huge success, Ladd continued to feel insecure, and he became an alcoholic. He died in 1964 at the age of 51, having consumed a cocktail of alcohol and sedatives. In *Rebel Without a Cause* there is a scene where the tiny teenager Sal Mineo opens his high-school locker and we see a picture of Alan Ladd stuck on the inside of the locker door. Yes, indeed, a small boy's idea of a tough guy.

BURT LANCASTER (1913–94)

Lancaster is hard to categorize but many of his roles have involved him in "tough guy" antics. His first film *The Killers* (1946) had him as an ex-gangster waiting stoically for his own demise at the hands of two goons. He played a very tough guy indeed in *Brute Force*, a liberal prison movie directed by Jules Dassin. Lancaster had been a circus acrobat before becoming an actor and he employed these talents in the swashbucklers *The Flame and the Arrow* and *The Crimson Pirate*. But he always sought to play a broad range of parts and this is reflected in the variety of movies he made in the 1950s: *From Here to Eternity*, *Come Back Little Sheba*, *The Rainmaker*, *Vera Cruz*, *Sweet Smell of Success*, *Gunfight at the OK Corral* and

Separate Tables. He followed these with *Birdman of Alcatraz* and *The Leopard*, which was directed by Luchino Visconti, the Italian director with a penchant for operatic effects.

Thrillers such as *Seven Days in May* and *Executive Action* suggest Lancaster's politics leant towards the liberal, and he was always interested in playing people from ethnic minorities, such as *Apache*, *Jim Thorpe – All-American* and *Valdez is Coming*. He had two successes in the 1980s: *Atlantic City* and *Local Hero*. He also played Moses for television, and so Lancaster, if he was a tough-guy actor, was certainly a versatile tough guy. He will always be remembered for his role as the cynical and corrupt newspaper columnist in *Sweet Smell of Success*.

ABOVE *Burt Lancaster as J.J. Hunsecker, a poisonous newspaper columinist in one of the best Hollywood movies of the 1950s,* Sweet Smell of Sucesss *(1957).*

KIRK DOUGLAS (b. 1916)

Douglas was at one time dubbed "the most hated man in Hollywood" because of his reputation for aggressiveness and egomania. Another jibe thrown at him was that he has always wanted to be Burt Lancaster. Certainly their careers have often coincided (*Gunfight at the OK Corral*, *The Devil's Disciple*, *The List of Adrian Messenger*, *Seven Days in May* and *Tough Guys*). Douglas's forte is portraying obsessed, self-destructive loners, which he proved in films such as *Champion*, *Ace in the Hole*, *Detective*

ABOVE *Steve McQueen loved doing his own stunts. In* The Great Escape *(1963) he fled from the German Gestapo by motorbike.*

Story, *The Bad and the Beautiful*, *Lust for Life* (as Vincent Van Gogh) and *Two Weeks in Another Town*. But he has also played various larger-than-life heroic roles, in particular in *Spartacus*, *Twenty Thousand Leagues Under the Sea*, *Paths of Glory*, *In Harm's Way* and *Cast a Giant Shadow*. His best part? Not everyone will agree, but my vote for this goes to his role in *Lust for Life*. Even after a series of strokes hampered his speech and movement, he fought back to continue acting in small parts.

STEVE MCQUEEN (1930–80)

Steve McQueen was a macho star who very often insisted on doing his own stunts. In the famous car chase in *Bullitt* he drove the car himself, and in the motorbike escape section in *The Great Escape* he

ABOVE *Jan Sterling tells Kirk Douglas, "I've met some hard-boiled eggs in my time, but you're six-and-a-half minutes!" in Billy Wilder's* The Big Carnival *(aka* Ace in the Hole, *1951).*

not only rode his own motorbike but the bike of his supposed pursuer as well. McQueen had an icy quality on screen, which many people liked and which just as many disliked. But enough movie-goers flocked to his films to make him a very big star indeed. He first made an impact in the 1960 western *The Magnificent Seven*, then he made *The War Lover* (1962), *The Great Escape* (1963), *Love with the Proper Stranger* (1963), *The Cincinnati Kid* (1965) and *The Sand Pebbles* (1966). Other hits included *The Thomas Crown Affair* (1968), *Bullitt* (1968), *Le Mans* (1971), *The Getaway* (1972), *Papillon* (1973) and *The Towering Inferno* (1974). He died of cancer at the age of 50 in 1980, and retains a legion of fans.

CLINT EASTWOOD (b. 1930)

Eastwood was the major macho star of the 1960s, 70s and 80s. He made his name in the spaghetti westerns *A Fistful of Dollars, For a Few Dollars More* and *The Good, the Bad and the Ugly*. He then struck another goldmine with a series of films in which he played psychopathic cop Harry Callahan: *Dirty Harry, Magnum Force, The Enforcer, Sudden Impact* and *The Dead Pool*. In between he made action movies such as *Where Eagles Dare* and *The Eiger Sanction*. He sang disastrously in *Paint Your Wagon* but other attempts to break the Eastwood mould have been more successful, notably in *Bronco Billy* and *Honky Tonk Man*.

Eastwood's acting style belongs, as someone once said, to "the Mount Rushmore school of acting" but audiences and critics seemingly approve. He has branched out into directing with films such as *Play Misty for Me, The Outlaw Josey Wales, Bird, White Hunter, Black Heart* and *Unforgiven*

ABOVE *Clint Eastwood played the vigilante cop Dirty Harry in the third movie of the series* The Enforcer (1976).

(for which he won the Best Director Oscar). He has continued to act and direct in movies such as *In the Line of Fire, The Bridges of Madison County, Absolute Power, Midnight in the Garden of Good and Evil* and *Space Cowboys*.

SYLVESTER STALLONE (b. 1946)

Stallone has specialized in characters whose biceps are infinitely bigger than their brains. His first and greatest success was with *Rocky*, which he wrote for himself to star in. Another "character" Stallone has spawned is Rambo, a vigilante who murdered hundreds in his three appearances. Declining audiences for his movies forced him to reassess, and he tried playing a gentler role in *Cop Land*, a role for which he was much over-praised. What do aging musclebound Hollywood stars do? They usually make movies that parody their former screen personas. Watch this space.

147

RIGHT *Sylvester Stallone's first big success was in* Rocky (1976) *playing a no-hoper heavyweight boxer who gets the chance to contend for the crown against all the odds.*

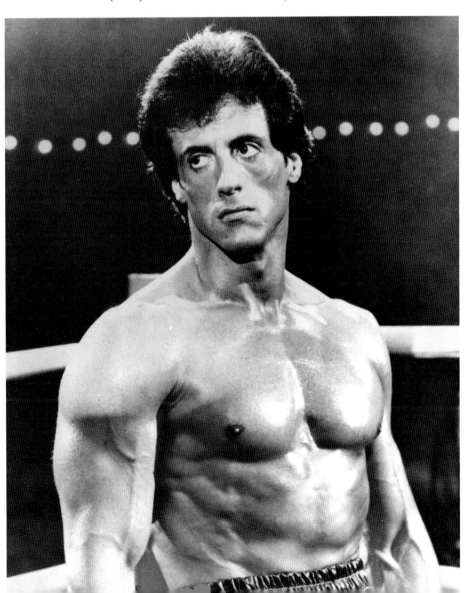

ABOVE *Schwarzenegger hands out the kind of arbitrary justice that his screen characters seem to indulge in, this time as the avenging angel in* The Last Action Hero *(1993).*

ARNOLD SCHWARZENEGGER (b. 1947)

Schwarzenegger was a Mr Universe before he started "acting". His first films featured him in his real-life role as a muscle-man: *Stay Hungry* and *Pumping Iron*, but soon he was playing roles such as *Conan the Barbarian* and *Conan the Destroyer*. *The Terminator*, *Commando*, *Red Sonja*, *Raw Deal*, *Predator* and *Total Recall* made him the favourite of the Saturday-night-video-and-takeaway circuit. He was also encouraged to show off his softer side in the truly cynical *Kindergarten Cop*. He is not as mindless as his roles might suggest; he was in the comedy *Twins*, with Danny De Vito playing his unlikely twin. Married to one of the Kennedy clan, Schwarzenegger is rumoured to have political ambitions. His career and the box-office returns from his movies have zoomed downwards since the mid-1990s; he won't be the first Hollywood star to turn to politics when his career waned.

MEL GIBSON (b. 1956)

Gibson (born of American parents but spending his formative years in Australia) first came to prominence in the *Mad Max* movies, which helped to put him and the new Australian cinema on the movie map. He was also very effective in Peter Weir's *Gallipoli* and *The Year of Living Dangerously*, and in the Fletcher Christian part in *The Bounty*. However, the movies that really catapulted him to world stardom were the *Lethal Weapon* quartet. Teamed with Danny Glover, Gibson starred as a flaky detective prone to self-destruction in these action movies that make few demands on the brain cells. *Bird on a*

BELOW *Mel Gibson as he appeared in the* Lethal Weapon *series.*

Wire with Goldie Hawn flopped at the box office, but there is no doubt that Gibson was now established as a major world star. He has also made a successful transition into a star/director role, firstly with *The Man Without a Face* and in the Oscar-winning *Braveheart*. He also played Hamlet in the 1990 Franco Zeffirelli version of the Shakespeare play. Critics on the whole were kind to him, but this did not encourage him to pitch for more serious roles. *The Patriot* was called stridently anti-British by British critics and won him few friends. *What Women Want* raised the hackles of feminists, but *Signs* was another hit for him. Gibson is probably a better actor than most of his film roles allow him to be, but he seems content to star in fairly mediocre movies that keep him in the very first rank of bankable stars.

BRUCE WILLIS (b. 1955)

Willis gives the impression on screen of being inordinately pleased with himself. Even when he is playing modest and shy, somehow it smacks of narcissism. The no-brainer *Die Hard* (1988) was a huge hit and really launched Willis into stardom; there have been sequels. He had an absolute disaster with *Hudson Hawk*, which might have stalled his career, but *Pulp Fiction*, *Twelve Monkeys*, *The Fifth Element* and *The Siege* brought it back on track. In *The Sixth Sense* and *Unbreakable*, he took on more vulnerable roles. For a number of years during the 1990s, Willis and his then-wife Demi Moore were seen as

ABOVE *Russell Crowe first came to the notice of the wider movie public through his role in* Romper Stomper, *an Australian film about racist skinheads directed by Geoffrey Wright.*

Hollywood's golden couple, which may or may not say something about Hollywood of that era.

RUSSELL CROWE (b. 1964)

Crowe is a New Zealander who started his acting career in Australian television soaps. Two notable Australian movies he made were *Proof* (1991) and *Romper Stomper* (1992). He gravitated to Hollywood and made the big time when he played the violent cop in *L.A. Confidential*. By contrast, he played a shy and inadequate whistle-blower in *The Insider*, before having a major triumph in *Gladiator*. He received Oscar nominations three years running with *The Insider* (1999), *Gladiator* (2000) – for which he won the Best Actor award – and *A Beautiful Mind* (2001).

LEFT Die Harder *was the unsubtle tagline for the second of the* Die Hard *movies that made Bruce Willis a star.*

BRUCE WILLIS DIE HARD 2 DIE HARDER

GET
READY
FOR...

LEFT *Keanu Reeves had a huge box-office hit with the out-of-control-bus thriller* Speed, *which also starred Dennis Hopper and Sandra Bullock.*

SAMUEL L. JACKSON (b. 1948)

Jackson was in Spike Lee's *Do the Right Thing* and *Jungle Fever*, as well as Scorsese's *GoodFellas*. It was his part in Tarantino's *Pulp Fiction* that finally established his screen persona as the tough guy, and he was also in that director's *Jackie Brown*. However, he is an actor with a fairly wide range and he has played different kinds of roles in *Trees Lounge* and *The Red Violin*, a movie that deserves to find a wider audience. Jackson is mostly used in actioners, but as he gets older, I would expect him to be cast more and more in parts that exploit his intelligence and fluency as an actor.

Jackson is one of Hollywood's growing number of major black stars, a trail blazed by Sidney Poitier and Dorothy Dandridge in the 1950s. He has a more powerful screen presence than Poitier, a wider acting range, and is certainly not as tied to dignified black roles as Poitier was.

KEANU REEVES (b. 1964)

Reeves became something of a cult figure with young audiences after movies such *Bill and Ted's Excellent Adventure, Point Break* and *My Own Private Idaho*, but it was in action movies such as *Speed, Chain Reaction* and *The Matrix* that he gained his largest audiences. For many, his appeal remains a matter of mystery.

ABOVE *Samuel L. Jackson played a character called Zeus (no, not God!) in* Die Hard with a Vengeance. *He has had more thoughtful roles, notably alongside Greta Scacchi and Don McKellar in* The Red Violin *and in* Trees Lounge, *directed by fellow actor Steve Buscemi.*

THE COMEDY ACTORS

Comedy actors are a different breed from comics like Chaplin and Keaton. Comedy actors are not really professional clowns, they play ordinary people who find themselves in difficulties, and the comedy arises as they try to extricate themselves from their predicaments. Comedy is a real test of an actor: think of Laurence Olivier – he was a brilliant comic actor and he usually brought a comic element even to tragic roles.

WILLIAM POWELL (1892–1984)

Debonair is the adjective most over-used about Powell, but he was an accomplished comedy actor in movies such as *My Man Godfrey, Love Crazy, Life with Father*, and in the *Thin Man* series with co-star Myrna Loy.

CAROLE LOMBARD (1908–42)

Lombard was an intelligent, tough comedy actress who was killed in an air crash in 1942, leaving Clark Gable a widower. She showed her prowess in *Twentieth Century, My Man Godfrey,* *Nothing Sacred, They Knew What They Wanted, Mr and Mrs Smith* and *To Be or Not to Be.*

ROSALIND RUSSELL (1908–76)

Russell was at her best in comedies such as *The Women, His Girl Friday, My Sister Eileen* and *The Velvet Touch*. She also played dramatic roles in *Night Must Fall, Sister Kenny* and *Picnic*. She was the screen's Auntie Mame.

CARY GRANT (1904–86)

British-born Archie Leach became Cary Grant and went on to establish himself as one of Hollywood's greatest stars. Picked by Mae West for *She Done Him Wrong* (1933), Grant was soon in demand as a comedy actor in movies such as *The Awful Truth, Bringing Up Baby, His Girl Friday* and *The Philadelphia Story*. His dark, good looks also qualified him for straight roles in *Gunga Din, Only Angels Have*

ABOVE *Alastair Sim (1900–76) was one of the most accomplished movie comedy actors. Here he appears as the headmistress in* The Belles of St Trinian's *(1954).*

Wings and *Suspicion* – the latter directed by Hitchcock who saw something more sinister behind those handsome features, which he exploited later in *Notorious*. Other important comedies were *I Was a Male War Bride, Monkey Business* and *Operation Petticoat*, which he mixed with straight roles in *North by Northwest, An Affair to Remember, Indiscreet* and *Charade*. Grant symbolized sophistication for many film-goers, but he was not afraid to show himself as ridiculous in his comedies. Married five times, Grant retired from movies in 1966 to devote himself to promoting cosmetics for an internationally known firm. He died at the age of 82 in 1986 after weathering the passage of time remarkably well.

151

ABOVE *Carole Lombard as she appeared in Ernet Lubitsch's* To Be or Not to Be *(1942). Lombard was one of the best comedy actresses Hollywood has ever produced.*

ABOVE *Cary Grant in drag in the Howard Hawks comedy* I Was a Male War Bride.

LEFT *One of Jack Lemmon's best screen roles was in Billy Wilder's* The Apartment, *in which he played an ambitious New York "Organization Man" willing to lend out his apartment to his philandering bosses.*

JACK LEMMON (1925–2002)

Lemmon was often accused of working too hard at the comic effects he aimed to achieve, and certainly he could never be said to underplay, but he was very effective in some movies such as *Some Like it Hot*, *The Apartment*, *How to Murder Your Wife*, *The Fortune Cookie*, *The Odd Couple* and *The Front Page*. Lemmon was particularly associated in the public's mind with characters in Neil Simon comedies such as *The Out-of-Towners* and *The Prisoner of Second Avenue*. In these movies he played the harassed American middle-class male, beset by problems of urban violence, bureaucratic red tape and the general hassle of 20th-century life. He also played straight roles in *Days of Wine and Roses*, *Save the Tiger*, *The China Syndrome*, *Missing* and *JFK*. His irresistible bantering relationship with co-star Walter Matthau in *The Odd Couple* was reprised in two *Grumpy Old Men* movies in the 1990s. Lemmon's speciality was the decent, average middle-class man all at sea in a world of dishonesty and brutality.

WALTER MATTHAU (1920–2000)

Born Walter Matthow, the son of Jewish-Russian immigrants to New York, Matthau achieved star status comparatively late in life. His

152

GRUMPY OLD MEN

ABOVE *Both Jack Lemmon and Walter Matthau indulged in misogynistic roles from time to time in movies such as* How To Murder Your Wife *(1965).*

Peter Sellers had a great popular success in the series of Pink Panther *movies, playing the hapless Inspector Clouseau.*

speciality was the cynical slob, and he played variations on this stereotype in *The Fortune Cookie, The Odd Couple, Plaza Suite, Kotch, The Sunshine Boys, The Bad News Bears, House Calls* and *California Suite.* He also played assorted villains in various movies and had the misfortune to play opposite Streisand in *Hello Dolly!* His critical and sarcastic comments about her indicated that his on-screen persona reflected a lot of his own personality. He directed one low-budget picture, *Gangster Story* in 1960.

PETER SELLERS (1925–80)

Sellers made his name in *The Goon Show* on British radio, then graduated to British movies such as *The Ladykillers, The Smallest Show on Earth, I'm All Right, Jack* and *Only Two Can Play.* When he went to Hollywood, his early films such as

Good friends Lemmon and Matthau appeared in Grumpy Old Men *(1993), a success for both actors late in their screen careers.*

Lolita, Dr Strangelove (in which he played three parts) and *The Pink Panther* held promise of a great international career. But his emotional problems and a disastrous run of bad films put his career into reverse. A near-fatal heart attack in 1964 seemed to increase his sour view of life, but he found steady work and success in the series of Inspector Clouseau films that

followed *The Pink Panther* after a ten-year gap – although they scarcely stretched him as a comedy actor. One last worthwhile film before he finally succumbed to his heart condition was *Being There* (1979). Sellers once said revealingly, "If you ask me to play myself, I will not know what to do. I do not know who or what I am." Sellers was a man who hid behind funny voices.

DANNY DEVITO (b. 1944)

Of diminutive stature, DeVito became a major comedy star in the 1980s in movies such as *Ruthless People, Wise Guys, Throw Momma from the Train, Twins, Tin Men, The War of the Roses* and *Other People's Money.* He was in *Batman Returns* and acted in and directed *Hoffa.* In the 1990s he remained a very busy actor; among the movies he acted in were *Get Shorty, Mars Attacks, L.A. Confidential* and *The Virgin Suicides.* He is quoted as saying that a person of his height and looks is forced to cultivate immense self-esteem and confidence, otherwise they would go under in a society that worships good looks and suavity.

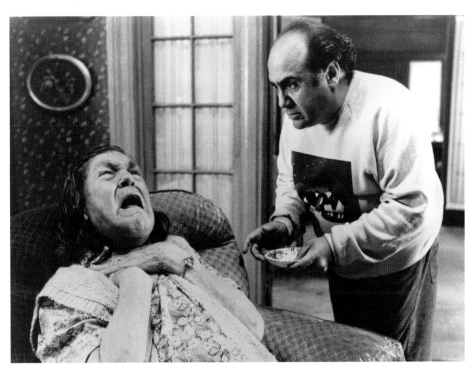

Danny DeVito, seen here with co-star Anne Ramsey, had a major success in the misanthropic comedy Throw Momma from the Train *(1987).*

LEFT *Robin Williams played perhaps the quintessential Robin Williams role in Hook as Peter Pan, the boy who never really grew up to be a man.*

of the Williams screen persona so he appeared as psychotics in *Insomnia* and *One Hour Photo*, which revealed him as an actor who can convey sinister depths. Let us hope he pursues this side of his talent as he goes into his 50s rather than the clownish kid aspect of his screen persona. Let the real Robin Williams stand up.

BEN STILLER (b. 1965)

Stiller is better known as a comic actor than as a director, but he has directed *Reality Bites* (1994), *The Cable Guy* (1996) and *Zoolander* (2001). As an actor he won a huge following after his success in the gross-out comedy *There's Something About Mary* (1998), but *Mystery Men* (1999) did not enhance his career much. He was amusing as the put-upon potential son-in-law Greg Focker in the hit film *Meet the Parents* (2000), and played Chas the international real estate whizz in *The Royal Tenenbaums* (2001).

154

ROBIN WILLIAMS (b. 1952)

Williams started out as a stand-up comedian, then went into the television series *Mork and Mindy*, which brought him fame and fortune and opened the door to Hollywood. His first really big hit was *Good Morning, Vietnam*, which was followed by *Dead Poets Society*. Both roles represented Williams as a life force bringing enlightenment into other people's lives. This has been the most irritating part of the Williams persona, that and the unending need to be loved by audiences. *Mrs Doubtfire* was another hit for the actor, but along the way he made some turkeys as well. His career reached a nadir with the quite nauseating *Patch Adams*. He must have realized he needed new direction because the public were clearly tiring

ABOVE *Ben Stiller shakes Robert De Niro's hand in* Meet the Parents (2000). *De Niro's character, an ex-CIA agent, has his prospective son-in-law investigated to see if he's up to scratch.*

THREE GREAT STARS

Marlon Brando, George C. Scott and Robert De Niro qualify for the accolade of all-time greats but they defy categorization, although some critics have tried to pigeon-hole them into certain sterotypes.

MARLON BRANDO (b. 1924)

Born in 1924 in Omaha, Nebraska, Brando played Stanley Kowalski in *A Streetcar Named Desire* on Broadway before starring in Elia Kazan's film version. This part created the Brando stereotype: the incoherent, primitive and rapacious male animal. However, the tabloids who peddled that stereotype conveniently ignored the range of parts that the "Method" actor undertook: the paraplegic in *The Men*

ABOVE *Marlon Brando as Don Corleone hears a plea for help from the local undertaker in* The Godfather *(1972).*

(1950), his first movie, the Mexican revolutionary in *Viva Zapata*, Mark Antony in *Julius Caesar* and the motorbike gang leader in *The Wild One*. His most memorable part in the early part of his film career was in *On the Waterfront*. Again he played an incoherent, potentially violent man, but Brando revealed reserves of tenderness and vulnerability in the character, thereby creating one of the all-time great screen performances.

Brando has never really hidden his contempt for his profession; perhaps his hatred is reserved more for the business end of the film business than for film acting itself, but his lack of care has led him into making some movie stinkers, including *Desirée, The Teahouse of the August Moon, Sayonara,*

LEFT *Marlon Brando (Marc Antony) emotes over the dead body of Caesar while James Mason (Brutus) addresses the Roman mob in the 1953 production* Julius Caesar.

155

Bedtime Story and *Candy*. But his range is staggering: from Shakespeare to musicals, from drama to comedies. He was a charming Sky Masterson in *Guys and Dolls* and an effete Fletcher Christian in *Mutiny on the Bounty*. It was *Bounty* that marked a break with the Hollywood moguls who complained about long delays in the shooting of the film because of Brando's whims. He directed *One-Eyed Jacks* in 1960, starred in *The Chase* and *Reflections in a Golden Eye* in the 60s, the only two decent movies he made in that decade, and then appeared as Don Corleone in *The Godfather* in 1972. When the Academy awarded him an Oscar, he sent a Native American woman to collect it in order to draw attention to the plight of contemporary Native Americans in the USA. Increasingly Brando has devoted himself to causes, and his later films have reflected his political leanings: *Queimada*, *Roots: the New Generation* (for television), *Apocalypse Now*, *The Formula* and *A Dry White Season*. He has had to deal with major traumas in his family life – including murder and suicide – but he continued to work in movies from time to time during the 1990s, none of them in any way memorable. "Acting is a useless and empty profession",

George C. Scott as fight promoter Gloves Malloy confers with director Stanley Donen in the amusing spoof of 1930s movies Movie Movie *(1978).*

Brando has been quoted as saying. He may or may not be right about that, but such an attitude has prevented him from achieving the heights he might have done.

GEORGE C. SCOTT (1926–99)

Scott was another great screen actor with something approaching contempt for his profession. His self-loathing, by his own testimony, brought him to the brink of total breakdown on numerous occasions and he had to fight periods when he just wanted to lose himself in a bottle. Yet on screen he was one of the most powerful presences ever seen because he had that quality of being like a coiled spring just about to release the rage that boiled under the surface.

LEFT *George C. Scott won an Oscar for his role as General Patton in* Patton *(1970). He later played Benito Mussolini in a 1985 TV series* Mussolini: The Untold Story.

He was first noticed as the prosecutor in *Anatomy of a Murder*, but really made his mark as the smooth but ruthless gangster in *The Hustler*. As the cold manipulator of the pool hustler Fast Eddie (Paul Newman), Scott excelled in Robert Rossen's fine movie. Scott's range as an actor was reflected in his comic portrayal of Buck Turgidson in *Dr Strangelove*, one of his greatest screen performances. One of the real tests of actors is whether or not they can play comedy convincingly – Olivier could, but Brando never showed that he was as good in comedy as he was in dramatic roles. Scott, however, played comedy brilliantly both on screen and on stage. A series of indifferent movies followed *The Hustler*, but Scott hit the jackpot again with his portrayal of George S. Patton in *Patton* (1970). Awarded an Oscar, he refused the honour, stating that he disagreed with actors being judged in competition with one another. This might have arisen from his deep disappointment from losing out for the Best Supporting Actor Oscar when he had first been nominated for *Anatomy of a Murder*, but whatever the reason, he stuck to his guns, which inevitably did not endear him to the Hollywood establishment. Solid performances in *The Last Run* and *The Hospital* followed, but again Scott seemed fairly indifferent to the movies he appeared in. *The Day of the Dolphin*, *Islands in the Stream* and *Movie Movie* were the best of the 1970s. In *Movie Movie* he again showed his talent for comedy, while in Paul Schrader's *Hardcore* he played a religious man looking for his lost daughter in a pornographic underworld. Over the last 20 years of his life, he generally made fairly worthless movies, merely taking on parts to pay bills and alimony. He starred in a television movie remake of 12 *Angry Men*, for which he won an Emmy award; true to form, he failed to pick up the award. The fact that he has made so few good movies is a matter of regret, but he was undoubtedly one of the most powerful screen actors that America has ever produced.

ROBERT DE NIRO (b. 1943)

De Niro first came to real prominence with his performance as Johnny Boy in Martin Scorsese's *Mean Streets*. Scorsese encouraged his actors to improvise and use aspects of their own personalities; this approach paid off, particularly in the scenes between De Niro and Harvey Keitel. Keitel and De Niro again appeared together in Scorsese's *Taxi Driver*, surely the best American film of the 1970s, and once more their improvisational technique paid dividends in terms of the realism of the scenes between them. In between these two movies, De Niro starred in *The Godfather Part II* in which he played the younger Don Corleone, Brando's part in *The Godfather*. Subtly mimicking the older actor's high-

RIGHT *De Niro played boxer Jake La Motta in Scorsese's* Raging Bull, *seen by many as De Niro's best screen performance and the director's major work.*

pitched voice from the first movie, De Niro made a convincing portrayal of the young Don Corleone learning to use the methods of his Mafia oppressors to create a comfortable life for his family.

It was appropriate that De Niro should play Corleone as a younger man because in many ways he is Brando's natural successor in Hollywood. De Niro exudes repressed and expressed violence (*Raging Bull*, *The Deer Hunter*, *Once Upon a Time in America*, *The Mission*, *The Untouchables*); he plays straight, intense, dramatic roles (*True Confessions*, *Angel Heart*, *Stanley and Iris*); he can play romantic roles (*Falling in Love*); he is also expert at comedy (*New York, New York*, *King of Comedy*, *Brazil*, *Midnight Run*). The actor goes to extreme lengths to prepare for his roles, for example adding 60 extra pounds to his frame to play Jake La Motta in *Raging Bull*. It may be that, like many actors, De Niro hides from himself in the parts he plays.

In more recent years, De Niro's movies have not really extended him. Even Scorsese's *Casino* seemed to

ABOVE *Robert De Niro, Brando's heir-apparent in Hollywood, played the young Don Corleone in the second of the* Godfather *trilogy (1974).*

demand only the retreading of familiar paths. However, he has been very successful in comedies such as *Analyze This* (1999), *Meet the Parents* (2000) and *Analyze That* (2002).

De Niro owns and helps to run a very expensive restaurant in Manhattan, and the desire to do really good work in the cinema may be draining away. At his very best, De Niro is a major acting talent.

157

BRITISH STARS

It may seem disproportionate to give a section over to British stars who have made it internationally, but those who appear here are difficult to categorize in terms of Hollywood archetypes. Each of them, with one exception, started in British films and then made it in Hollywood – but remained essentially British in the parts they played.

JAMES MASON (1909–84)

Mason made his name in a series of Gainsborough melodramas such as *The Man in Grey*, *The Seventh Veil* and *The Wicked Lady*. He gave a fine performance as an IRA gunman in *Odd Man Out*, then went to Hollywood and starred in *Caught*, *Pandora and the Flying Dutchman* and as Rommel in *The Desert Fox*. He was Brutus in *Julius Caesar* and the self-destructive star in *A Star is Born*, one of his finest performances. He was the villain in Hitchcock's *North by Northwest* and Humbert Humbert

in *Lolita*. Excellent performances followed in *The Pumpkin Eater*, *The Deadly Affair*, *Autobiography of a Princess* and *The Shooting Party* (1984), his last film. Mason was one of the most accomplished screen actors Britain has ever produced.

DEBORAH KERR (b. 1921)

Scots-born Kerr made *The Life and Death of Colonel Blimp*, *I See a Dark Stranger* and *Black Narcissus* before going to Hollywood and starring in *King Solomon's Mines*, *Quo Vadis*, *From Here to Eternity*, *The King and I*, *Tea and Sympathy*, *Heaven Knows, Mr Allison* and *Separate Tables*. Her most notable films after that were *The Sundowners*, *The Innocents*, *The Night of the Iguana*, *The Gypsy Moths* and *The Arrangement*. She received an Honorary Oscar for career achievement in 1994.

VIVIEN LEIGH (1913–67)

Blessed with outstanding beauty, Leigh also found her looks somewhat of a handicap when it came to being taken seriously as an actress. Married for many years to Laurence Olivier, she

ABOVE *Deborah Kerr (far left) with co-star Van Jonson on location for the 1955 version of Graham Greene's* The End of the Affair. *Too often Kerr was cast as a genteel wife, when her real talent was for earthier parts.*

ABOVE *James Mason was already a big movie star in Britain before he left for Hollywood after the war. Here is a poster for* The Night Has Eyes *(1942).*

ABOVE *Vivien Leigh starred as Lady Hamilton with husband Laurence Olivier as Lord Nelson in Alexander Korda's production of* Lady Hamilton *(aka* That Hamilton Woman*).*

may also have suffered from being perceived as "Mrs Olivier". However, she was excellent as Scarlett O'Hara in *Gone with the Wind* and had successes with *Waterloo Bridge* and *Lady Hamilton*. Her more serious film roles in *Caesar and Cleopatra* and *Anna Karenina* did not bring her critical praise. Her last important screen role was as Blanche Dubois opposite Brando in *A Streetcar Named Desire*. After that, she made only three films: *The Deep Blue Sea*, *The Roman Spring of Mrs Stone* and *Ship of Fools*. Ill-health shortened her life and she died at the age of 54 in 1967.

TREVOR HOWARD (1916–88)

Howard had a powerful screen presence that very few other British actors have possessed. He was excellent in *Brief Encounter* and *The Third Man*, and his performances in *Outcast of the Islands* and *The Heart of the Matter* are two of the best ever in British films. He made some

ABOVE Two of the most popular post-war British stars were Trevor Howard and Kenneth More, here seen in The Clouded Yellow *(1950).*

Hollywood movies, notably as Captain Bligh in the Brando *Mutiny on the Bounty*, but he never became a Hollywood star. Other notable films he starred in include *Sons and Lovers*, *The Charge of the Light Brigade* and *Ryan's Daughter*. He played Pope Leo in *Pope Joan*, Richard Wagner in *Ludwig* and King Arthur in *Sword of the Valiant*.

JEAN SIMMONS (b. 1929)

Simmons's best-known British films are *Great Expectations* (as Estelle), *Black Narcissus* (as an Indian girl), *The Blue Lagoon* (shipwrecked on a desert island with Donald Houston) and *Hamlet*, Olivier choosing her to be his Ophelia. Hollywood gave her a string of mediocre parts until *Guys and Dolls*, *The Big Country*, *Elmer Gantry*, *Spartacus*

BELOW Olivier chose a 17-year-old Jean Simmons to play Ophelia to his Hamlet in the 1948 film he also directed, which won the Best Picture Oscar for that year.

and *The Grass is Greener*. Then her career seemed to stagnate. Husbands included Stewart Granger and Richard Brooks, the director, both of whom rather domineered her. She also had a

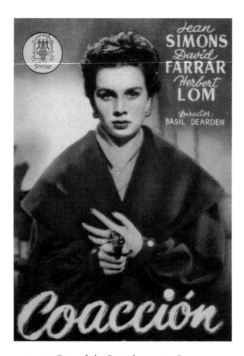

ABOVE *One of the British movies Jean Simmons starred in before moving permanently to Hollywood was the 1950 thriller* Cage of Gold.

long-lasting battle with the bottle. In the 1980s and 90s she made numerous television appearances, and was part of the ensemble cast of the movie *How to Make an American Quilt* (1995).

JOHN MILLS (b. 1908)

Mills never made it in Hollywood, probably because he was so irretrievably British. A succession of war movies established him as the archetypal British officer, stiff upper-lip and terribly, terribly decent: *In Which We Serve, We Dive at Dawn, The Way to the Stars, Morning Departure, The Colditz Story, Above Us the Waves, Dunkirk* and *Ice Cold in Alex*. He was also a military man in *Tunes of Glory* and *Oh! What a Lovely War*. In between war heroics, he played *Scott of the Antarctic* and Mr Polly in *The History of Mr Polly*. Hollywood movies included *War and Peace, King Rat, Ryan's Daughter* (playing a deaf mute, for which he won an Oscar for Best Supporting Actor) and *Oklahoma Crude*. But for many film fans, he will be remembered as the secret weapon the Germans never had.

AUDREY HEPBURN (1929–93)

Hepburn was Belgian-born of Irish-Dutch parentage, but she ranks as a British star since she made her start in British pictures such as *Laughter in Paradise* and *The Lavender Hill Mob*. *Roman Holiday* made her a star in Hollywood and this success was followed by a string of important films: *Sabrina, War and Peace, Funny Face, The Nun's Story, Breakfast at Tiffany's, Charade* and *My Fair Lady*. She usually played child-women, an archetype that won her many ardent fans but which made it more difficult for her to get worthwhile parts in the 1970s and 80s. She played the angel Hap in *Always*, Spielberg's 1990 remake of *A Guy Named Joe*.

ABOVE *Audrey Hepburn epitomized a kind of elfin, gamin charm for her many fans. After appearing in small parts in British movies, she made it big starring with Gregory Peck in* Roman Holiday *(1953).*

DIRK BOGARDE (1921–99)

Dirk Bogarde first came to prominence as the young gunman who shoots down copper Jack Warner in *The Blue Lamp* (1948). Bogarde's employers, however, believed he had a future as a leading man and starred him in a succession of war movies such as *They Who Dare* (1953) and *The Sea Shall Not Have Them* (1954) as well as harmless comedies such as the *Doctor* series in which he played the young doctor Simon Sparrow. Bogarde played Sidney Carton in the 1958 version of *A Tale of Two Cities* and even survived playing Franz Liszt in *Song Without End* (1960). He had two successes working with director Joseph Losey: *The Servant* (1963) and *Accident* (1967). Bogarde was now in a different league of movie star, being used by Luchino Visconti in *The Damned* (1969) and *Death in Venice*

LEFT *Alec Guinness (1914–2000) was one of the most popular British stars, appearing in a number of Ealing comedies such as* The Man in the White Suit *(1951).*

ABOVE *Dirk Bogarde occasionally won better parts than his usual romantic hero in British movies. In* Hunted *(1952) he played a criminal on the run.*

(1971). He also worked with Alain Resnais in *Providence* (1977) and Bernard Tavernier in *These Foolish Things* (1990). He died in London in 1999.

JULIE ANDREWS (b. 1935)

Andrews made her name in the stage version of *My Fair Lady* but lost out to Audrey Hepburn when the film came along. She has tried hard to cast off

the squeaky-clean image she then gained from *The Sound of Music* and *Mary Poppins*, determinedly trying to create a sexual image for herself in *The Americanization of Emily, Darling Lili, 10, S.O.B., Victor/Victoria* and *The Man Who Loved Women*. However, her essential scrubbed English nanny persona has never really deserted her. She has appeared in several movies directed by her husband, Blake Edwards. She battled cancer in the late 1990s and had a triumphant return to the Broadway stage.

ABOVE *Julie Andrews's biggest success on screen was as the singing governess in* The Sound of Music *(1965).*

RICHARD BURTON (1925–84)

At times Burton was more famous for his off-screen antics than his on-screen performances: his drinking bouts, his marriages to Elizabeth Taylor, and his consumption of luxury goods when he and Taylor were "hot property" in Hollywood. After appearing in a number of forgettable British films, Burton made *My Cousin*

ABOVE *One of Richard Burton's better screen roles was as a British spy in the film version of Len Deighton's* The Spy Who Came in from the Cold *(1965).*

ABOVE *Hollywood occasionally remembered that Richard Burton had once been a highly distinguished stage actor. He played famous American actor Edwin Booth in* Prince of Players *(1955).*

162

Rachel in Hollywood, then the first CinemaScope film *The Robe*, followed by *The Desert Rats*, *Alexander the Great* and *Bitter Victory*. His career took an upturn with *Cleopatra* and his marriage to Taylor – he then became the male half of the Taylor–Burton industry. But decent movies were still few and far between. Possible exceptions, depending on taste, were *Who's Afraid of Virginia Woolf?*, *The Spy Who Came in from the Cold*, *The Taming of the Shrew* and *The Comedians*. He played the hero in *Where Eagles Dare* opposite Eastwood, hammed it up as Henry VIII in *Anne of the Thousand Days*, and was awful in awful movies such as *Blackbeard*, *Exorcist II* and *The Wild Geese*. His last film, 1984, gave him a decent part and he was effective in it. His was a lost talent.

LAURENCE OLIVIER (1907–89)

Olivier was a great stage and screen actor. One of the few actors to master both mediums, he appeared in British movies such as *Fire over England* and *The Divorce of Lady X* before going to Hollywood to star in *Wuthering Heights* (during the shooting of which Sam Goldwyn complained about this "dirty British actor"). Hollywood, or Greta Garbo, had already rebuffed him by turning him down for a part in *Queen Christina*. He played Max De Winter in *Rebecca* and Darcy in *Pride and Prejudice*, then he starred in and directed *Henry V* and *Hamlet*. Later film triumphs included *Carrie*, *Richard III* (which he also directed), *Spartacus* and *The Entertainer*. *Sleuth* and *Marathon Man* were the best of the movies he made in the latter part of his movie career, when he tended to take parts for the money, including playing Neil Diamond's father in *The Jazz Singer*. Olivier could have remained a matinée idol, because he had the looks and style for that role, but he wanted to be much more than that.

BELOW *Laurence Olivier as* Hamlet *in the 1948 version of Shakespeare's play, a movie he also directed.*

PETER O'TOOLE (b. 1932)

O'Toole is another of those British actors famous for their drinking and generally self-destructive ways. He became a star after playing *Lawrence of Arabia* in David Lean's film, then played Henry II to Burton's Becket in *Becket*, but also appeared in some stinkers such as *What's New, Pussycat?*, *Casino Royale* and *Goodbye Mr Chips*. *The Lion in Winter* was one of his more

BELOW *Peter O'Toole's big break came when he played Lawrence in* Lawrence of Arabia, *the 1962 epic directed by David Lean.*

SEAN CONNERY (b. 1930)

There is a lot more to Sean Connery than the James Bond tag. Incomparably the best of the Bond actors (although when you consider the competition, that's not saying much), Connery has also worked for Hitchcock in *Marnie*, for Martin Ritt in *The Molly Maguires* and for John Boorman in *Zardoz*. He played an Arab chieftan in *The Wind and the Lion*, where he got away with his Scottish brogue in the desert, and was an elderly Robin Hood in *Robin and Marian*. He returned to the Bond part in 1983 (*Never Say Never Again*), but his career received a great boost with *The Name of the Rose*, *The Untouchables* and *Indiana Jones and the Last Crusade*, in which he played Harrison Ford's father. In the 1990s he remained a top box-office draw, quite an achievement for a man in his 60s whose career had been written off. Movies such as *The Hunt for Red October*, *First Knight*, *The Rock* and *Entrapment* kept him in the first rank. One of the few Scottish actors to make it internationally, Connery has ploughed some of his vast earnings back into helping deprived Scottish youth get a decent start in life.

notable films, but a succession of box-office failures, together with his reputation for boozing, put his film career in jeopardy. On stage he was so bad as *Macbeth* at the Old Vic that people queued to see him go over-the-top every night. His film career was rescued to a certain extent by *The Stunt Man* and *My Favourite Year*. He had something of a success in Bertolucci's *The Last Emperor*, but the movies he made in the 1990s were almost all forgettable. He returned to the London stage with some success in the play about an alcoholic columnist, *Jeffrey Bernard is Unwell*. Omar Sharif called him "the prototype of the ham" and this is an accurate summation, except to say that hamminess sometimes works in particular roles on screen. In 2003 O'Toole was awarded a Lifetime Achievement Oscar.

RICHARD HARRIS (1930–2002)

Harris was a notorious hellraiser, which is usually a euphemistic description used to disguise a harsher reality. After having featured parts in *The Long and the Short and the Tall* (1961) and *Mutiny on the Bounty* (1962), Irish-born Harris achieved star status playing an inarticulate rugby player in Lindsay Anderson's *This Sporting Life* (1963). This gave Harris credibility as a serious actor, and Italian director Antonioni used him in the enigmatic *The Red Desert* (1964). Thereafter,

ABOVE *Richard Harris became a star after his performance in* This Sporting Life *(1963), which was adapted from the novel by David Storey. For many years he lived a life of excess, but he cleaned up his act in the 1980s.*

Harris's career spiralled downwards in terms of the quality of the movies he appeared in, although he was in some commercial successes: *The Heroes of Telemark* (1965), *Camelot* (1967), *A Man Called Horse* (1970) and *Cromwell* (1970). A multitude of mediocre movies followed, the only exceptions being *The Field* (1990), *Unforgiven* (1992) and *Gladiator* (2000). Pauline Kael, the movie critic, wrote of Harris, "He hauls his surly carcass from movie to movie, being dismembered." However, he had a late success as Dumbledore, the wizard headmaster in the first two *Harry Potter* movies.

ABOVE *Albert Finney played Albert Seaton, a working-class rebel, in Karel Reisz's* Saturday Night and Sunday Morning *(1960). The actress is Shirley Ann Field.*

ALBERT FINNEY (b. 1936)

Finney's stage and screen career has been inconsistent because he has decided that there are more things to life than being a successful and famous actor. Hence, his screen appearances have been spasmodic, although some of his performances reveal that he has what it takes to be a really expert movie actor. His first big success was as Albert Seaton, the archetypal working-class rebel figure in *Saturday Night and Sunday Morning*. He was the first of the British stars who could play working-class men with authenticity; hitherto we had to suffer Johnny Mills or Stewart Granger going down-market. Finney had a popular success with *Tom Jones*, but none of his other 1960s

LEFT *Vanessa Redgrave as she appeared in Antonioni's* Blow-Up. *Redgrave has alternated between stage and screen, but has never really established herself as a first-rank movie star.*

movies made much of a mark – including the underrated *Charlie Bubbles* which he directed himself. He was amusing in *Gumshoe*, excruciating as Hercule Poirot in *Murder on the Orient Express*, but compelling in *Shoot the Moon* and *The Dresser*. Too many movies like *Scrooge*, *Annie* and *Under the Volcano* have restricted the number of decent performances he has given on screen. He made *Miller's Crossing* with the Coen brothers, was Julia Roberts' mentor in *Erin Brockovich*, and starred as Winston Churchill in the TV drama *The Gathering Storm*. Finney is a physical actor of great potential; a few times that potential has been tapped.

JULIE CHRISTIE (b. 1941)

Christie came to prominence in the 1963 *Billy Liar* and then won an Oscar for her performance in *Darling*. Her career reached something of a peak with *Doctor Zhivago*, but she was woefully miscast in *Far from the Madding Crowd*. Two better roles came her way in *Petulia* and *The Go-Between*. She co-starred with Warren Beatty in *McCabe and Mrs Miller*, definitely one of her better films, as was Nicolas

ABOVE In her early days in British movies, Julie Christie had small parts in comedies such as The Fast Lady. *Here she is with the star of the movie, James Robertson Justice.*

Roeg's *Don't Look Now*. *Shampoo* and *Nashville* were two further hits for her. *Heaven Can Wait*, *Demon Seed*, *Heat and Dust* and Kenneth Branagh's *Hamlet* (in which she played the Queen) were other notable movies.

MICHAEL CAINE (b. 1933)

Caine is a screen actor of extremely limited range who can be effective in some roles. He was best suited to parts such as Harry Palmer in *The Ipcress File* and *Funeral in Berlin*. Other very popular movies he appeared in include *The Italian Job* and *Get Carter*. There was a period in the late 1970s and early 80s when it seemed his career had been sunk by too many bad movies, but *Educating Rita* rescued it. *Hannah and Her Sisters* (for which he won an Oscar), *Dirty Rotten Scoundrels*, *Blood and Wine*, *Little Voice*, *The Cider House Rules* (his second Oscar) and *The Quiet American* have balanced the bad movies he has continued to make. He has survived at the top in the business.

JUDI DENCH
(b. 1934)

Dench is by no stretch of the imagination a big movie star, but her infrequent screen appearances have garnered her much praise and not a few awards, including Oscars. Her film career

ABOVE Michael Caine made a real impact as Harry Palmer, Len Deighton's rebellious British agent, in The Ipcress File *(1965).*

did not really take off until the 1980s when two adaptations of British novels, *A Room with a View* and *A Handful of Dust* reminded movie-makers she could act on screen. She was 007's handler in the most recent James Bond movies, *GoldenEye*, *Tomorrow Never Dies*, *The World Is Not*

BELOW Judi Dench as she appeared in 84 Charing Cross Road *(1986). She played second lead to Anne Bancroft and Anthony Hopkins in this movie, but went on to carve out a secure niche in the film world as well as continuing her distinguished stage career.*

Enough and *Die Another Day*, played Queen Victoria in *Mrs Brown* and Elizabeth I in *Shakespeare in Love*, for which she was unaccountably given an Oscar. Other movies include *Tea with Mussolini* and *Chocolat*.

ANTHONY HOPKINS (b. 1937)

Hopkins has only intermittently taken his profession totally seriously in the sense of pursuing the great roles and taking care about what he does on screen. He has spoken caustically of the preciousness and pretentiousness of the British theatre and actors, which is refreshing, but too often he has involved himself in crass movie projects; indeed, far too often for a man of his immense talent. His screen career did not really start to take off until he made *Magic* for Richard Attenborough in 1978 and *The Elephant Man* for David Lynch in 1980. He was a convincing Captain Bligh in *The Bounty* (1984), but really made an impression as Hannibal Lecter in *The Silence of the Lambs*. *Howards End*, *The Remains of the Day* and *Shadowlands* were three of his better movies and he also scored playing Nixon in the Oliver Stone movie of that name. Appearing in movies such as *Meet Joe Black*, *The Mask of Zorro* and more appearances as Lecter in *Hannibal* and *Red Dragon* no doubt pays the bills, but these are not worthy of his talents.

EMMA THOMPSON (b. 1959)

Thompson's usual role in movies is that of the eminently sensible but feeling woman, as she showed in *The Remains of the Day*, *Howards End* and *In the Name of the Father*. At one time married to Kenneth Branagh, they seemed for a while to be British filmland's "golden couple", although comparisons with Oliver and Vivien Leigh were surely far-fetched. She played the Bloomsbury Group painter Carrington in the movie of the same name and adapted Jane Austen's *Sense and Sensibility* for the screen in 1995, a movie she also starred in. She was chosen to play the Hillary Clinton-type character in *Primary Colors* (1998).

KENNETH BRANAGH (b. 1960)

Branagh has been involved in a multitude of enterprises, both on stage and on screen. After forging for himself a high-profile career in serious theatre, he directed and starred in *Henry V* (1989), which led to inevitable comparisons with Laurence Olivier and his 1944 movie of Shakespeare's play. He then went to Hollywood and directed a quasi-tribute to *film noir*, *Dead Again*, before acting in and directing the indulgent *Peter's Friends*. A second Shakespeare movie, *Much Ado About Nothing*, was another success, which was followed by a full-length *Hamlet*, packed full of Hollywood and British stars. His acting career rocketed with critically acclaimed performances in two television dramas, *Conspiracy* (2001) and *Shackleton* (2002), followed by a movie role in *Harry Potter and the Chamber of Secrets* (2002).

LEFT *Anthony Hopkins will be remembered as Hannibal Lecter in* The Silence of the Lambs, Hannibal *and* Red Dragon.

ABOVE *Emma Thompson starred alongside Hugh Grant and Kate Winslet in* Sense and Sensibility. *Her script won her an Oscar.*

PIERCE BROSNAN (b. 1951)

Brosnan had made *The Fourth Protocol* and *Mrs Doubtfire* before being chosen as James Bond in succession to Timothy Dalton and appearing in *GoldenEye* (1995). He has followed that up with more Bond movies, *Tomorrow Never Dies* (1997), *The World Is Not Enough* (1999) and *Die Another Day* (2002). An Irishman, he usually plays suave on screen, but has sent up that image in *Doubtfire* and *Mars Attacks!* The 2003 *Evelyn* was an attempt to break away from the Bond image: he played a father fighting for custody of his daughter.

HELENA BONHAM CARTER (b. 1966)

At the start of her screen career, Bonham Carter was closely associated with Merchant-Ivory productions, such as *A Room with a View*, *Where Angels Fear to Tread* and *Howards End*. She usually plays a slightly neurotic variation of the English rose and can be irritatingly affected doing it. She was in the Branagh-directed *Mary Shelley's Frankenstein*, Woody Allen's *Mighty Aphrodite* and a film version of Henry James's *Wings of a Dove*. Generally associated with period movies, she has tried to break free from that image in *Fight Club*, *Women Talking Dirty* and *Planet of the Apes*.

ABOVE *Helena Bonham Carter with co-star Rupert Graves in a scene from* Where Angels Fear to Tread *(1991), a film adaptation of E.M. Forster's first novel.*

RALPH FIENNES (b. 1962)

Fiennes is one of the outstanding British stage actors to have emerged since around 1990, and he has carried that success over into his screen roles. He first made an impact as Heathcliff in the 1992 *Wuthering Heights*, but made his major screen breakthrough in Spielberg's *Schindler's List* playing a sadistic Nazi. He was then directed by Robert Redford in *Quiz Show* as an Ivy League intellectual caught up in the grubby corruption of 1950s American

ABOVE *Ralph Fiennes' performance as a Nazi officer in* Schindler's List *won him a well-deserved Oscar nomination.*

game shows, and won international acclaim as the burned plane-crash victim in *The English Patient*. The one blot on his screen record is playing John Steed in *The Avengers*, but *Onegin* and *The End of the Affair* put him back on track. He was also excellent in *Sunshine*, a European co-production directed by Istvan Szabo in which he played three parts, each a member of a different generation of a Hungarian Jewish family. He is a fine, intelligent actor equally at home on stage or screen. He needs to avoid movies like *Maid in Manhattan* (2003), however.

KATE WINSLET (b. 1975)

Winslet's big break came with the success of *Sense and Sensibility* (1995), but she really hit the big time starring with Leonardo DiCaprio in *Titanic*. She also played Ophelia to Branagh's Hamlet in the 1996 movie, but movies such as *Hideous Kinky*, *Holy Smoke*, *Quills* and *The Life of David Gale* have not done much for her career.

JUDE LAW (b. 1972)

Law played Lord Alfred Douglas opposite Stephen Fry's Oscar Wilde in the 1997 *Wilde*, then had successes in *Gattaca* and *eXistenZ*. He was very good as a nasty, spoiled rich kid in *The Talented Mr Ripley*. Law is not afraid to play unsympathetic parts, as he further showed in *Road to Perdition*. With his talent, he should be an enduring star.

EWAN MCGREGOR (b. 1971)

McGregor had major successes in two movies directed by compatriot Danny Boyle: *Shallow Grave* (1994) and *Trainspotting* (1996). He managed to survive being miscast in *Emma* (and wearing a terrible wig) and followed that with *Brassed Off*, *A Life Less Ordinary*, *Velvet Goldmine*, *Little Voice* and *Rogue Trader*. He then took the Hollywood shilling by appearing as the young Obi-Wan Kenobi in the first episodes of the *Star Wars* series. He also appeared in *Black Hawk Down* directed by Ridley Scott. McGregor shows no inhibitions on screen at all and he dared to sing in *Moulin Rouge* (2001), emerging with credit.

CATHERINE ZETA-JONES (b. 1969)

Zeta-Jones emerged from the musical stage and appeared in *Christopher Columbus: The Discovery*, *Splitting Heirs*, *Blue Juice* and *The Phantom*. She followed that with *The Mark of Zorro*, *Entrapment*, *Traffic* (the one worthwhile movie she has starred in) and *America's Sweethearts*. She made a well-publicized marriage to American star Michael Douglas in 2000 and won a Best Supporting Actress Oscar for her singing role in *Chicago* (2002).

167

ABOVE *Welsh-born Catherine Zeta-Jones as she appeared in the 1996 Paramount movie* The Phantom.

FRENCH STARS

JEAN GABIN (1904–76)

Jean Gabin could play proletarian heroes, tough guys and members of the officer class. He starred in some of the great French classics: *La Grande Illusion, Le Quai des Brumes, La Bête Humaine* and *Le Jour Se Lève*. He frequently played gangsters in movies such as *Touchez pas au Grisbi* and *The Sicilian*. He also played Inspector Maigret in a series of movies, but there is no doubt that it will be for the pre-war movies that Gabin will be best remembered. In these films he seemed to typify something essentially French: style and toughness mixed with tenderness, honesty and a romantic aura.

YVES MONTAND (1921–91)

Gabin's natural successor, Montand started as a singer, then graduated to serious roles. He first came to international prominence in *The Wages of Fear* (1953). He made *Let's Make Love* (1960) with Marilyn Monroe and had a much-publicized affair with her. However, his Hollywood career did

BELOW Yves Montand took over the mantle of Jean Gabin and became for many the screen's archetypal Frenchman. In actual fact Montand was born Ivo Levi and was Italian by birth. When he died, France went into mourning.

not take off and he returned to Europe to make films such as *The War is Over, Vivre pour Vivre, The Red Circle* and *Le Sauvage*. He returned to Hollywood in 1970 to make *On a Clear Day You Can See Forever* with Streisand and Vincente Minnelli. In the latter part of his career he had great success with *Jean de Florette* and *Manon des Sources*. Montand died in 1991 at the age of 70. The French mourned him deeply; most people remembered him as the young protégé of Edith Piaf, the errant but loving husband of Simone Signoret and as a French Bogart.

SIMONE SIGNORET (1921–85)

One of those French actresses who seemed to symbolize something eternally French, Signoret had a long and distinguished career in French movies from 1942 to 1982. Her best-known films are *La Ronde, Casque d'Or, Les Diaboliques* and *La Mort en ce Jardin*. Foreign films included *Room at the Top, Ship of Fools, The Deadly Affair* and *Games*.

ABOVE Brigitte Bardot first came to prominence in Roger Vadim's And God Created Woman. Here she is seen with co-star Curt Jurgens.

BRIGITTE BARDOT (b. 1934)

Bardot became a sex symbol in the 1950s, largely due to her roles in movies directed by her then-husband, Roger Vadim: *And God Created Woman* and *Heaven Fell That Night*. Dubbed a "sex kitten", Bardot never managed to break free from that stereotype, although she tried in movies such as *The Truth, Contempt* and *Shalako*. In her latter years she practically disowned her movie career, preferring to battle for the rights of animals and being connected with extreme right-wing politics in France.

PHILIPPE NOIRET (b. 1930)

Noiret has become better known internationally through performances in recently successful films, *Life and Nothing But* and *Cinema Paradiso*, but he has had a screen career spanning four decades. He was in *La Grande Bouffe (Blow Out)*, Francesco Rosi's *Three Brothers* and Tavernier's *The Clockmaker*. He has appeared in Hitchcock's *Topaz, Justine, Murphy's War* and *Round Midnight*. He had a success in *Il Postino* in 1994. He has become almost as recognizable a symbol of Frenchness as Gabin was in his day.

ABOVE *Philippe Noiret's most famous movie is probably* Cinema Paradiso. *Here he is on the set of the movie (far left) with co-stars Salvatore Cascio and Jacques Perrin.*

JEANNE MOREAU (b. 1928)

Moreau came to prominence with *Les Amants* (1958) and *Les Liaisons Dangereuses* (1959). Antonioni used her beautiful but ravaged features in *La Notte* and Truffaut saw her as a symbol of femininity in *Jules et Jim*. She worked with Luis Buñuel in *Diary of a Chambermaid* and Orson Welles in *Chimes at Midnight*. She has continued to work in movies well into her 70s.

GÉRARD DEPARDIEU (b. 1948)

Depardieu has graduated from animalistic parts to portraying more sensitive men in *Le Dernier Métro, The Woman Next Door, Danton, Jean de Florette, Trop Belle pour Toi, Cyrano de Bergerac, Green Card* and *Uranus*. Indeed, the hulk has turned out to be a fine screen actor. He was unable to

ABOVE *Gérard Depardieu had a huge success starring in* Jean de Florette *(1986), directed by Claude Berri.*

avoid *1492* being the turkey it was, however, but *Tous les Matins du Monde, Germinal, Colonel Chabert* and *The Horseman on the Roof* were better for him and he has remained at the top.

CATHERINE DENEUVE (b. 1943)

Deneuve became a symbol of French beauty in art-house movies such as *Les Parapluies de Cherbourg, Les Demoiselles de Rochefort, Mayerling* and *The Hunger*. Polanski used her rather differently in *Repulsion*. Luis Buñuel also gave her more opportunity than usual in *Belle de Jour* and then in *Tristana*, while François Truffaut starred her in *Le Sauvage* and *Le Dernier Métro*. She has performed in several American movies including *Mayerling* and *The April Fools*, but she has never seriously threatened to become a Hollywood star. She had a success with *Indochine* and was not reluctant to play her age and an alcoholic in *Place Vendôme* (1998).

ISABELLE HUPPERT (b. 1955)

Huppert emerged as one of the leading screen actresses in France in the 1970s and 80s. Her first big success was as the victim heroine of *The Lacemaker*, then she had a change of pace as the murderer, *Violette Nozière*. Cimino followed this change of style by casting her as the gun-toting madame in *Heaven's Gate*. Her lack of classical beauty and her limited English may mean that international stardom will elude her, but she still commands strong parts, as she showed playing the title role in Claude Chabrol's version of Flaubert's classic novel, *Madame Bovary*. She was kept busy in French movies in the 1990s and should still be cast in leading roles because she is an accomplished actress.

JULIETTE BINOCHE (b. 1964)

Binoche first came to international attention when she appeared in *The Unbearable Lightness of Being* (1988), which she followed with *Les Amants du Pont-Neuf*. Louis Malle directed her as the havoc-causing heroine of *Damage*.

ABOVE *Juliette Binoche starred in Krzysztof Kieslowski's* Three Colours *trilogy – Blue (1993),* White *(1994) and* Red *(1994).*

169

She won an Academy Award for *The English Patient* (1996) and had a great success with *Chocolat* (2000). She was also very effective in the fine period drama *Widow of Saint-Pierre* (2000). Because of her looks, she is sometimes not taken very seriously by critics, but the fact is that she is an intelligent and effective actress when the role is right.

DANIEL AUTEUIL (b. 1950)

It was with *Jean de Florette* and *Manon des Sources* that Auteuil made his name, but since then he has played convincingly in *Un Coeur en Hiver, My Favourite Season* and *La Reine Margot*. Auteuil can communicate power and vulnerability on screen and is certainly one of the very best screen actors around.

ITALIAN STARS

ANNA MAGNANI (1907–73)

Magnani played powerful, passionate women to the hilt. There was never underplaying when she was on screen, but she was highly effective in Rossellini's *Open City* and De Sica's *The Miracle*. In her Italian movies she seemed to encapsulate the incendiary, sensual stereotype of Italian womanhood, but in fact she was an able actress. Hollywood tried to make an international star of her in movies such as *The Rose Tattoo*, *Wild is the Wind* and *The Fugitive Kind* (with Marlon Brando), but she could never really be fitted into the Hollywood mould. After her Hollywood efforts, she failed to regain her former status in her domestic industry and died at the comparatively early age of 66. She was seemingly as incendiary off-screen as she was on-screen.

GINA LOLLOBRIGIDA (b. 1927)

"La Lollo", as she was known, was, unlike Magnani, never accused of overacting; indeed, the debate was whether she ever acted at all. She played mindless, busty and plastic beauties in a succession of movies of which *Fanfan la Tulipe*, *Les Belles de Nuit*, *Bread, Love and Dreams*, *Beat the Devil*, *Trapeze*, *Solomon and Sheba* and *Woman*

of *Straw* were the most successful. As she advanced in years, her career fizzled out, having had no track record as an actress to sustain it. Her screen image must have set back the cause of the liberation of Italian women for many years.

LEFT *Anna Magnani was one of the most powerful actresses of the Italian cinema, but Hollywood didn't utilize her talents properly.*

BELOW *Gina Lollobrigida was one of the most popular Italian stars of the 1950s and 60s. At her peak, she was the Italian glamour star.*

ABOVE *Here Gina Lollobrigida is seen with French co-star Daniel Gelin in the 1954 production* Woman of Rome.

MARCELLO MASTROIANNI (1923–96)

A romantic star who was also an intelligent actor, Mastroianni worked memorably with Fellini in *La Dolce Vita* and 8½ and Antonioni in *La Notte*. Other important films included *The Stranger, Yesterday, Today and Tomorrow, Casanova '70, La Grande Bouffe* and, with Fellini again, *Fred and Ginger*. There is no doubt that Mastroianni occasionally took roles he could amble through, but he generally brought a skilful technique to his screen appearances. Perhaps his good looks meant that he would inevitably be cast in rather silly romantic stories, but at his best he could be very effective when working with able directors who recognized what he was capable of.

SOPHIA LOREN (b. 1934)

"La Loren" has her supporters who say she is a talented actress. These fans cite movies such as *Desire Under the Elms, Two Women* and *The Condemned of Altona* as evidence of this. But the public mostly remember her for her exposure in movies such as *Boy on a*

ABOVE *Marcello Mastroianni was at his most effective on screen when he made movies with directors such as Antonioni. Here he starred in* La Notte (1961) *opposite Jeanne Moreau. The movie is a bleak picture of a loveless marriage.*

ABOVE *Sophia Loren had a great success appearing opposite Peter Sellers in a film version of Bernard Shaw's play,* The Millionairess (1960).

ABOVE *Carlo Ponti married Sophia Loren twice (1957 and 1966) and he produced many of her movies, including* Ghosts Italian Style (1968).

Dolphin, Heller in Pink Tights, El Cid, The Millionairess, Arabesque and *Man of La Mancha*. Married to producer Carlo Ponti, Loren has had her difficulties with the Italian tax authorities, spending a short spell in jail. She has a cold quality on screen which prevents her, for some, from being watchable. However, she was an international star for a number of years. Even in her 70s, La Loren still flaunts it and is always more than capable of arousing fan frenzy among those who worship her.

LINO VENTURA (1919–87)

Italian-born Lino Ventura made as many French movies as Italian, starring in some of Jean-Pierre Melville's most memorable gangster flicks: *Second Wind (Le Deuxième Souffle), Le Samouraï* and *The Red Circle*. His deadpan style was very well suited to the ultra-cool anti-heroes of Melville's fables of the criminal world. Claude Lelouch also used Ventura in *La Bonne Année*, which cast Ventura in a more romantic role. Ventura was in the Bogart mould and the enduring image one has of him is in a trench coat in shadowy rooms or walking down dark streets.

171

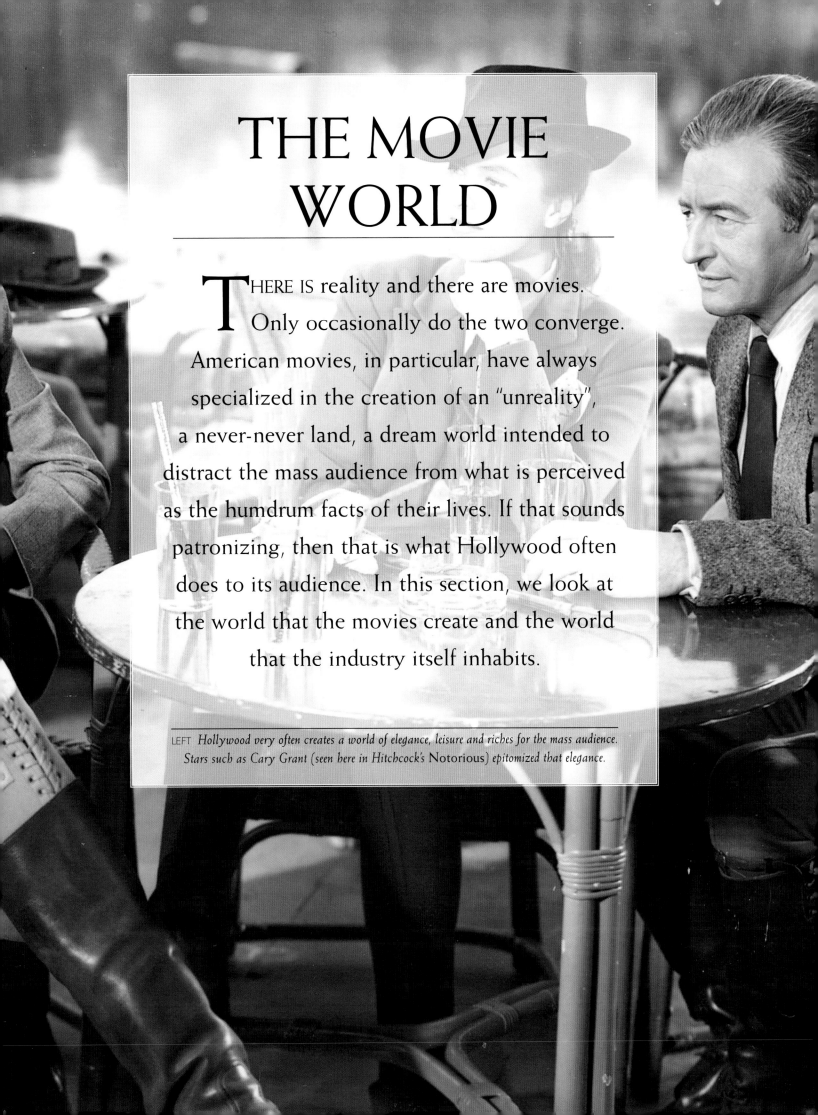

THE MOVIE WORLD

THERE IS reality and there are movies. Only occasionally do the two converge. American movies, in particular, have always specialized in the creation of an "unreality", a never-never land, a dream world intended to distract the mass audience from what is perceived as the humdrum facts of their lives. If that sounds patronizing, then that is what Hollywood often does to its audience. In this section, we look at the world that the movies create and the world that the industry itself inhabits.

LEFT *Hollywood very often creates a world of elegance, leisure and riches for the mass audience. Stars such as Cary Grant (seen here in Hitchcock's* Notorious) *epitomized that elegance.*

INTRODUCTION

In his excellent book, *America in the Dark*, David Thomson writes about "Hollywood and the gift of unreality". His argument is that Hollywood created a separate reality, indeed an alternative reality, which obeyed different rules from that of everyday life. The prime function of the movies was to create unreality for the masses. Whenever films did touch on social issues or life as we know it, Hollywood managed to distort the reality of things to provide reassuring messages and resolutions. In life, there may be a few happy endings; in Hollywood, there is almost always a happy ending. Its staple fare is the "feel-good" movie. It sells hope and solace. From Busby Berkeley musicals to Steve Martin comedies, from Bette Davis melodramas to gross-out comedies, the message has remained much the same: trust in the American Way of Life and, even though things may appear hopeless, a happy ending will somehow be conjured up for you.

ABOVE *Greta Garbo became a major asset for the industry in the 1930s, starring in lavish MGM productions such as* Marie Walewska.

However, not even Hollywood can provide endlessly carefree movies of the Andy Hardy and *Lassie Come Home* variety. There have to be bumpy rides along the way before the uplifting chords of the final reprise of the score usher us out of the cinema to face real life again. You can fool most of the people a lot of the time, but not all of the customers all of the time,

so signs of social conflict or contradictions must be represented in some movies. And that is where genre movies come in: the westerns, the musicals, the gangster movies, the horror flicks, the science fiction epics, the adventure films, the swashbucklers, the screwball comedies, the war pictures, the epics and the social issue movies.

Genres made commercial sense because the studios could sell an easily identifiable product to a mass audience accustomed to buying that product. However, genre movies were also a useful means of representing a conflict within society, often between an individual and the community, and of reaching a compromise resolution

that reinforced the values of the community. Thus, a western such as *Shane* (1953) could show the conflict between a greedy rancher and small homesteaders, and resolve the conflict through the figure of Shane, the buckskin-clad, loner hero (Alan Ladd), who has to move on when, through his special skills as a gunman,

LEFT AND BELOW *Biopics were a staple genre of all the major studios. Examples include the Cary Grant movie* Night and Day, *supposedly about the life of Cole Porter (below), and* Rommel, Desert Fox, *starring James Mason as the German World War II general (left).*

he has made the valley safe for the homesteaders to grow their families and crops. Message: you need a professional, specially skilled military person to defend the rights of ordinary citizens against bullies of one kind or another (perhaps a particularly useful message for the Cold War era).

Courtroom dramas are almost a separate genre of their own; in *12 Angry Men* Henry Fonda played the

ABOVE *The Big Clock (1948) starred Charles Laughton and Ray Milland and was an example of film noir, which was granted genre status by movie critics.*

classic role of the liberal in the cream suit who gently persuaded his fellow jurors that they were wrong to find a Hispanic youth guilty of murder, thereby condemning him to the electric chair. In the movie, all the conflicts and dissensions among the jury members are smoothed over and the American system of justice is triumphantly vindicated by the end of the film. The issue of the rights and wrongs of capital punishment is not even addressed. However, the

ABOVE *Disaster movies keep getting made; witness the recent* Titanic. *One of the most successful disaster movies at the box office was the 1974* The Towering Inferno.

audience feels reassured by the proceedings and, indeed, grateful to such a wonderful judicial system and leaves the cinema with the thought that there will always be a Henry Fonda around to prevent injustice. Oh, yeah? Well, it only happens in the world of the movies, that world of unreality.

Hollywood, someone once said, is a state of mind rather than a place. However, it is a place as well, although only one studio, Paramount, now physically remains there. Every year the workers and executives of this mythical or real place, depending on your point of view, come together to present prizes to one another in the

Oscars ceremony. As usual with Hollywood, the business end of things is the driving force behind the hype of this orgy of congratulation.

The Oscars achieve massive publicity for the American film industry, and the winning actors and directors find that their value in the market place has increased considerably. However, the publicity that Hollywood courts and actively co-operates with also has its down side, and that is the possibility of scandal. The publicity hounds who eat up Hollywood hype can also bite the hands that feed them, and many a star or film personality has succumbed

ABOVE *Errol Flynn acts out a scene with his co-stars during the shooting of the 1939 western* Dodge City.

to the pressures of living their lives in the endless limelight of fame. Hollywood may try to arrange itself and its movies to convey a rosy and wholesome image, but occasionally Superman is found without his cape on and looks like a sleazy creature from the sewers.

LEFT *Irwin Allen's* The Day the World Ended *starred important Hollywood stars like Paul Newman and William Holden, but the stars and script played second fiddle to the special effects of the disaster genre.*

BELOW *David Cronenberg is sometimes called the thinking man's horror movie director. This 1987 remake of the 1950s Vincent Price version of* The Fly *starred Jeff Goldblum as the guy who turns into a fly.*

THE SILENT YEARS

Irving Thalberg is quoted as saying there never was any such thing as a silent movie. He described how at MGM in the pre-sound days he would sit with other executives in the screening room and watch MGM's latest offering in despair at what he saw, wondering what kind of product they had to sell to the public. Then they would put the movie into a cinema, either with a fully fledged orchestra or pianist to provide musical accompaniment, and suddenly there was drama, excitement and magic on the screen. The music did more than simply underscore the narrative the audience was seeing; it told them what to feel and how to react. When we talk about "the silents" we should always bear Thalberg's dictum in mind. Indeed, when silents are revived now for theatrical showings, they usually have an added soundtrack of specially written music.

However, when Georges Méliès, theatre owner in Paris at the end of the 19th century, began making films,

ABOVE *Georges Méliès dealt in cinematic magic, as this shot of the moon getting one in the eye demonstrates.* 2001 *it isn't, but to turn-of-the-century audiences coming fresh to this new art, this was spectacle indeed.*

musical accompaniment was not part of his plans. He merely saw film as an extension of his skill as an illusionist. But the movies he made caught on, and in 1900 he filmed the story of Cinderella. Along the way he discovered the use of fades and dissolves, slow (and fast) motion and animation, especially in his science fiction films *A Trip to the Moon* and *An Impossible Voyage*. The first real "movie" is generally reckoned to be

The Great Train Robbery. It was made by Edwin Porter, one of a group of American pioneers who were inspired by the likes of Méliès to use the new invention as a means of narrative. Porter's films became regular features in the fare served up to audiences by the nickelodeons.

In the beginning, films were photographed with a stationary camera, which recorded what happened in front of it in an unbroken sequence. Movies did not seem all that different from stage plays, except that the actors were not actually performing there in the theatre. Close-ups and editing techniques were slow to come, until Griffith got to work moving the technique of the motion picture towards what we recognize as the art of the cinema nowadays. His use of close-ups, editing techniques, cross-cutting and composition within the frame was to reach its apotheosis in *The Birth of a Nation*. The cinema would never be the same again.

THE CREATION OF STARS

The actors who appeared in those early movies were largely anonymous, until a certain Florence Lawrence broke the barrier because of her popularity with audiences. She became known as "The Biograph Girl" – a star had been born and producers

began to realize that you could sell movies by association with big names. Famous stars would provide what the producers desperately needed – "product identification" – and competition for the hottest new properties increased dramatically. Mary Pickford, for example, who joined Biograph in 1909, became a favourite of the masses, was dubbed "America's Sweetheart", and ended up earning more than half-a-million dollars a year from Paramount.

LEFT *One of the top female stars of the silent era was Lilian Gish, who was in Griffith's* The Birth of a Nation (*1915*).

Movies were now attracting famous stars from the stage and vaudeville, including John Barrymore, Walter Hampden, Gaby Deslys the opera star, Geraldine Farrar and W.C. Fields. Mary Pickford was the highest-paid, but sweetness was not the only draw: Theda Bara became the first screen "vamp", a female who devoured men. Charlie Chaplin also shot to fame from a debut in a Keystone comedy; he was shortly signed by the Essanay company for 1250 dollars a week. Douglas Fairbanks became an instant star with his first film, *The Lamb*, and William S. Hart was the first screen western hero.

SILENT COMEDY

What most people remember from the silent years are the comedies: the Mack Sennett Keystone Kops series, Charlie Chaplin, Buster Keaton, Fatty Arbuckle, Harold Lloyd, Ben Turpin and Laurel and Hardy.

Sennett's comedies comprised mad chases, wild mayhem and surreal slapstick involving violence that never seemed to hurt anyone. Indeed, these movies resembled crazy, out-of-control dream sequences where everyday stability was turned upside down. Their function was eventually taken over by cartoons. By way of contrast, the slapstick in Chaplin's silent comedies was minimized. His main talents were as a mime and a kind of comic ballet dancer. His character as the "little tramp" or vagabond was milked for every drop of pathos. The other great comedian of the 1920s, Buster Keaton, was less interested in making his audiences feel sorry for the incompetents and unfortunates he impersonated, and instead specialized in amazing stunts and acrobatics. All the same, "Old Stoneface" as he was known, gained the audience's sympathy by more subtle means.

ABOVE *Florence Lawrence (1886–1938) was known as "The Biograph Girl" and was one of the first stars of silent movies.*

ABOVE *Mary Pickford (1892–1979) was "America's Sweetheart". She and Douglas Fairbanks were Hollywood's first golden couple.*

Fatty Arbuckle was nearly as big a star as Chaplin at the time of his downfall. Harold Lloyd made a living out of appearing to hang out of tall buildings, whilst Ben Turpin's cross-eyed comedian act made up in gusto for what it lacked in comic nuance. Many people see Laurel and Hardy as effectively silent comedians, and among the very greatest of them. Even though most of their films were talkies, they were still basically visual comedians.

Nothing dates faster than comedy, but many of these silent comedies and actors stand the test of time, principally because they are silent. Perhaps visual comedy is more timeless than comedy that depends on dialogue or the witty one-liner. At any rate, television regularly shows compilations of the best sequences from the Hollywood silent comedies, and the sales of videos of some of the best of the silent comedies reflect a continuing public interest. It is interesting to note that only silent comedies made by Hollywood survive to this day. No other national cinema ever rivalled the American film industry in making the world laugh at the antics of these mute lunatics on the screen.

177

WILLIAM FOX PRESENTS
Theda Bara
CLEOPATRA

LEFT *Theda Bara (1885–1955) may seem faintly ridiculous now, but in her heyday she was known as the Vamp.*

ABOVE *The Big Four who established United Artists: Douglas Fairbanks, Mary Pickford, Charles Chaplin and D.W. Griffith.*

THE EUROPEANS

When it came to artistic advances, the real progress was taking place in Europe, particularly in Germany, Russia, France and

ABOVE *Louise Brooks, one of the great silent stars, appeared in German director G.W. Pabst's* Pandora's Box *(1929). But her career did not survive long into the sound era.*

Scandinavia. In Germany the Expressionist movement strongly influenced directors such as Fritz Lang in *Die Niebelungen* (1924), *Metropolis* (1927) and *Spies* (1928). Similarly, Robert Wiene's *The Cabinet of Dr Caligari* (1919) showed the influence of Cubist painting. F.W. Murnau, another distinguished German director, made important films in *The Last Laugh* (1924) and *Faust* (1926).

In Russia, the leaders of the Revolution soon realized the propaganda value of the infant medium. Sergei Eisenstein became the most famous director in the world, and an important film theoretician as well.

ABOVE *A famous shot from Eisentein's* The Battleship Potemkin *(1925).*

His films, *Strike* (1924), *The Battleship Potemkin* (1925) and *October* (1928), reflected his belief in the power of montage sequences – the editing of film in a succession of closely controlled shots to produce a specific effect on the cinema audience.

"A COLLAR BUTTON UNDER A
LENS AND THROWN ON A SCREEN
MAY BECOME A RADIANT PLANET."
SERGEI EISENSTEIN

In France, Abel Gance produced *Napoléon* (1927), a film shot for multiple projectors throwing images on a triple screen. Jean Renoir, the son of the Impressionist painter, began his long film career with *The Water Girl*

(1924) and *Nana* (1925). In Sweden, Mauritz Stiller made *The Emigrants* (1921), *Gunnar Hedes Saga* (1922) and *The Saga of Gosta Berling* (1924), which launched the film career of a rather chubby young woman, Greta Garbo. In Denmark, Carl Dreyer became known worldwide for his movies *The Parson's Widow* (1920), *Master of the House* (1925) and *The Passion of Joan of Arc* (1928).

RIGHT *Abel Gance was a French director who thought big, and if he had been alive in the 1950s he would have been handed many an epic to direct. Napoléon (1927) ran for six hours and was meant to be one of six films – but the other five were never made. It traces Napoleon's career from a schoolboy to his invasion of Italy in 1797. Napoléon is still regularly revived today – note the "Francis Coppola presents" heading for this re-release.*

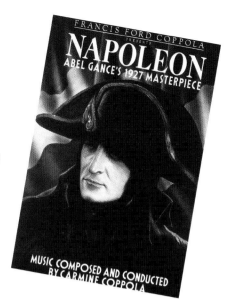

THE SILENT 20s IN HOLLYWOOD

LEFT *Al Jolson initiated sound in the movies in* The Jazz Singer *(1927).*

The great comedians Chaplin and Keaton helped to give screen comedy a new status. Chaplin with *The Gold Rush* (1925) and *The Circus* (1928), and Keaton with *The Navigator* (1924) and *The General* (1927), earned themselves serious attention as creative artists. Douglas Fairbanks achieved huge success with *The Three Musketeers* (1921), *Robin Hood* (1922), *The Thief of Bagdad* (1924) and *The Black Pirate* (1926), which was a very early exercise in colour film.

Fans who liked their stars larger-than-life adored Rudolph Valentino in *The Sheik* (1921), *Blood and Sand* (1922) and *The Eagle* (1925). Alla Nazimova, starring in *Salome* (1923) and *The Redeeming Sin* (1925), tried her utmost to be exotic and other-worldly enough to satisfy the fantasies of millions of men.

Then on October 6, 1927, the première of *The Jazz Singer* took place. Al Jolson was heard speaking one line: "You ain't heard nothing yet, folks. Listen to this." The sound film was born and two years later silent movies were finished.

179

BELOW *Zasu Pitts in Erich von Stroheim's silent masterpiece,* Greed. *Stroheim originally shot 50 reels of film but reduced it to a four-hour running time before an exasperated Irving Thalberg cut it to around 100 minutes.*

Hollywood was producing its own masterpieces in the last years of the silents. Erich von Stroheim was a highly extravagant maverick director who eventually found it impossible to operate within the Hollywood system which put such a premium on making a cost-effective product with an assembly-line production method. Before his directorial career was eclipsed, however, he made *Foolish Wives* (1922), *Greed* (1923) and *The Wedding March* (1928). The Swede Victor Sjöström directed Lillian Gish in *The Scarlet Letter* (1926) and *The Wind* (1928). D.W. Griffith directed the melodrama *Broken Blossoms* with Lillian Gish and Richard Barthelmess in 1919, followed by *Way Down East* (1920), *Orphans of the Storm* (1922) and *America* (1924).

THE STUDIOS

From the mid-1920s on, Hollywood film production functioned within the studio system. The system established a factory production style, in essence no different from a Ford assembly line except that what rolled off the production line were not automobiles but movies. To the moguls who ran the studios, and the money men who controlled the finances in New York, movies were first and foremost a business.

In fact, the "Big Five" (MGM, Paramount, Fox, Warner Brothers and RKO) had more money invested in real estate than in film production. This real estate was in the form of first-run cinemas in the best positions in the principal cities of America. The studios had to make enough major features to service these cinemas and also the affiliated chains with which they had special agreements. As we have seen, each of the five majors was involved in the three aspects of the movie business: production, distribution and exhibition.

None of the majors made enough top-notch features in a year to service their own cinemas, which normally required weekly changes of programme, so the cinemas they owned showed the products of other studios as well. For example, if MGM had a huge hit on its hands, the other companies would benefit from that success through the box-office returns from the cinemas they owned that showed the MGM movie. The major studios were nominally in competition with one another, but in fact they formed an oligopoly that dominated the American film industry and successfully blocked entry to lesser fry. It would be the late 1940s before the American government would act decisively to force the majors to divest themselves of their exhibition function and thereby end the monopoly that had lasted more than 20 years.

The other large studios, Columbia, Universal and United Artists (the company formed by Pickford, Fairbanks, Chaplin and Griffith) were known as the "Little Three". They were prevented from competing with the five majors because they did not have the control over the exhibition side of the business that the majors wielded. However, they were still big studios capable of producing major films.

In addition, there were the "Poverty Row" outfits such as Republic and Monogram, and independent producers who would hope to sell their product to one of the majors.

By 1919, the American film industry had established a dominant position in the world film markets. It is a position that has never seriously been challenged. American cinema is dominant and that dominance had its foundations in the studio system. Even though that system began to break up in the 1950s, the studios survive in some form to this day, despite the many changes in ownership and function. However, their role has changed completely.

MGM

MGM is probably the most famous of all the Hollywood studios. Its proud boast that it had more stars than there are in heaven typifies the studio's general approach: give the public glamour, gloss and glitz. MGM film-makers had a motto they were meant to subscribe to: "Make it good, make it big, give it class." "Ars Gratia Artis" was the legend that appeared above Leo the Lion, MGM's trademark, which is loosely translated as "Art for art's sake"; but art had nothing to do with MGM movies if Louis B. Mayer had anything to do with it. The mogul who ran MGM for 25 years was more interested in providing corny, "family" entertainment to draw the public in.

THE BEGINNINGS
MGM came into being in 1924 with the merger of Metro Pictures, Goldwyn Pictures (minus Sam Goldwyn) and Louis B. Mayer's company. It was the Studio production arm of Loew's Inc., headed by Marcus Loew in New York, which is where all the financial decisions were made.

Louis B. Mayer and the "boy wonder" Irving Thalberg were in charge of production at Culver City, the home of MGM. From the start they put their faith in stars and in top technicians. Curiously, MGM was never a particularly happy hunting-ground for directors: the studio's producers and the heads of the various technical departments were more powerful. Their main task was to create showcases for the glamorous stars MGM took enormous trouble to groom and market. Thalberg would work very closely with his producers and with the writers to produce vehicles for these stars, and only when they had the "product" right did they assign a director to a picture.

1925–1940

Two silent hits for MGM were the 1925 version of *Ben-Hur*, with Ramon Navarro, and King Vidor's *The Big Parade*, a war movie of the same year. The 1929 musical *The Broadway Melody* was the first talking picture to make big bucks for the studio. Garbo was an MGM star, and she starred in her first sound film *Anna Christie* in

ABOVE *British star Robert Donat starred with Greer Garson in the classic MGM movie* Goodbye, Mr Chips *(1939). This was Garson's film debut.*

1930, and in 1932 *Grand Hotel* featured a roster of MGM luminaries: Lionel Barrymore, Joan Crawford, John Barrymore and Wallace Beery. The latter, along with child star Jackie Cooper, also made audiences weep in the aisles in *The Champ* (1931).

The "look" of MGM films was glossy – "stars shot through cellophane wrapping" – but two of their most popular stars in the 1930s went against the house style: Wallace Beery and Marie Dressler. Garbo was the ultimate ethereal star and MGM exploited her in *Queen Christina* (1933) and *Camille* (1936), with Robert Taylor as Armand. Two other major stars emerged in the 1930s: Clark Gable and Joan Crawford. These two were teamed together in eight movies, almost all of them entirely forgettable.

LEFT *Greer Garson was groomed by MGM to be the "great lady" of the screen. She was meant to represent class and gentility among a galaxy of stars that MGM was constantly boasting about.*

ABOVE *"Make it big!" was part of MGM's credo, and they didn't come any bigger in the 1940s than David Selznick's production of* Gone with the Wind.

Gable made a lot of money for the studio in *Mutiny on the Bounty* (1935), with Charles Laughton as Captain Bligh going well over the top, and in *San Francisco* (1936). The decade ended with the première of *Gone with the Wind* (1939), which David Selznick produced for MGM.

1940–1960

MGM had found a gold mine in the series of Andy Hardy pictures they had started in the late 1930s, featuring Mickey Rooney. The family entertainment these movies offered (and their endorsement of American small-town values) warmed Louis B. Mayer's heart and filled Loew's coffers. Under producer Arthur Freed, the Freed Unit at MGM produced a series of "teenage musicals" with Mickey Rooney and Judy Garland, and then graduated to elaborate technicolor

RIGHT *Hurd Hadfield on the set of* The Picture of Dorian Gray, *the 1945 MGM adaptation of Oscar Wilde's novel. MGM prided itself on its "classy" products and often adapted literary works for the screen.*

musicals that created new standards for the genre: *Meet Me in St Louis* (1944), *On the Town* (1949), *An American in Paris* (1951), *Singin' in the Rain* (1952) and *The Band Wagon*

(1953). MGM's musical stars were the best in the business: Gene Kelly, Fred Astaire, Judy Garland and Cyd Charisse. They also employed the most talented directors of musicals: Vincente Minnelli, Gene Kelly, Stanley Donen and Charles Walters.

However, musicals were expensive to produce and did not bring great returns on investment during a period in which MGM badly needed an upturn in its profits. In 1951 Mayer was replaced as head of production by Dore Schary, but the more radical and adventurous former RKO man did not manage to halt MGM's downward slide, although *Quo Vadis?* (1951), *Cat on a Hot Tin Roof* (1958), *Gigi* (1958) and *Ben-Hur* (1959) all did well for the studio. By then, musicals, MGM's pride, were going out of fashion and they had become too expensive to make anyway.

MGM musicals were the pride of the studio. Most of the best musicals, such as Singin' in the Rain, *were produced by the Freed Unit under the supervision of producer Arthur Freed.*

1960 ONWARDS

In the mid-1960s MGM had a few good years, based on the box-office returns of some major hits: *How the West was Won* (1962), *Doctor Zhivago* (1965), *The Dirty Dozen* (1967) and *2001* (1968). The early 1970s saw new owners selling off backlots and studio props and cutting back to four or five movies a year, but the studio had recovered sufficiently by the early 80s to be able to purchase United Artists after the debacle of *Heaven's Gate* helped to ruin the studio. In 1986 Ted Turner, at that time the owner of the CNN television news channel, bought MGM/UA. One attraction for Turner was that he was able to buy the MGM and United Artists film library; thus the Turner Classic Movies television channel (TCM) had an Aladdin's Cave of film goodies to source it. Since then, the ownership of MGM/UA has changed hands several times; it is still in the movie-making business but the great days of Gable, Garbo, Kelly, Astaire, Tracy and Hepburn are gone forever.

The doyen of the studio system at its zenith, MGM produced the most wish-fulfilling of all the fantasies of the dream factory.

By the 1980s MGM imported most of the films they gave their name to, like this 1988 George Lucas production Willow, *which starred Val Kilmer and Joanne Whalley. It did not wow the box office.*

PARAMOUNT

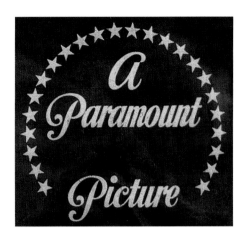

Paramount was born in 1916 from the merging of Adolph Zukor's Famous Players Film Company with Jesse Lasky's company and the Paramount distribution company. Zukor would become one of Hollywood's most hard-nosed moguls, building the empire that would eventually make Paramount Hollywood's biggest studio. As a businessman he realized that you could only play in the ballpark if you were heavily involved in the three major aspects of the film business: production, distribution and exhibition. Thus Paramount, like the other four majors, became a vertically integrated business that wielded enormous influence in the film market.

1916–1929

Zukor set great store by star names, as is evidenced by the name of his first company: Famous Players. Among the stars he had in the early years were Douglas Fairbanks, Mary Pickford, Wallace Reid, Billie Burke and William S. Hart. In the 1920s Valentino made huge profits for the studio in *The Sheik* and *Blood and Sand*. Cecil B. De Mille directed his first version of *The Ten Commandments* in 1923, whilst Ronald Colman made an early version of *Beau Geste* in 1926. *The Covered Wagon* in 1923 was the first epic western. *Wings* (1927) was a spectacular "flying" movie set in World War I.

THE 1930S

Paramount in the 1930s was the studio where the Marx Brothers, Mae West and W.C. Fields exploited their particular forms of comic mayhem. The western was also one of Paramount's favourite genres: the laconic Gary Cooper starred in *The Plainsman* (1936) whilst Joel McCrea strapped on the gun holsters for *Wells Fargo* in 1937. De Mille donned his religious hat to direct *The Sign of the Cross* (1932) and *The Crusades* (1935), and in between these efforts he miscast Claudette Colbert as *Cleopatra* in 1934. Prestige productions came in the form of Preston Sturges's comedies, Frank Borzage's *A Farewell to Arms* (1932) starring Gary Cooper and Helen Hayes, and the exotic fantasies

ABOVE *These are the famous Paramount Pictures gates, through which all hopefuls had to pass if they wanted to make it with the studio. Some never got past the gatemen.*

dreamed up by Josef von Sternberg for Marlene Dietrich: *Morocco* (1930), *Shanghai Express* (1932) and *The Scarlet Empress* (1934). But it was in the musical field that Paramount really

ABOVE *Paramount was appalled with the Austrian's director's extravagance in movies such as* Greed *and* Queen Kelly. *Von Stroheim was never allowed to direct a movie in the sound era.*

ABOVE *Cecil B. De Mille was one of Paramount's most successful directors. His religious epics netted the studio huge profits over the years, with their queasy mixture of religiosity and sex.*

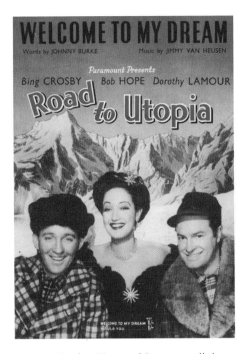

ABOVE *Crosby, Hope and Lamour spelled box-office riches for Paramount in the series of* Road *movies.*

competed. Jeanette MacDonald starred with Maurice Chevalier in three musicals, including the delightful *Love Me Tonight* directed by Rouben Mamoulian. Bing Crosby was a major Paramount star, as were Bob Hope, Betty Grable, George Raft and Dorothy Lamour.

1940–1960

With their series of *Road* pictures, Hope and Crosby boosted Paramount profits enormously in the 1940s and 50s. Other major Paramount stars were Alan Ladd with *This Gun for Hire, The Glass Key* and *The Blue Dahlia.* Victor Mature and Hedy Lamarr wooed the audiences away from their television sets in 1949 with

"AN EXECUTIVE CANNOT EXPECT LOVE – EVER!"
DARRYL ZANUCK

Samson and Delilah, while Bing Crosby and Barry Fitzgerald did a good P.R. job for the Catholic church in *Going My Way.* Without Crosby, Hope made big bucks with *The Paleface* and *Son of Paleface.* An all-star cast including James Stewart and Betty Hutton made De Mille's *The Greatest Show on Earth* (1952) a huge success. Alan Ladd had the greatest role of his career in the 1953 *Shane,* whilst De Mille could not avoid preaching again in the extremely vulgar *The Ten Commandments* of 1956 with Charlton Heston as Moses parting the Red Sea. Critical plaudits as well as box-office success came with Hitchcock's *Rear Window* (1954), starring James Stewart with Grace

185

ABOVE *A box-office winner for Paramount was Danny Kaye in a series of inventive comedies. Here he is with Glynis Johns in* The Court Jester (1956), *in which he explains, "The pellet with the poison's in the vessel with the pestle, the chalice from the palace has the brew that is true."*

Kelly, and *Psycho* in 1960. Among famous directors who worked at Paramount during this period were Billy Wilder (*The Lost Weekend* and *Sunset Boulevard*), Preston Sturges (*The Miracle of Morgan's Creek, Hail the Conquering Hero*) and William Wyler (*The Heiress*).

THE 1960S ONWARDS

The Carpetbaggers (1964) gave Paramount a hit movie and the studio also did very well with *Rosemary's Baby* (1968), directed by Roman Polanski, and the glutinous *Love Story* in 1970. However, it really hit the jackpot in 1972 with *The Godfather*, directed by Francis Coppola. *The Godfather Part II* also did well in 1974, but not on the scale of *Saturday Night Fever* (1977) and *Grease* (1978), both starring John Travolta. These box-office receipts were eclipsed in the 1980s by the Indiana Jones movies *Raiders of the Lost Ark* and *Indiana Jones and the Temple of Doom*. Eddie Murphy arrived as a major star in *Beverly Hills Cop* and Paul Hogan surprised the studio by making it a lot of money with *Crocodile Dundee*. Other hits included *Top Gun, Terms of Endearment, Trading Places*, the *Star Trek* movies and *An Officer and a Gentleman*.

186

ABOVE *Robert Evans was the golden boy of the Paramount production executives in the 1970s, helping to bring to the screen the* Godfather *movies and* Chinatown. *His fall from grace was spectacular, however, and his career never recovered.*

PARAMOUNT NOW

In 1966 Gulf & Western took over Paramount. The days of Adolph Zukor and the great movie entrepreneurs were long gone. Paramount became part of a much larger company that had had no previous experience in the film industry. In 1993 Paramount was bought by the conglomerate Viacom. The studio has continued to have its successes and seems set to remain a major presence in the industry for as long as movies survive.

ABOVE *Rosemary's Baby, directed by Roman Polanski and starring Mia Farrow, was a huge hit for Paramount in 1968.*

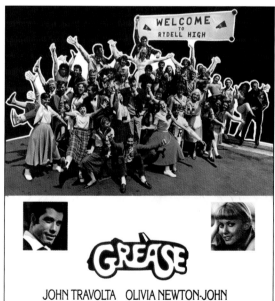

ABOVE *Grease (1978) was a major box-office hit for Paramount. It starred John Travolta and Olivia Newton-John. With* Saturday Night Fever *and this hit, Travolta's career was riding high.*

20th CENTURY FOX

William Fox began in nickelodeons, then built picture palaces, moved into film distribution and finally production. He was one of the entrepreneurs who challenged the monopoly of the Motion Picture Patents Company. Fox's first film was made in 1914 (*Life's Shop Window*), but it was the emergence of Theda Bara as a major star that helped establish the Fox Film Company. In the mid-1920s Fox managed to acquire cinemas in prime sites and strengthened the company's position in relation to its main rivals.

However, hard times followed when the stock-market crash of 1929 hit the company; Fox was forced to sell his shares. Five years later Fox merged with 20th Century Pictures under Darryl Zanuck and Joseph Schenck: 20th Century Fox was created.

THE PRE-1940 FOX MOVIES

What Price Glory?, *Sunrise* and *Seventh Heaven* were three of the more memorable Fox silents. Janet Gaynor was the studio's top silent star, and she was joined in the 1930s by Spencer Tracy (until he went to MGM), Warner Baxter, Will Rogers, Alice Faye, Sonja Henie, Don

ABOVE *Tyrone Power was a major star for Fox for many years.* The Razor's Edge *(1946) was Fox's film version of the Somerset Maugham novel.*

Ameche, Tyrone Power and the biggest box-office attraction of them all, Shirley Temple. *Little Miss Marker* (1934), *The Littlest Rebel* (1935), *Dimples* (1936), *Wee Willie Winkie* (1937), *Rebecca of Sunnybrook Farm* (1938), *The Little Princess* (1939) and several others starring the diminutive but resistible moppet, made Fox big money: she was the envy of other moguls, including Louis B. Mayer at MGM, who, according to Judy Garland, was obsessed with Temple. Alice Faye, Don Ameche and Sonja Henie were the musical stars, and Tyrone Power was the romantic leading man in *In Old Chicago*, *Alexander's Ragtime Band*,

ABOVE *Tyrone Power, Ava Gardner, Mel Ferrer, Errol Flynn and Eddie Albert starred in this 1957 Fox film version of Hemingway's novel* The Sun Also Rises.

Rose of Washington Square, The Rains Came and *Jesse James.* John Ford directed Henry Fonda in *Drums Along the Mohawk* in 1939.

1940 ONWARDS

The 1940s started auspiciously for Fox with John Ford's adaptation of Steinbeck's *The Grapes of Wrath,* and *The Oxbow Incident,* directed by William Wellmann. Betty Grable and Carmen Miranda starred in a series of brash musicals whilst Jennifer Jones attempted to raise the tone somewhat in *The Song of Bernadette* (1943). Clifton Webb was a huge hit in *Cheaper by the Dozen* and Olivia de Havilland suffered in *The Snake Pit* (1948). Cary Grant and Ann Sheridan sparred in *I Was a Male War Bride.* In the 1950s, with a decrease in audiences hitting Hollywood, Fox led the industry in

ABOVE Cleopatra, *the 1962 Taylor–Burton version, was so expensive to make that it nearly bankrupted the studio and scarcely made its money back at the box office.*

introducing CinemaScope with *The Robe* (1953). They now had Marilyn Monroe as a star, and she helped make *How to Marry a Millionaire, Gentlemen Prefer Blondes* (both 1953) and *The Seven Year Itch* (1955) successful. Film versions of stage musicals such as *South Pacific* and *The King and I* featured in the 1950s. In the early 60s Fox had a major disaster with the 38-million-dollar *Cleopatra* starring Elizabeth Taylor. Fox's finances were helped hugely, however, by the stupendous success of *The Sound of Music* (1965). *Butch Cassidy and the Sundance Kid* (1969), *M*A*S*H* (1970) and *Patton* (1970) with George C. Scott were also hits.

The *Star Wars* series brought Fox enormous box-office returns in the late 1970s and early 80s, as did the Damien trilogy, starting with *The Omen* (1976). *Alien* and *Aliens,* with new star Sigourney Weaver, did well

188

LEFT *Marilyn Monroe had an ongoing stormy relationship with the Fox studio. Here she starred with Lauren Bacall and Betty Grable in a very successful musical comedy,* How to Marry a Millionaire.

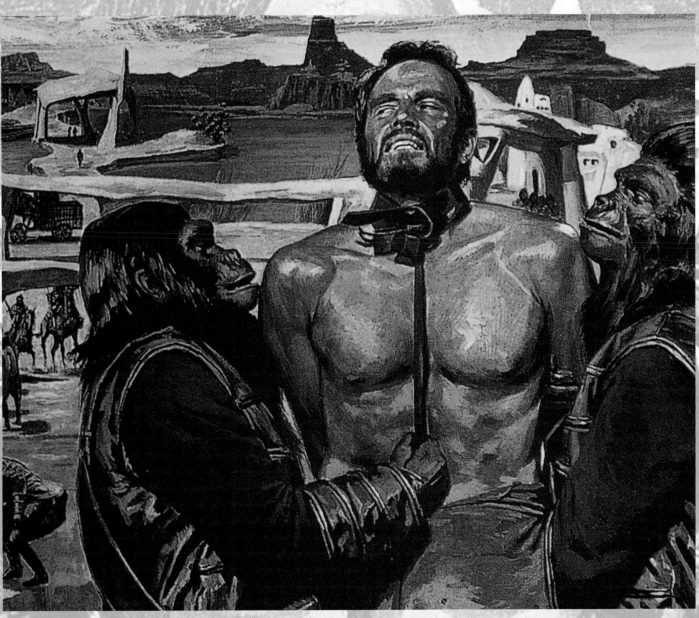

ABOVE *The original* Planet of the Apes *series ran to five movies. The first of the series (1968) was by far the best of them, and very much better than the 2001 remake.*

RIGHT Wall Street, *directed by Oliver Stone and starring Michael Douglas as Gordon "Greed is good" Gekko, was a prodigious hit for Fox in 1987.*

but were surpassed at the box office by the truly awful *Porky's* series. However, times were rocky for the studio by this time and, as if to prove it, Rupert Murdoch was able to purchase it in 1985. Fox had become part of the conglomerate News International, just another arm of a vast media-owning multinational.

WARNER BROTHERS

There were four Warner brothers: Albert, Harry, Sam and Jack. The whole family helped run a nickelodeon, then the brothers branched out into distribution. Soon they were into production and Warner Bros. came into being in 1923. Among their first successes were the *Rin Tin Tin* movies starring a lovable dog, while Ernst Lubitsch, a director of sharp comedies, gave the studio's productions some tone during the silent years. It was Warners' *The Jazz Singer* and its huge success that revolutionized Hollywood. Warner Bros. had truly arrived.

WARNER BROTHERS AND THE DEPRESSION

Warners attempted to build on the success of the Al Jolson movie with a number of musicals, but the public soon tired of this fare. Warners then turned to gangsters and social realism, and if there is one studio associated with the Depression and the New Deal, it is surely this one. Whereas MGM and Mayer were associated with a devout Republicanism, the Warner brothers were more sympathetic to the Democratic president, Roosevelt. Criticism of a society indifferent to poverty and hardship was implicit in the movies that starred Edward G. Robinson, James Cagney and Paul Muni. Movies such as *Little Caesar*, *I Am a Fugitive from a Chain Gang* and *The Public Enemy* reflected the underside of the American Dream and made criminals anti-heroes. Then the studio's products changed course, partly due to condemnation from official sources and pressure groups. In 1933 Busby Berkeley made three musicals for the Depression, *42nd Street* (directed by Lloyd Bacon), *Gold Diggers of 1933* and *Footlight Parade*. They offered audiences eroticism and spectacle whilst acknowledging in passing the reality of poverty and deprivation in contemporary America.

Errol Flynn was a major Warners star in the 1930s and 40s with movies such as *Captain Blood* (1935), *The Adventures of Robin Hood* (1938) and

ABOVE *Errol Flynn starred in this 1938 Warner Brothers production of* The Adventures of Robin Hood, *directed by Michael Curtiz. The movie was a huge hit for Warners and Flynn, and is a fine example of a Hollywood action movie.*

The Sea Hawk (1940). Paul Muni scored in *The Story of Louis Pasteur* (1936), *The Good Earth* (1937), *The Life of Emile Zola* (1937) and *Juarez* (1939). Bette Davis became a major star in *Of Human Bondage* (1935), *Jezebel* (1938), *Dark Victory* (1939), *The Old Maid* (1939) *The Private Lives of Elizabeth and Essex* (1939), *The Letter* (1940), *The Great Lie* (1941), *The Little Foxes* (1942), *Now Voyager* (1942) and *Old Acquaintance* (1943). She was the undisputed queen of the melodramas.

LEFT *James Cagney was a big Warners star in the 1930s. Here he is with Frank McHugh in* The Roaring Twenties *(1939), a typical gangster story about the Prohibition Era.*

190

ABOVE *Warners stars were expected to do their part in publicizing the studio's movies. Here Errol Flynn, Humphrey Bogart and Gilbert Roland board the "Dodge City Special" (probably unwillingly) to publicize the western* Dodge City *(1939).*

Warners returned to its "social conscience" style with the 1939 *Confessions of a Nazi Spy* with Edward G. Robinson, which was clearly anti-American isolationist in intent.

FROM PEARL HARBOR ON

With America's entry into the war, Warners rallied to the flag with stirring, patriotic movies such as *Sergeant York* (1941), *Yankee Doodle Dandy*, *Across the Pacific* and *Casablanca* (all 1942). The last of these became one of the most famous cult pictures ever shot and made Humphrey Bogart a major star, while doing no harm to the career of Ingrid Bergman. Bogart went on to star in *The Maltese Falcon* (1941), *To Have and Have Not* (1945, with his future wife, Lauren Bacall), *The Big Sleep* (1946) and *The Treasure of the Sierra Madre* (1948). Meanwhile, Joan Crawford had moved over to Warners from MGM, leaving her glamour-girl persona behind her and settling for maternal roles. She shone

in *Mildred Pierce* (1945), *Humoresque* (1946) and *Possessed* (1947), suffering dramatically at the hands of husbands, lovers and children.

Alfred Hitchcock made three movies for the studio: *Rope* (1948), *Under Capricorn* (1949) and *Dial M for Murder* (1954). Judy Garland made her "comeback" film for Warners, *A Star is Born* (1954), whilst director Elia Kazan made James Dean a star in *East of Eden*. Nicholas Ray used Dean again in *Rebel Without a Cause* (1955) and George Stevens directed the new star in Dean's last picture, *Giant* (1956), before he was killed in a car crash. In the 1960s the studio scored with *Who's Afraid of Virginia Woolf?* (1966), *Bonnie and Clyde* (1967), and *Bullitt* (1968). Its production of *My Fair Lady* (1964), however, failed to make the impact expected of it.

A demonic thriller, *The Exorcist* (1973), and the first *Superman* movie (1978) made big profits in the 1970s, as did the disaster movie *The Towering Inferno* (1974). Clint Eastwood did well with *Every Which Way But Loose* (1978) and *Any Which Way You Can* (1980), and Barbra Streisand and Kris Kristofferson helped make the third version of *A Star is Born* (1976) a major hit. The story of the uncovering of the Watergate scandals gave Alan Pakula, the director, and Dustin Hoffman and Robert Redford, the stars, opportunities to shine in *All the President's Men* (1976), whilst Streisand again and Ryan O'Neal helped make *What's Up, Doc?* (1972) a success. In the 1980s Steven Spielberg's influence on *Gremlins* (1984) and *The Goonies* (1985) helped create hits. The follow-up *Superman* movies did well at the box office, as did the dire series of *Police Academy* movies.

WARNER BROTHERS TODAY

In 1989 Time Inc. bought Warners and formed Time Warner. In 1996 Time Warner ate up the Turner Broadcasting System to become the

ABOVE *Christopher Reeve was a superhero in the first of the Superman series (1978). As with the later* Batman *(1989) and* Dick Tracy *(1990), Hollywood believed it could only resurrect comic book heroes if they indulged in affectionate send-up. Reeve's performance as the quick-changing defender of the American Way of Life is in line with the series' tongue-in-cheek quality.*

world's largest media conglomerate. The original Warner brothers have all long vanished from the scene, but the studio's great movies with Bogart, Davis, Crawford, Flynn and Cagney are still favourites with all true cinema lovers.

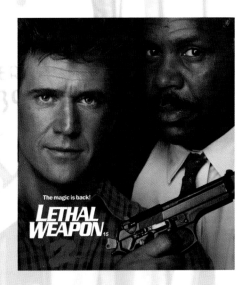

ABOVE *The* Lethal Weapon *series brought immense rewards at the box office for Warners. Critics were less generous.*

RKO

Citizen Kane *has repeatedly topped many film critics' lists of the greatest movies of all time.*

CITIZEN KANE

Hollywood Greats

RKO is an abbreviation for the Radio-Keith-Orpheum Corporation, which was the result of various mergers between a small movie production and distributing company and the Radio Corporation of America. Hence RKO–Radio Pictures.

David Selznick was an early production chief at the studio and he set himself the difficult task of injecting RKO movies with some quality whilst keeping the budgets very tight. In the 1930s producer Pandro S. Berman made the series of Astaire–Rogers musicals including *Top Hat* (1935), *Swing Time* (1936), *Shall We Dance?* (1937) and *Carefree* (1938). Another famous producer, Merian C. Cooper, produced the classic *King Kong* (1933) which teamed an outsize ape with Fay Wray. Other quality pictures included *Alice Adams* (1935) with Katharine Hepburn and *The Informer* (1935) with Victor McLaglen, directed by John Ford. *The Hunchback of Notre Dame* (1939), directed by William Dieterle and starring Charles Laughton as Quasimodo, also brought critical and commercial success. Even in the 1930s RKO took some commercial risks backing projects whose sure-fire commercial success was not always assured.

RKO was also notable for the number of independent productions it financed. Orson Welles's *Citizen Kane* (1941) and *The Magnificent Ambersons* (1942) were both independent productions which the studio lost money on, but these two movies alone ensured that the RKO name would live on. Yes, RKO executives interfered disastrously with the final cut

King Kong *(1933) is perhaps, along with* Citizen Kane, *the most famous movie that RKO produced.*

RKO, still RKO-Radio at the time of the release of Sinbad the Sailor *(1947), specialized in small-budget adventure actioners like this swashbuckler that starred Douglas Fairbanks Junior.*

ABOVE *Hitchcock made one of his best movies for RKO in 1946,* Notorious, *which starred Cary Grant and Ingrid Bergman. The film was a spy thriller involving a post-war Nazi plot to create an atomic bomb.*

of *The Magnificent Ambersons*, but perhaps the studio should be given some credit for giving Orson Welles his chance in the first place. RKO was the smallest of the Big Five studios, it did not have the financial depth of the other four majors, so this perhaps in part explains why they took more chances with their productions.

During the war, RKO did its bit with John Wayne in *Back to Bataan* (1945) and Gregory Peck as a brave Russian resistance fighter in *Days of Glory* (1944). After the war RKO was one of the leading producers of what came to be known

as *film noir*: *Out of the Past* and *Crossfire*, both released in 1947 and both starring Robert Mitchum, have become noted films of this genre. The movie that brought in the most revenue for the studio, however, was the sickly sweet *The Bells of St Mary's* (1944) with Bing Crosby. Cary Grant and Ingrid Bergman starred in Hitchcock's *Notorious* (1946), but James Stewart in *It's a Wonderful Life* (1947), directed by Frank Capra, failed to attract the expected customers. Now *It's a Wonderful Life* has become everybody's favourite Christmas movie, but in 1947 it rang no bells at the box office.

HOWARD HUGHES ARRIVES
In 1948 Howard Hughes bought the ailing studio and proceeded to indulge his obsessions to the

detriment of the studio's product and finances, although Fritz Lang managed to direct *Rancho Notorious* (1952) and *While the City Sleeps* (1956) at the studio during Hughes's reign. RKO stars in the 1950s included Jane Russell, with whom Hughes was infatuated, Robert Ryan, Jane Greer and Dana Andrews. But too many RKO movies were sub-standard action and war flicks, and finally Hughes sold out to General Teleradio, who were no better at making successful movies. Finally, in 1958 the studio was sold to Desilu, owned by Lucille Ball and Desi Arnaz, who used it to churn out episodes of *I Love Lucy*. It was a sad ending to the film studio that had made the Astaire–Rogers series, the Orson Welles classics and some of the best of *film noir*.

COLUMNBIA

Founded by brothers Jack and Harry Cohn in 1924, Columbia was for 20 years a comparatively minor studio, partly because it owned no cinemas itself and was therefore squeezed by the majors' monopolistic practices. The 1948 divorcement decree that forced the majors to sell their cinemas helped Columbia establish itself on an equal par with the giants of the industry.

Harry Cohn was the dominant figure in Columbia for many years. Even by the standards set by other movie moguls such as MGM's Louis B. Mayer and Fox's Darryl Zanuck, Cohn was reckoned to be an extremely tough character indeed. Giving no quarter and treating stars, directors and producers alike with total disdain, he brooked no opposition to his rule. He forced female stars such as Rita

RIGHT Gilda starred Rita Hayworth and Glenn Ford in an erotic film noir that played with concepts of sexual identity.

Hayworth to change their appearance to fall in line with what he thought a Columbia star should look like. Generally, Cohn behaved like a medieval autocrat, but he got away with this behaviour because so many people were ambitious to climb the greasy pole of success in Hollywood.

Not that the studio under Harry Cohn did not have its successes: its first great hit was the 1934 *It Happened One Night* with Gable and Colbert. How many times have you seen that clip on television where Gable tries to hitch a lift for Colbert and himself, until Colbert steps forward, hitches her skirt above the knee and brings the traffic screeching to a halt? Yes, movie-goers were easily titillated in those days because the Hays Office imposed such an iron control on what they considered prurient content. Comedy scored again for Columbia in the far superior *Twentieth Century* (1934) with John Barrymore and Carole Lombard. But Columbia was also the studio for cheaply produced series such as the *Blondie* films, serials such as *Batman* and *The Three Stooges* comedy shorts. On a more prestigious level, Jean Arthur and Gary Cooper starred in Frank Capra's *Mr Deeds Goes to Town* (1936). The screwball comedy *His Girl Friday*, with Cary Grant and Rosalind Russell, was a hit in 1940.

Rita Hayworth was the studio's only big star in the 1940s and she made *Cover Girl* with Gene Kelly in 1944 and *Gilda*, the steamy *film noir*,

ABOVE Rita Hayworth as she appeared in the 1948 Columbia production The Lady from Shanghai. *Her then-husband Orson Welles directed the movie.*

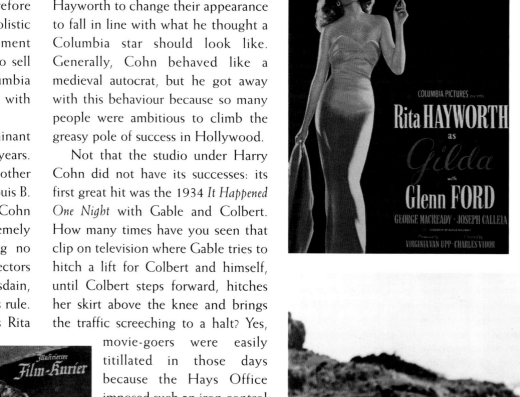

with Glenn Ford in 1946. Harry Cohn took a very personal interest in Hayworth, forcing her to undergo painful beauty treatments that altered her appearance quite dramatically. The studio made big bucks with *The Jolson Story* (1946) and *Jolson Sings Again* (1949). In the late 1940s and 50s the studio produced a string of quality pictures: *All the King's Men* (1949), *Born Yesterday* (1950), *From Here to Eternity* (1953), *On the Waterfront* (1954) and *The Bridge on the River Kwai* (1957). Winners for the studio from the 60s and 70s included *A Man for all Seasons* (1966), *Guess Who's Coming to Dinner* (1967), *Funny Girl* (1968) and *Easy Rider* (1969), whilst post-1970,

> "IT'S NOT A BUSINESS,
> IT'S A RACKET."
> *HARRY COHN*
> HEAD OF COLUMBIA

Close Encounters of the Third Kind (1977), *Kramer vs. Kramer* (1979), *Tootsie* (1982), *Ghostbusters* (1984) and *The Karate Kid* series ensured that Columbia stayed in the major league. Columbia was bought by the Coca-Cola company in 1982, then in 1989 Coca-Cola sold the studio to the Sony Corporation. In 1994 Sony reported a financial loss largely due to the poor performance of films made by the Columbia studio. The studio then became part of Sony Pictures Entertainment. The studio founded by the detestable mogul, Harry Cohn, had come a long way from its Poverty Row beginnings.

ABOVE *Columbia won several Oscars with this 1979 production* Kramer vs. Kramer, *which starred Dustin Hoffman and Meryl Streep as parents battling over custody of their son. Some critics saw the movie as a male backlash against feminism.*

BELOW *A big success for Columbia was the 1953 movie* From Here to Eternity. *Here Burt Lancaster and Deborah Kerr are on the beach in the most famous scene of the movie.*

195

UNIVERSAL

In 1915 Carl Laemmle, the founder of Universal, bought a large piece of land in the Hollywood Hills and named it Universal City. It became a factory for churning out films, very few of which were at all memorable. Erich Von Stroheim, however, made *Foolish Wives* there before Laemmle's general manager, Irving Thalberg, sacked him from his next movie. Irving Thalberg quickly moved on to greater things and became Mayer's right-hand man at MGM. Once Universal studio adapted to sound, they produced *All Quiet on the Western Front* in 1930. This was a rare prestige production in a steady stream of routine dross.

However, the studio was best known for its horror movies and its horror stars, Boris Karloff and Bela Lugosi. *Dracula* (1931), *Frankenstein* (1931), *The Mummy* (1932) and several sequels, *The Bride of Frankenstein* (1935) and *The Invisible Man* series all made profits. In the 1940s the studio's only big money-maker was Claudette Colbert in *The Egg and I* (1947). But in the 50s Universal had big hits with a series of melodramas produced by Ross Hunter and directed by Douglas Sirk: *Magnificent Obsession* (1954), *Written on the Wind* (1956), *The Tarnished Angels* (1958) and *Imitation of Life* (1959). *Winchester 73* (1950) and

ABOVE *Universal was also well known for its horror movies in the 1950s. This was one of the most successful,* The Creature from the Black Lagoon *(1954).*

ABOVE *A 1930 advertisement for the Universal movie* All Quiet on the Western Front, *directed by Lewis Milestone and starring Lew Ayres. The film not only brought an unusual realism to the subject of war but, unlike many other war movies, it also treated German soldiers sympathetically.*

The Glenn Miller Story (1953), both starring James Stewart, also earned money. Anthony Mann made a series of westerns for Universal all starring James Stewart: apart from *Winchester 73* they included *Bend of the River* (1952), *The Naked Spur* (1953), *The Far Country* (1955) and *The Man from Laramie* (1955). Some addicts rate these Anthony Mann-directed Universal-produced westerns among the best ever made.

The studio's roster of stars also included Rock Hudson and Tony Curtis, who starred in westerns and action movies that were churned out for double bills: *The Lawless Breed* (1953), *The Golden Blade* (1953), *Back to God's Country* (1953), *Taza, Son of Cochise* (1954), *Son of Ali Baba* (1952), *The Black Shield of Falworth* (1954) and *The Purple Mask* (1955) were typical. Usually totally forgettable, these films were invariably in

technicolor and had risible scripts, but they brought in the customers in fairly lean times for the industry. A Universal movie of this type will be well-remembered by any film-goers who regularly went to the Odeons or ABCs in the UK in the 1950s. Good value double bills were one of the ways the studios fought against decreasing audiences, and Universal was in the forefront of producing this cheaply-made programme fodder.

However, double bills became a feature of the past and Universal was ready to lose its status as an also-ran in Hollywood. Gradually Universal-International, as it was now known, began climbing into the big league. It was able to employ important stars such as Paul Newman, Burt Lancaster, Steve McQueen and many more, and top directors as well. Its investment in big-budget projects and expensive stars began to pay off. They had a gigantic hit with the 1969 *Butch Cassidy and the Sundance Kid*, which starred Paul Newman as Butch Cassidy and the comparative newcomer Robert Redford as the Sundance Kid. Initially, the studio wanted Steve McQueen for the part, but McQueen wanted top billing over Newman, so Redford was drafted in. His career, and the future of the studio, never looked back.

Universal now entered a period of great success: *Airport* (1970), *The Sting* (1973) and *Jaws* (1975) ensured this. *Jaws* caused the executives at Universal some worries because the costs mounted and stories drifted back to the studio that the mechanical shark around which the movie revolved would not function properly. Executives began to think about replacing the young director Steven Spielberg to whom they had entrusted all this money. But when they saw the finished product, read the reviews and

ABOVE *This double-bill of Universal features from 1952 is typical of the kind of movies Universal produced at this time. Note that this double bill was "to celebrate Universal's 40th anniversary!"*

ABOVE *Tony Curtis played a Scarlet Pimpernel-type figure in this 1955 Universal swashbuckler, The Purple Mask.*

saw the queues of customers lining up to be scared, then their doubts vanished and they knew they were on to a winner and had discovered a major new directing talent who could deliver critical and commercial success. *Jaws* went on to become one of the all-time biggest money spinners of Hollywood history.

However, even these box-office successes were eclipsed in the 1980s by Steven Spielberg's *E.T.* (1982) and Robert Zemeckis's *Back to the Future* (1985). *Out of Africa* was another major hit for the studio in 1985. Universal was no longer an also-ran in the Hollywood stakes.

MCA took over Universal, and ownership of the studio in turn passed to Matsushita, the Japanese conglomerate, which bought the parent company MCA as well. Universal is now a massive presence in film and television production, eating up its rivals. For a long time excluded from the top table in Hollywood, Universal now hands out the invitations and has seen once mighty rivals struggle and even disappear from the scene.

BELOW *An unusual movie for Universal was the 1982 Missing, which dealt with political events in Chile under a fascist dictatorship. Here, director Costas-Gavras lines up a shot.*

ABOVE **The Sting** *(1973) paired Paul Newman and Robert Redford again in a Universal movie. It was one of the studio's biggest commercial successes.*

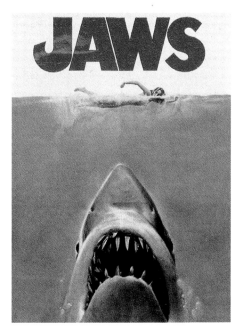

ABOVE *During the shooting of* Jaws *(1975), Universal executives were worried that the young Steven Spielberg was about to ruin the studio; however, the movie made a fortune.*

197

UNITED ARTISTS

United Artists was formed by Mary Pickford, Douglas Fairbanks, Charlie Chaplin and D.W. Griffith in 1919 to protect their financial and artistic interests. Griffith left the company in 1924, and his place as a partner was taken by Joseph Schenck, who added some much-needed business acumen. By 1928 the balance sheet was in the black, with Chaplin's *The Circus*, Fairbanks's *The Gaucho* and *The Iron Mask*, and Keaton's *Steamboat Bill Jr* adding to the profits.

In the 1930s the studio produced *The Front Page* (1931), *Les Misérables* and *The Call of the Wild* (both 1935), *Dodsworth* (1936) and *Dead End* (1937). Other memorable pictures included *Stella Dallas* (1937) and *The Prisoner of Zenda* (1937) with Ronald Colman. Laurence Olivier starred in both

RIGHT **The Graduate** (1967) *introduced Dustin Hoffmann to the screen and made a lot of money for United Artists.*

LEFT *United Artists backed Joseph L. Mankiewicz's movie about Hollywood, the* 1954 *The Barefoot Contessa, which starred Humphrey Bogart as a burnt-out director and Ava Gardner as a Rita Hayworth-like movie star who marries an aristocrat.*

Wuthering Heights (1939) and *Rebecca* (1940). Alexander Korda, the British producer, was associated with United Artists, making *Things to Come* (1936) and *The Man Who Could Work Miracles* (1937). Westerns included John Ford's classic *Stagecoach* (1939) and the lamentably bad but notorious *The Outlaw*, the Howard Hughes–Jane Russell fiasco, which was made in 1941 but not released until much later.

Chaplin continued to make films for his company: *The Great Dictator* (1940) and *Monsieur Verdoux* (1947). Selznick produced two hit films for UA in the 1940s: the wartime family drama *Since You Went Away* (1944) and

Hitchcock's *Spellbound* (1945). Hard times followed until the early 1950s produced such hits as *The African Queen* (1951) and *High Noon* (1952). Another mega-hit was Mike Todd's *Around the World in Eighty Days* (1956), which made its money from the publicity Todd produced for the movie rather than the quality of the movie itself. By the mid-50s both Chaplin and Pickford had sold their shares in the company. The concept of "the lunatics taking over the running of the asylum" – that is, the artists themselves running a major studio rather than businessmen – had largely been forgotten.

The *Bond* movies, *West Side Story* (1961), *Tom Jones* (1963) and *Midnight Cowboy* (1969) helped make the 1960s a profitable decade for UA, who were taken over in 1967 by the Transamerica Corporation, an insurance conglomerate. Heavy losses were incurred in the early 70s until hits such as *One Flew Over the Cuckoo's Nest* (1975) the *Rocky* series, the *Pink Panther* series and 10 (1979), which starred Bo Derek and Dudley Moore, turned the tide. In the 80s UA continued to finance the *Bond* series and also to profit from *Rocky* and the Stallone persona. Woody Allen is one director/star who makes his movies for

the "new" United Artists. It was MGM that took over United Artists in 1981; thus, the company that was set up to protect artists from the tentacles of the majors at last succumbed to one of the giants of the industry. Ownership of UA has since passed through several hands as the game of Hollywood musical chairs continues.

BELOW *Woody Allen is one director/star who has regularly been funded by United Artists. Here he is seen in his send-up of Tolstoy's* War and Peace, *the 1975* Love and Death.

HOOT GIBSON · BOB STEELE
THE UTAH KID
A MONOGRAM PICTURE

LEFT *Monogram Pictures was one of the studios located on what was known as Poverty Row in Hollywood because of the cheaply shot quickies they churned out. In this 1944 masterpiece,* The Utah Kid, *the good guy in the orange shirt comes up against a rather elderly sheriff. "B" movie westerns still have their addicts:* The Utah Kid *lives on!*

MOVIE GENRES

In the heyday of Hollywood each of the major studios resembled a factory. The aim of these factories was to make a product – movies – that could be shown in cinemas all over the world. The studios had to make enough movies to allow for weekly changes of programme and, at various times in cinematic history, for double-feature bills. When 90 million people in the United States alone were going out to the cinema each week, there seemed to be an unceasing demand for the Hollywood product. To satisfy this demand, movies were produced by a mode of production that was close to an assembly line.

Each worker in that assembly line knew exactly what his or her specific job was. In 1941 a film industry publication calculated that there were 276 separate crafts involved in making a motion picture, and most of those crafts formed guilds that protected their members' right to perform their specific tasks. Studio heads, after their initial misguided opposition to these craft guilds, realized that this kind of "demarcation" philosophy suited their purpose, which was to make the product they required to service their cinemas in sufficient quantity and as cheaply as possible.

"If you've seen one, you've seen 'em all!" is a frequent complaint about the movies, and it is true that movies, certainly in the old days, fell into definite categories, frequently called "genres". Genres made sense economically because a studio could re-use the same sets, locations, actors, directors, costumes and even plots to churn out more westerns, musicals, crazy comedies, war movies, horror flicks, swashbucklers, etc, an assembly line approach which produced economics of scale and which also bred a sense of familiarity in the mass audience. Audiences would know what to expect if they paid their money to see a musical, and if you added Gene Kelly or Judy Garland, then they would have two sets of expectations at least – of the genre and the star. Genres and stars were a means of product differentiation and a way of persuading the customer to come back for more. As a way of producing movies relatively cheaply and encouraging customer loyalty, genre films were good news for the studios. However, talented directors were able to use the generic form to create art.

WESTERNS

The western is the most cinematic of the genres because no other art form can hope to emulate the cinema's power to represent the myths of the American frontier in such an all-embracing manner. But why have westerns been so popular with the public in the past, and why have they largely disappeared from our cinema screens? The answer lies in the way westerns deal in mythology. They present a view of America's frontier and agrarian past that feeds the American Dream: the rugged individual striking out for the unknown, Man against raw Nature, the pursuit of an independent way of life, the acquiring of land and wealth, the conquering of hostile elements in the shape of Indians, and building communities out of the wilderness based on simple values and hard work.

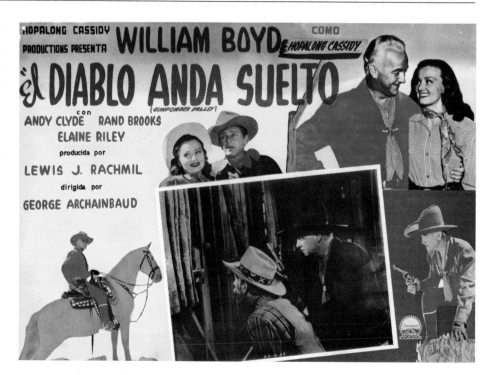

ABOVE *William Boyd as Hopalong Cassidy starred in innumerable "B" westerns and found himself a large fan base especially among the devotees of the Saturday morning Cinema Clubs of the 1940s and 50s.*

ABOVE *William Wellmann's production of* Yellow Sky *(1948) was loosely based on Shakespeare's play* The Tempest, *and starred Gregory Peck and Richard Widmark.*

As the memories of that trail-blazing past recede, the American public may feel less need for frequent doses of western mythology, hence the drastic drop in the number of westerns produced in the last 20 to 30 years. In addition, perhaps too much reality has broken through the mists of legend to sustain the western myths any longer. For example, most Americans now accept that a form of genocide was practised against the Indian population in order for the white man's civilization to flourish. In an era where so-called heroes turn out to be mere mortals after all, it is also difficult to suspend our disbelief when watching these larger-than-life western heroes create law and order out of chaos. Cinema-goers are more interested in the new heroes, the urban guerillas of Jean-Claude Van Damme and Quentin Tarantino movies than the straight-shooting, honest cowboys of yesteryear.

The great days of the western are undoubtedly over. Western fans, however, will debate earnestly which are the truly great westerns: *Stagecoach, My Darling Clementine, Red River, Shane* and *The Searchers* would probably be on most fans' list, although many would speak up for the spaghetti westerns directed by Sergio Leone. Apart from Leone, most western fans would probably rate John Ford, Howard Hawks, Anthony Mann and Clint Eastwood as the top directors of the genre. The western still has life in it, as *The Outlaw Josey Wales, Dances with Wolves* and *Unforgiven* reflect. The western as a genre will never recapture its pre-eminent position, but it will resurface from time to time and still find an audience.

201

ABOVE The Man Who Shot Liberty Valance *(1962) was one of John Ford's last westerns. It has an elegiac tone as the movie mourns the passing of the old west.*

ABOVE *Daniel Day-Lewis starred as Hawkeye in the 1992* The Last of the Mohicans, *directed by Michael Mann.*

MUSICALS

The musical is another genre that Hollywood took over and made its own. When sound came to Hollywood, the studios poured out film after film with people singing and dancing rather inexpertly, and audiences seemed to love these happy films. However, the public soon tired of the new phenomenon – perhaps it was the onset of the Depression, perhaps it was just that there was such a surfeit of musicals.

RIGHT *Fred Astaire and Cyd Charisse starred in the MGM musical* The Band Wagon, *directed by Vincente Minnelli and with a script by Betty Comden and Adolph Green. The plot is a retread of* Singin' in the

they served up. Berkeley, using the camera to create his elaborate and rather soulless fantasies, was the ace director and choreographer who delivered the goods. Astaire and Rogers had no such truck with reality in their RKO musicals, however; Astaire was debonair and usually rich, Rogers was simply Rogers, the average young woman catapulted into opulent settings and wearing fancy clothes. The black-and-white Art Deco sets, the sumptuous costumes, the vision of society life, the exotic locations – all these elements combined to create pure escapist fantasies for the masses, who were struggling with the realities of unemployment and poverty.

ABOVE *Gene Kelly revolutionized the movie musical in* On the Town (1949), *when he filmed himself and his co-stars Vera Ellen, Frank Sinatra, Betty Garrett, Ann Miller and Jules Munshin singing and dancing against a real New York.*

It took Astaire and Rogers and Busby Berkeley to seduce the customers back into the cinemas to watch musical extravaganzas. Warner Bros., Berkeley's studio, sensed that people needed glamour, hope and extravagance plus an acknowledgement that there were hard times out there, so that's what

ABOVE *After the heyday of the MGM musical, studios invested in only sure-fire hits that had already been proven on stage.* West Side Story (1961) *was one of the more successful transitions of stage musicals to the screen.*

ABOVE *Another stage musical that made it to the big screen was* Hello, Dolly! *(1969) which starred Barbra Streisand.*

Musicals are inherently "utopian" – they concoct an alternative vision of reality that panders to our dreams. The search for love and popularity, success and wealth, is always celebrated in them. Love leads to marriage, putting on a show leads to massive popularity and success, the coupling of boy-and-girl strengthens the community and reinforces role models and orthodoxy. All movie genres are conservative in the values they espouse, and none more so than the musical. In the 1940s and 50s, the heyday of the MGM musical, some more adult elements were introduced to the storylines, but the resolution was always the same: Kelly would win Garland, Charisse or Caron, Astaire would woo Hepburn, Vera-Ellen or Hayworth and be showered with not only success in love but worldly success as well. Love and success went hand-in-hand in the world of musicals. Vincente Minnelli, director of *Meet Me in St Louis* (1944), *The Pirate*

(1948), *An American in Paris* (1951) and *The Band Wagon* (1953), raised the musical genre to new heights, as did Gene Kelly and Stanley Donan when they directed *On the Town* (1949), *Singin' in the Rain* (1952) and *It's Always Fair Weather* (1955).

Musicals were among the first genres to be discarded with the break-up of the studio system in the 1950s. They were expensive to make, required a large body of permanent employees to produce, and were deemed commercially risky if written especially for the screen. When MGM divested itself of stars such as Kelly, Garland and Astaire, then the writing was on the wall. From the mid-50s on, the only musicals made, by and large, were film versions of Broadway hits. Since the heyday of musicals, there have been talented individuals such as Bob Fosse (*Cabaret*) and Barbra Streisand (*Funny Girl*) working in the genre, but there has been no group of people to match the

greats of the MGM musical years. The dancing MGM musical vanished with the demise of the studio as a major movie-producing factory. However, in the last few decades the musical has partly reinvented itself in movies such as *Saturday Night Fever, Pennies from Heaven, Flashdance, Dirty Dancing, A Chorus Line, Moulin Rouge* and *Chicago. Moulin Rouge* (2001) was a radical reworking of the movie musical: its stars were not singing and dancing specialists; there was practically no original music written for the movie; and the superfast editing techniques did not allow the audience to dwell on any shortcomings of performance. Yet somehow, it worked. *Chicago* (2002) capitalized on this new interest in musicals, winning a Best Picture Oscar.

BELOW *Bob Fosse directed* Cabaret *(1972), starring Liza Minnelli and Michael York. Fosse brought a fresh style to the movie musical, but he never really repeated the success he had with this movie.*

GANGSTER MOVIES

Between 1930 and 1932 Hollywood produced a number of gangster movies that were genuinely more radical in spirit than those of other genres. The three best known are *Little Caesar* (1931), *The Public Enemy* (1931) and *Scarface* (1932). They are morality tales, a kind of Horatio Alger success story but turned upside down and viewed from the point of view of the dispossessed of society, who have to steal and murder their way to the top because all other "normal" avenues are cut off for them. The authorities were disturbed by the social undertones of these films and forced the studios to attach moral homilies to the movies: *Little Caesar* ends with titling on the screen saying, "Rico's career had been a skyrocket, starting in the gutter and ending there." Soon, the Hays Office, set up by the movie moguls themselves to stave off external censorship and to answer increasing

protests about the moral depravity of movies, was clamping down on the manner in which gangsters were portrayed on film. Criminals were to be represented as psychopathic and isolated individuals, whom all decent citizens should despise and help the authorities to destroy.

However, the public loved the exploits of Cagney, Muni, Bogart and Raft on the screen, and all these actors became major stars, largely through their impersonations of real-life gangsters such as Al Capone and John Dillinger. The gangster genre has never been as popular again as it was in the 1930s, but since then it has produced some of Hollywood's best movies, including *The Asphalt Jungle* (1950), in which a character states that "Crime is merely a left-handed form of human endeavour", *Bonnie and Clyde* (1967), a glamorizing and myth-making treatment of the story of

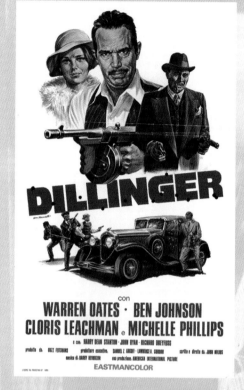

ABOVE *Warren Oates played famous gangster John Dillinger in the 1973 movie* Dillinger, *which was directed by John Milius.*

1930s gangsters, and *The Godfather* and *The Godfather Part II* (1972 and 1974). All four of these films seem to imply that society is hypocritical in its attitude to crime and that the boundaries between "respectable" business, the forces of law and order, and organized and "disorganized" crime are very thin indeed. In the 1980s, movies such as *Scarface* (1983), starring Al Pacino, and *Once Upon a Time in America* (1984), directed by Sergio Leone, reflected the continuing fascination with gangsterdom and what criminals tell us about the society in which we live.

Martin Scorsese's reworking of the gangster genre in movies such as *GoodFellas* (1990), *Casino* (1995) and *Gangs of New York* (2002) have been

LEFT *James Cagney in a familiar pose as the gangster as hero. Have Hollywood movies glamorized the gangster figure?*

been given a new lease of life, for example in *Lock, Stock and Two Smoking Barrels* and *Snatch*. The French have always found Hollywood gangsters irresistible, and movies such as *Rififi*, *Le Samouraï* and *La Balance* show their debt to the Hollywood originals. Jean-Pierre Melville's gangster movies, such as *Le Doulos* and *Le Deuxième Souffle*, pay homage to the Hollywood prototype and have more to do with style than reality. His romanticized representations of honourable criminals appeal to us, but don't expect to meet anyone like that in the real criminal world.

welcomed by audiences, whilst Warren Beatty's *Bugsy* (1991) was more in the traditional mould of the genre. These are very violent films and portray criminals as ruthless homicidal individuals who will stop at almost nothing to make their way in the world. Scorsese's gangster movies in particular push the representation of sadistic violence to uncomfortable extremes. It is reasonable to question whether this is acceptable in terms of showing it how it is or whether the audience is being invited to enjoy the violence on a prurient level. The same issues arise when the movies directed by Quentin Tarantino are discussed: *Reservoir Dogs* (1992) and *Pulp Fiction* (1994) seem to invite audiences to enjoy scenes of sadistic torture. British gangster films never had the resonance of their Hollywood

counterparts, although some British attempts at the genre have shown a tougher approach: *Get Carter*, *Villain*, *The Krays* and *The Long Good Friday*. Cockney gangsters have recently

205

ABOVE *Warren Beatty turned to the gangster genre again with* Bugsy, *which was about real-life gangster Bugsy Siegel, one of the criminal fraternity who brought us the doubtful bonus of Las Vegas.*

ACTION/ADVENTURE MOVIES

Adventure movies, or "action films", exist in various guises but inevitably involve a resourceful hero, and occasionally a heroine, who come up against incredible odds and win through in the last reel. Under "adventure" we could classify the wild fantasies of the James Bond movies, the swashbucklers, historical extravaganzas, "jungle" and "desert"

ABOVE *Burt Lancaster made several swashbucklers early in his career, including* The Flame and the Arrow *(1950), directed by Jacques Tourneur.*

epics, and a whole range of "actioners" including disaster movies. Universal, when it was still a minnow studio in the 1940s and 50s, produced a series of adventures supposedly set in exotic desert locations but actually shot in local sandpits; these movies were irreverently known as "tits and sand" in the trade, because of the opportunity they gave the studio to put its glamorous stars in skimpy costumes and to shoot cheaply on the back lot.

Just as weepies were intended to appeal predominantly to a female audience, so action films were perceived as appealing to men, hence the creation of major male stars who stood for adventure in the public mind: Douglas Fairbanks Senior and Junior, Clark Gable, Errol Flynn, Tyrone Power, Gary Cooper, Stewart Granger, Charlton Heston, Alan Ladd, Sabu, Cornel Wilde, John Payne, Sean Connery, John Wayne and Harrison Ford. Women inevitably played second fiddle to the male stars in these movies, but female names such as Yvonne De Carlo, Rhonda Fleming, Paulette Goddard, Susan Hayward, Dorothy Lamour, Maureen O'Sullivan and Maria Montez would appear above the title in many a routine actioner.

If particular stars were associated with action movies, so were individual directors who acquired a reputation for being able to keep the action moving while providing enough thrills and spills to please audiences. Among these were Irwin Allen (*The Lost World, The Poseidon Adventure, The Towering Inferno*), Cecil B. De Mille (*Reap the Wild Wind, Unconquered, Northwest Mounted Police*), Henry Hathaway (*Lives of a Bengal Lancer, Prince Valiant, North to Alaska*), Howard Hawks (*Only Angels Have Wings, Hatari, The Big Sky*), John Huston (*Moby Dick, The Treasure of the Sierra Madre,*

RIGHT *Bullitt is one of the best cop action movies ever made, with a stunning car chase up and down the hills of San Francisco at the heart of it.*

The African Queen), Zoltan Korda (*Sanders of the River, Elephant Boy, The Four Feathers, The Thief of Bagdad*) and Raoul Walsh (*They Drive by Night, They Died with their Boots On, Gentleman Jim, Captain Horatio Hornblower*). Subgenres under the umbrella of action films would also include boxing movies, motor-racing films and movies adapted from novels by John Buchan and Rider Haggard.

The Hollywood actioner could always be relied upon to throw up some absurd casting, for example Alan Ladd as a knight of the Round Table (*The Black Knight*) or Tony Curtis as an Arab in a tale of Arabian adventure (*Son of Ali Baba*) or as a Viking (*The Vikings*). Saturday morning serials were basically actioners stretched thinly over countless episodes (*The Perils of Pauline, Flash Gordon, Captain Marvel* and *Batman*). Each episode would leave the hero or heroine in

ABOVE *The 1985 sequel to* Romancing the Stone, The Jewel of the Nile *scarcely takes itself seriously in the vein of modern adventure movies.*

some dreadful predicament from which no apparent escape was possible. The Indiana Jones series was Spielberg's affectionate tribute to the good old days of Saturday morning cinema when you cheered the goodies and hissed the baddies. The *Mission Impossible* movies took their inspiration, if that is the word, from a 1960s television show, whilst the *Jurassic Park* movies harked back to movies such as *King Kong* and *The*

ABOVE *The dinosaurs in* Jurassic Park *were computer-generated, but they still scared the hell out of movie-goers.*

207

Lost World. Comic-book heroes such as Batman, Dick Tracy, Superman and Spiderman have found their adventures transferred to the big screen as what was once despised as low culture has become respectable. These comic-book hero movies mostly have a knowing, self-conscious, parodying tone to them, as though the film-makers are saying to

LEFT *John Woo graduated from making action movies in Hong Hong to big-budget Hollywood movies such as* Mission Impossible II *(2000), which again starred Tom Cruise as the good guy, Ethan Hunt.*

the audience, yes, we know this is ridiculous, but just share the joke with us. The *Men in Black* movies took this self-mocking tone that much further and the result was almost a total parody of the genre. *Spider-Man* (2001) was treated more respectfully, but intrinsic to these movies is an inevitable element of sending-up. We cannot take our heroes totally seriously in a real world that consistently exposes them as fraudulent.

COMEDIES

Abbott and Costello, Laurel and Hardy, the great comedians of the silents, Martin and Lewis, The Three Stooges, Fernandel, Bob Hope, Sid Field, the *Carry On* series, the *Doctor* series, the *Pink Panther* series, screwball comedy, Red Skelton, Hepburn and Tracy comedies, Preston Sturges, Ealing comedies, Mel Brooks, Woody Allen, W.C. Fields, Danny Kaye, Ernst Lubitsch, the Marx Brothers, Neil Simon, Frank Tashlin, Billy Wilder, Gene Wilder, the Farrelly brothers, Jim Carrey, Mike Myers: all these and many, many more make up some kind of Hall of Fame for cinematic comedy.

ABOVE *Groucho Marx, the only really funny Marx brother, is the one in the middle. Harpo is on the left and Chico, decidedly unfunny, is on the right.*

Comedy divides opinion like no other type of movie. Woody Allen is the funniest man alive for some people; others find that his angst-ridden attempts to provoke laughter leave them entirely unmoved. Many people still laugh at Abbott and Costello when their movies are shown on television, while many other people wonder what anyone could have ever seen in the little fat guy and his straight-man partner, although at their peak in the 1940s they were No. 1 box-office stars in America.

The fact is that nothing dates as fast as comedy, and often what people cling to when watching old comedies again is the memory of their youth and what made them laugh in the good old days. Try telling a

contemporary young person why you think Danny Kaye movies are funny and watch the incredulous look appear on their face. And how to explain the awful fascination that *Three Stooges* movies can have with their nose-twisting, ear-pulling, thumb-wrenching sadism? Did we really find that funny in those days? Was Jerry Lewis always as inane? Did anyone, anywhere, ever find Red Skelton funny? Yes, obviously they did, because Skelton was big at the box office for a time in the 1940s. There's no accounting for taste in comedy.

For example, I have tried to appreciate the comic genius that Preston Sturges is supposed to have poured into comedies such as *The Great McGinty*, *Sullivan's Travels* and

LEFT *Bud Abbott (the thin one) and Lou Costello (the fat one) were the top box-office comedy team in the 1940s. They still have their fervent fans today.*

ABOVE *Marilyn Monroe, Jack Lemmon and Tony Curtis starred in many people's favourite comedy, Some Like it Hot.*

ABOVE *Mel Brooks had a huge hit with the western spoof* Blazing Saddles *in 1974. Despite recent flops, he has retained his place at the top of the screen-comedy tree.*

Hail the Conquering Hero, but, for the life of me, I just can't see it. The *Carry On* series leaves me absolutely cold and leaves, I suspect, the rest of the world outside Britain the same way, but every time those comic epics crop up on television they get decent audiences, so somebody out there must like them. My own favourite type of Hollywood comedy, the screwball variety, is a taste that many people do not share. But for me, movies such as *Bringing Up Baby,*

ABOVE **Carry on Cleo** *(1965) was meant as a spoof of the infamous Liz Taylor movie of* Cleopatra, *which almost bankrupted 20th Century Fox. Here, Sid James as the unlikeliest Roman is seen with a very unlikely Cleopatra, Amanda Barrie.*

His Girl Friday, Ball of Fire, I Was a Male War Bride, Monkey Business, Twentieth Century, Love Crazy and numerous others had an anarchic tone and a paciness to them that made them the most enduring of screen comedies. I admire some Ealing comedies such as *The Ladykillers* and *The Man in the White Suit,* but generally find the view of British life represented in the majority of these films too cosy and self-congratulatory. Many, many would disagree.

Since the 1990s Hollywood has moved the boundaries of what was once thought to be acceptable in comedy. Now we have the gross-out comedy served up in "masterpieces" such as *There's Something About Mary, Dumb and Dumber,* the *Ace Ventura* movies, the *Police Academy* and *American Pie* series, where the main focus is on bodily functions and the grosser aspects of teenage sex. The object seems to be to make the audience groan with disgust, and this alone is deemed to be intrinsically comedic.

Only a small proportion of films survive the passing of years to impress future generations with the same impact as when they were first released. But for comedies, the job is even harder. In 2020, will Peter Sellers as Inspector Clouseau seem funny to people for whom Sellers is just a vague

ABOVE *The Monty Python team graduated from television to the big screen and had a success in 1983 with* The Meaning of Life. *Here Eric Idle, Michael Palin, Graham Chapman and Terry Jones play overgrown schoolboys, while John Cleese provides discipline.*

name from the past? Is Woody Allen's appeal a particularly contemporary one, relevant only to the 1980s and 90s? Will anyone still be watching *Three Stooges* movies in 2020? Perhaps we should leave these questions to the academics and just enjoy what we enjoy when we enjoy it.

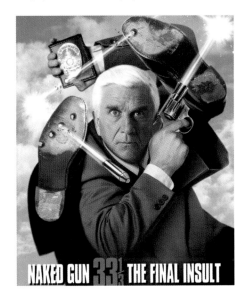

ABOVE *Leslie Nielsen resurrected a flagging screen career when he started to appear in the* Naked Gun *series of movies as Frank Drebin, the dumbest cop of them all.*

ROMANTIC COMEDIES

Romantic comedy is a sub-genre of comedy, and in the heyday of Hollywood was staple fare in the movie houses of the world. In the 1930s stars such as Joan Crawford, Margaret Sullavan, Katharine

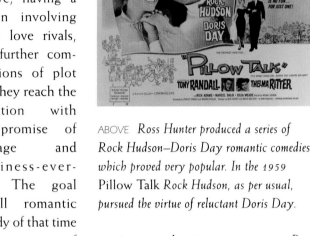

ABOVE *An early example of romantic comedy. Laurence Olivier (before he became a "serious" actor) and Merle Oberon starred in the British movie* The Divorce of Lady X *(1938).*

Hepburn, Myrna Loy, Claudette Colbert, Cary Grant, Clark Gable and William Powell were regularly cast in romantic comedies, which were big at the box office. Consider these 1930s movies: *It Happened One Night, The Shop Around the Corner, Quality Street, Alice Adams, Sylvia Scarlett, The Divorce of Lady X, Shopworn Angel, Dancing Lady, Wife versus Secretary* and *Bringing Up Baby* (a screwball romantic comedy). The plot consisted of variations on

hero and heroine "meeting cute" (for example, they bump into each other or get tangled in each other's clothes), falling in love, having a misunderstanding often involving one or more potential love rivals, then further complications of plot until they reach the resolution with the promise of marriage and happiness-ever-after. The goal of all romantic comedy of that time was the marriage of the hero and heroine.

By the 1940s and 50s, the sex war had sharpened and exchanges between the sexes on screen became slightly franker and more edgy. The Spencer Tracy–Katharine Hepburn comedies – *Woman of the Year, Adam's Rib, Pat and Mike* and *The Desk Set* – represented the relationship of the sexes in a transitional stage in which women were breaking free from more traditional roles and the men were resisting these changes. Judy Holliday made romantic comedies in which even her dumb-blonde persona was seen to be making progress

RIGHT *Woody Allen adopted the persona of Humphrey Bogart to help him in his wooing of Diane Keaton in the* 1972 Play It Again, Sam.

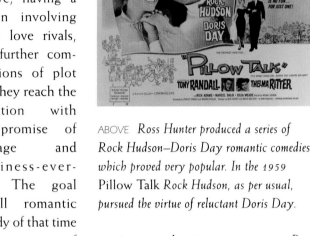

ABOVE *Ross Hunter produced a series of Rock Hudson–Doris Day romantic comedies which proved very popular. In the* 1959 Pillow Talk *Rock Hudson, as per usual, pursued the virtue of reluctant Doris Day.*

against male intransigence: *Born Yesterday, The Marrying Kind, It Should Happen to You, Phffft!* and *The Solid Gold Cadillac* are examples. Whatever good fortune befell the heroine, however, her ultimate wish was represented as being married to a good man and having a family.

This, indeed, was the raison d'être of the women played by Doris Day in a series of mainly Ross Hunter-produced comedies in the late 1950s and 60s. Her character's main object was to resist the lascivious advances of a male lothario and attain a state of marriage without losing her virginity. Day's virtue was threatened by various male stars such as Clark Gable, Rock Hudson, Cary Grant and Rod Taylor in movies such as *Teacher's Pet, Pillow Talk, Lover Come Back, Move Over Darling, That Touch of Mink* and *Send Me No Flowers.*

Just as the Audrey Hepburn-starring *Roman Holiday* had been the romantic comedy of the 1950s (Hepburn played a Princess Margaret-type character on the loose in Rome), so *Breakfast at Tiffany's* with Hepburn paired with George Peppard became the most famous of Hollywood romantic comedies in the 1960s. Hepburn also starred with Albert Finney in *Two for the Road*, directed by Stanley Donen.

If the lovers in these romantic comedies never made it to bed, that is not the case with recent examples of the sub-genre: the problem is not whether the hero and heroine have sex together, but whether their relationship will survive beyond that. Doris Day's resolute defence of her virginity has long since been forgotten; now in the movies it is just as likely that the heroine will make

the first moves and it is the hero who feels his freedom under threat. Romantic comedy can still be very big at the box office indeed, as *When Harry Met Sally...*, *Four Weddings and a Funeral*, *Notting Hill*, *As Good As It Gets*, *Sliding Doors*, *You've Got Mail* and *Bridget Jones's Diary* have shown. The stars of romantic comedy now are Tom Hanks, Meg Ryan, Gwyneth Paltrow, Hugh Grant, Julia Roberts,

ABOVE *Meg Ryan and Billy Crystal discuss the nature of relationships between men and women in the hit romantic comedy* When Harry Met Sally... (*1989*).

Helen Hunt, Renée Zellweger and Reese Witherspoon. Romantic comedy has caught up with the mores of the times, but essentially it exploits the same subject matter it has always done: love between two people.

BELOW *Hugh Grant and Andie MacDowell meet for the first time in the hugely successful British romantic comedy* Four Weddings and a Funeral (*1994*).

EPICS

The cinema has always tried to provide spectacle for mass audiences. After all, the camera can go anywhere and record scenes of enormous vistas and in great detail. Through the skills of their set and costume designers, the technological and material resources of cinema can recreate any period of history, any imaginary world, any vision of writers and directors. Nowadays, "epic" backgrounds such as vast amphitheatres filled with bloodthirsty crowds can be generated through computer technology. Think of the savings the producers can make from not employing all those thousands of extras! Ever since they became a mass entertainment, movies have tried

ABOVE *The 1956 version of* The Ten Commandments *was director Cecil B. De Mille's second attempt to film this biblical story. Charlton Heston was Moses and Yul Brynner was The Pharaoh. It was a toss-up who was the more wooden.*

to provide spectacles that no other art or entertainment medium can rival in their size, authenticity and sheer opulence.

The Birth of a Nation was the cinema's first great spectacle and from then on many producers and directors have attempted to impress us with the grandness of their designs, the extravagance of their concepts, their devotion to reproducing a historical period and to rewriting history itself.

Unfortunately, along the way, authenticity was often the first casualty, so we saw such errors of taste as John Wayne as a Roman centurion at the foot of the Cross mouthing, "Truly, this was the son of Gawd." Tony Curtis, complete with Brooklyn accent, would play Roman slaves, and Victor Mature would

ABOVE *Victor Mature pulls down the temple in the 1949 epic* Samson and Delilah, *which also starred Hedy Lamarr.*

wrestle with stuffed lions. Epics would become the excuse for excessive religiosity in Cecil B. De Mille's spectacles or for viewing female stars in skimpy costumes as with Lana Turner in *The Prodigal.* Somehow scripts tended to be more leaden for epics – as Howard Hawks said about the dreadful *Land of the Pharaohs,* which

ABOVE *Tolstoy's* War and Peace *received the Hollywood epic treatment in 1956. It starred Audrey Hepburn, a miscast Henry Fonda and Mel Ferrer.*

ABOVE Spartacus (1960) was one of the few literate Hollywood epics. It managed to be about something other than violent action set against a Roman background.

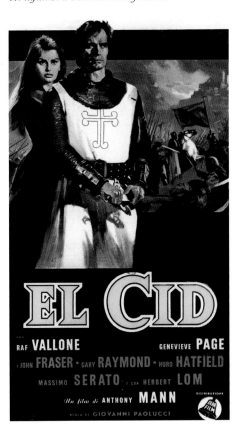

ABOVE El Cid (1961), directed by Anthony Mann, starred Charlton Heston and had a fine musical score by Miklós Rózsa.

he directed, "I never knew how a Pharaoh talked." How does Moses talk; how does a Roman slave leading a rebellion against the Roman Empire talk? Indeed, does Ben-Hur need to talk at all? There have been few literate epics but, then, the mass movie audience don't want Shakespeare when they pay their money to see an epic. They want size, action, spectacle, thrills, good triumphing over evil, and romance.

Only a handful of epics stand up to any test of real quality; the vast majority are best enjoyed as cinema at its most ostentatious and its most vulgar. You do not go to an epic to be educated about a historical period or learn how people lived in past times. You go to an epic to be impressed by the size of things and to wonder at the effort that went into the enterprise.

We usually think of epics as taking place in the distant past, produced by De Mille and starring the inevitable Charlton Heston, but movies such as Titanic are epics in a light disguise: the object is to serve up great spectacle, currently with the lavish use of special computer-generated effects. This was also true of Gladiator, which is in the tradition of Spartacus and The Last Days of Pompeii. The Lord of the Rings series, adapted from J.R.R. Tolkien's books, are epic in scale and embrace legend, myths and spirituality while telling a simple tale of the struggle of good and evil. Indeed, not many epics have room to allow for shades of grey: delineation of character and motive is not a top priority in this genre.

With the success of Gladiator and Titanic, other epics will follow fast on their heels. However, those overtly religious epics such as The Ten Commandments and The Greatest Story

ABOVE Boris Pasternak's novel Doctor Zhivago was given epic screen treatment in the 1965 MGM movie directed by David Lean and starred Julie Christie, Omar Sharif and Rod Steiger.

Ever Told (1965) are unlikely to make a reappearance, unless the religious right's influence in Hollywood and America in general takes a grip. It is a fact that epics are conservative in the political and social attitudes they embrace: Spartacus was one of the few liberal epics ever made. Generally epics take the side of nice kings and queens as opposed to nasty rebels.

ABOVE Gladiator (2000) was the first Roman epic Hollywood made for many years. It proved that this kind of epic still had legs at the box office.

213

FILM NOIR

Strictly speaking, *film noir* is not a genre. It is a body of films that emerged from Hollywood between 1941 and 1958 that shared stylistic and thematic concerns. The term was first used by French critics when they noticed the "blackness" of look and theme common to the American movies released in France after the Liberation. Perhaps because they had

ABOVE *Tyrone Power had one of his best screen roles in* Nightmare Alley (1947).

been cut off for four years from American films, the critics remarked on how different these movies were from the standard pre-war Hollywood product with its glossy, high-key lighting and upbeat, reassuring message. These *films noirs* were bleak social documents, turning a disenchanted eye on the contemporary American scene and uncovering a society full of anxieties and divisions.

The film-makers who made the *films noirs* were perhaps influenced by German Expressionism and Italian Neo-realism. Expatriate European directors such as Wilder, Preminger, Ophuls, Siodmak and Curtiz made some of the best-known *noirs* with

their determinedly shadowy images and nihilistic view of human nature. However, an opposing view of Hollywood *film noir* points to the war-time and immediate post-war restrictions placed on American film-makers by the US government. Hollywood had to cut down on its use of lighting and sets because resources were needed for the war effort. Thus, the shadowy, dark look of wartime movies came not from the film-makers' gloomy view of the world, but from technological necessity: they could not use extensive lighting, so they used dark sets lit by a few lights or filmed at night. One additional effect of the muted lighting was that it

ABOVE *Gene Tierney played a neurotic woman under the control of an evil psychiatrist, Jose Ferrer, in the 1950* Whirlpool.

disguised the reuse of old sets again and again because of the restrictions on set-building.

Whatever the origins of *film noir*, certain thematic concerns and familiar plot lines are apparent in the body of

ABOVE *Humphrey Bogart and Lauren Bacall try to work out the plot in the 1947 thriller* The Big Sleep. *The stars married in real life but Bogart died prematurely in 1957.*

Falcon, *Double Indemnity*, *The Big Sleep*, *Out of the Past*, *Crossfire* and *Touch of Evil*.

If you are being pedantic, the term *film noir* can only really be applied to those black-and-white movies that were made between, say, 1941 (*The Maltese Falcon*) and 1958 (*Touch of Evil*). However, *film noir* remains an influence on movie-makers around the world. In recent years, two movie hits have self-consciously paid homage to *film noir*: *The Usual Suspects* and *L.A. Confidential*.

BELOW Touch of Evil (1958), *directed by Orson Welles, is often identified as the last movie made that truly belonged to the authentic* film noir *tradition.*

ABOVE The Third Man (1949) *was a brilliant British* film noir *directed by Carol Reed, and starring Orson Welles.*

films dubbed *noir*. Very often a *film noir* is about a male protagonist encountering a femme fatale, for example, who uses her sexual attractiveness to manipulate him into murder. She then double-crosses the sap until order is restored by the destruction of this powerful female figure, often at the cost of the hero's life. Perhaps *film noir* is misogynist in its general representation of women: the women are beautiful but duplicitous, predatory and promiscuous. This trend in wartime and post-war American movies may have had something to do with the uncertain relationship between the sexes due to wartime dislocations and suspicions about what had gone on while the boys were away at war. In addition, millions of women had their first opportunity to work during the war years, and this fed male paranoia that women were breaking out and refusing to play their "correct" roles in society as mothers and wives. This anxiety was fed into the movies that Hollywood made in order to "cheer" wartime audiences.

Film noir was often the product of the "B" picture system, whereby the studios produced low-budget films to fill the lower half of double bills. As a result these "B" pictures were not given the same scrutiny as the "A" pictures, which allowed creative directors and writers the freedom to experiment and handle themes that would have been out of bounds on more expensive products. The result was masterpieces such as *The Maltese*

RIGHT *A late* film noir *is Roman Polanski's* Chinatown (1974), *a deliberate homage to the tradition of the genre.*

HORROR MOVIES

Audiences love to be scared, and film-makers have learned to serve up ready-made nightmares on demand. Horror films came out of the tradition of European Gothic novels by way of Mary Godwin and Bram Stoker. Cinema, of all the art forms, is nearest to the dream state: we sit in the dark watching huge figures on a screen enact our fantasies and fears. Horror films deal with our nightmares, the fears of mankind, the horror of the irrational and the unknown, and the horror of man himself. They embrace the classic demonic myths of Frankenstein and Dracula, the concept of nature that turns abnormal, and the horror of human personality. Horror is the

ABOVE *Tod Browning directed the strange* Freaks (1932) *and* The Devil-Doll (1936). *There is still a certain fascination about these movies, as this re-release of a Browning double bill reflects.*

creature, the blood-sucking vampire, the fiendish scientist, the ghoul, or Freddy with the murderous, nightmarish nails. Horror is all around us in the everyday world: it is a shadow on the walls of a deserted swimming-pool (*Cat People*), it is a hesitant, shy and psychopathic young man in a motel (*Psycho*), or it is a man with "love" and "hate" tattooed on his hands (*The Night of the Hunter*).

Some observers see the horror film as an expression of our subconscious wish to smash the norms that oppress us. For example, many horror films are located within the family situation. In horror films the underside of normality is exposed and the irrational chaos beneath respectability and convention explodes and threatens to engulf society. As in all genres, however, the monstrous has to be defeated and the norms restored. We are able to indulge our rebellious instincts for a while before the status quo wins through. While watching the horror movie, we half-long for the

LEFT *Val Lewton was one of the best-known horror movie producers. The* Curse of the Cat People *was the 1944 sequel to the highly successful but subtly scary* Cat People (1942).

forces of chaos to win, but fear at the same time what that chaos will reveal about ourselves.

In the 1950s the British company Hammer Films began to rework the myths of Dracula, Frankenstein, werewolves, vampires and all the other elements of the classic horror movie. Their models were clearly the Universal Studios' horror movies of the 1930s, but Hammer mostly shot in colour and with reasonable budgets for sets and costumes. The result is

ABOVE *In the 1950s and 60s the British company Hammer Films reworked some of the old Universal horror movies. Here is one their more successful efforts,* Horror of Dracula (*aka* Dracula, 1958).

ABOVE *The other face of horror: a Hammer zombie relaxes and smiles for the camera in his lunch hour during the shooting of* The Mummy's Shroud *(1967).*

BELOW *Joan Crawford carved out for herself a mini-career late in her life as the heroine, or otherwise, of horror movies such as* I Saw What You Did, *directed by horror specialist William Castle in 1965.*

ABOVE *Christopher Lee was a star of Hammer Films. In the 1970* Scars of Dracula *he played Count Dracula yet again.*

that the early Hammer productions look fairly sumptuous, so whatever tosh the story serves up, the movies at least look good. Two major horror stars emerged from this cycle of Hammer movies: Peter Cushing (much the better actor of the two) and Christopher Lee. Cushing's first effort in the horror stakes was *The Curse of Frankenstein* (1957), then came *Horror of Dracula* (1958), *The Revenge of Frankenstein* (1958) and *The Hound of the Baskervilles* (1959). Cushing became a star of horror movies and he went to make many other Hammer films, as well as working for other producers of the genre. Lee took the title role in *Horror of Dracula* (he and Cushing were very often paired in these movies), then made *Corridors of Blood, The Man Who Could Cheat Death* and *The Mummy* in quick succession. He, like Cushing, acquired a wide fan base of horror addicts, and he has scarcely strayed from the genre since. He also played Dr Fu Manchu in a couple of undistinguished movies and Dracula in several sequels.

Since the early 1980s Hollywood has continued to mine the horror genre: in the *Halloween* series, the *Freddy Kruger/Nightmare on Elm Street* movies, a succession of movies adapted from Stephen King sources (*Carrie, Christine, The Shining, Misery*), reworkings of the ghost story (*The Sixth Sense, The Others*) and a knowing send-up of the genre in the *Scream* series of movies. The genre will never die out, as long as there is a teenage audience out there who want to be alternatively frightened and amused by the nightmares that the makers of horror movies can think up.

217

ABOVE *Donnie Darko (2002) is a half-horror, half sci-fi movie, but it deals with familiar content: the alienation of a teenager which manifests itself in horrific imaginings and dark deeds.*

SCIENCE FICTION MOVIES

Bug-eyed monsters, aliens with incredibly high IQs, invaders that act suspiciously like Cold War enemies, insubstantial jelly-like creatures that mean no harm to us earthlings, E.T., the translucent beings who emerge from the gigantic spaceship in *Close Encounters of the Third Kind*, the nasty alien out to get Mel Gibson and family in *Signs*: all of these are cinematic manifestations of our dreams about space and those unknown creatures that may or may not inhabit it.

In the 1950s, aliens – whether invading the earth or encountered when explorers ventured into space – were invariably hostile and subversive. A notable exception was Michael Rennie as Klaatu in *The Day the Earth Stood Still*: he spoke like an Englishman who had been to a public school (perhaps he had been to Eton?), was very cool and collected

ABOVE *Forbidden Planet (1956) is loosely based on Shakespeare's* The Tempest *and is rated as one of the better sci-fi movies of the 1950s.*

ABOVE *Ed Wood's* Plan 9 from Outer Space *(1959) was so bad that it won itself a multitude of fans. It is definitely one of the worst movies ever made.*

even when faced with the wickedness of earthlings, and showed extreme politeness to one and all as he tried to save us from ourselves.

However, this was the exception to the rule. Most aliens in 1950s movies were bad, and I mean really bad. This comic-book view of extra-terrestrials perhaps suited the politics of the Cold War, which was its height then, when anybody thought to be "un-American" was suspected of Communism and subversion. The 1940s and 50s was

the era of the McCarthyite hearings in Hollywood when liberal film-makers suspected of subversion had their careers ruined by association with Communism. SF films in the 50s were employed as parables for their times: to warn against alien beings taking over the minds and territory of Americans, or as a reminder of the dangers of conformity and paranoia, as in *Invasion of the Body Snatchers* (1956). In actual fact, that movie can be interpreted in two ways: as a

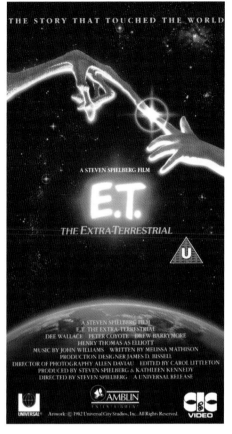

ABOVE *The third of the* Planet of the Apes *series,* Escape from the Planet of the Apes *(1971), is rated as the best of the sequels in this science-fiction series.*

warning against a spreading virus of intolerance and hysteria, or about how communities can be taken over by subversives right under the noses of honest citizens.

However, by the 1970s and 80s, with the Cold War receding, aliens began to be represented as benevolent. In the 1950s the military and government agencies had been represented as saving the USA from alien invasion. Now the individual had to protect him or herself against these very agencies in order to make contact with the aliens. Consider Spielberg's movies *Close Encounters of the Third Kind* and *E.T.* In *Close Encounters* the Richard Dreyfuss character and like-minded people have to fight the oppression of the authorities in order to meet the friendly aliens. When those wobbly creatures leave the spaceship at the end of the movie, they bypass the government personnel who have been trained to go into space with them, instead heading for the ordinary joes and jills who have only

good will in their hearts and a desire to leave everything behind them for a jaunt into another galaxy. Similarly, in the same director's *E.T.*, it is not the sinister government technicians and scientists who save the cuddly extra-terrestrial and treat him like a human being (well, not exactly, but you get the idea), but the empathizing youngsters who learn how to fly their bicycles in the process of saving him.

However, old attitudes die hard, and *Independence Day* (1996), *Mars Attacks!* (1996) and *Signs* (2002) have resurrected the evil alien figure to

ABOVE *E.T. (1982) was one of the most successful sci-fi movies ever made, and it represented aliens as well-disposed beings.*

trouble our daydreams. But now that old enemies have become new friends and the Cold War is officially dead, how will future cinematic aliens be represented, and who will they stand for in our dreams about the vast, unknowable reaches of space?

219

ABOVE *The* Star Wars *series went back in time for the beginning of the saga in a galaxy far, far away with* Episode 1: The Phantom Menace *(1999).*

LOVE STORIES

By "love stories" or "romantic movies", one usually means movies in which the main interest is in the romantic involvement of the two leads. Some people, on that basis, would argue that *Gone with the Wind* is a love story about Scarlett O'Hara and Rhett Butler rather than a civil-war epic. Similarly, *Casablanca* is about the tragic love between Bogart and

ABOVE The Seventh Veil (1945) may be a perverse love story, but a love story it is under all the psychological melodrama. In the final reel Ann Todd, a disturbed pianist, realizes she has been in love with her guardian, the sadistic James Mason, all the while.

Bergman rather than a thriller involving the Nazis, Claude Rains as a Vichy policeman and the Resistance. Some love stories are located in specific periods and are enacted amidst important events, such as *The Way We Were*, which deals with the McCarthyite period in Hollywood

but is more about the on-off romance between Streisand and Redford's characters. Who remembers very much about the Spanish Civil War from *For Whom the Bell Tolls*? But everyone remembers the Gary Cooper–Ingrid Bergman love affair.

Romantic love is a staple element in almost all Hollywood movies, even in genres such as horror, sci-fi, war or western movies. The producer would always say, "Where's the love interest?" The idea was that if there was a love story between the hero and heroine, then the appeal of a genre movie could be widened and, specifically, a female audience could be wooed into the cinema. I wish I could say things have got more sophisticated since the 1990s, but there is little evidence of that. Love interest is still pretty high on any self-respecting producer's list, even when the story and subject matter do not naturally call for it.

The British have made their share of romantic movies, but until the 1960s they were usually of the tight-lipped, blouse-buttoned variety – such as the most famous of them, *Brief Encounter*, where Celia Johnson is appalled when Trevor Howard arranges for them to borrow a friend's flat for some adulterous love-making. Oh,

LEFT The most famous love story of the British cinema is Brief Encounter (1946), directed by David Lean from a script by Noel Coward. It starred Celia Johnson and Trevor Howard as very genteel, illicit lovers.

the shame of it all! Indeed, lovers had to be very discreet in the movies right until the early 60s when the Production Code that ruled what you could and could not show in movies began to break down. British movies such as *Room at the Top*, *The Girl with Green Eyes* and all those films about Swinging London swept most of the restrictions aside. But romance was not about sex and bedroom scenes: it was about Katharine Hepburn being swept off her feet by Rossano Brazzi in *Summer Madness*; it was about Montgomery Clift and Elizabeth Taylor in *A Place in the Sun*; it was Jennifer Jones waiting on a windy hill for the return of William Holden in *Love is a Many Splendored Thing*; it was Joan Fontaine in *Rebecca* and *Letter from an Unknown Woman*, expiring of love for Laurence Olivier and Louis Jourdan.

ABOVE The 1973 The Way We Were was one of the most successful love stories of the 1970s. Starring Barbra Streisand and Robert Redford, it was partly set against Hollywood in the 1940s.

For a while now, there have been few movies that are straight romances. There has been lots of explicit sex in movies, but straightforward romance has seemed to decline. There have been a few movies that portray gay or lesbian love affairs, but they have generally failed to attract a wider audience. Perhaps the relationships between men and women were too fraught during the period that saw a battle for equal rights by women for conventional romantic movies to be that popular. There has been a

continuing obsession with sex in the movies, but even sex is shown to be a dangerous and potentially destructive instinct when indulged (*Fatal Attraction*, *Jagged Edge*, *The Morning After*). One 1980s love story, *Falling in Love* with Robert De Niro and Meryl Streep as the lovers, failed disastrously at the box office. In many ways, this movie was a throwback to the days of the great movie love story with two of the biggest contemporary stars playing opposite one another, but it failed to click with the general public.

However, in this post-feminist era, the time may once more be ripe for the return of the hankie-sodden

ABOVE The Age of Innocence (1993) *was adapted from Edith Wharton's novel, and starred Daniel Day-Lewis, Michelle Pfeiffer and Winona Ryder. It was an example of a subtle love story that exposed the hypocrisies of respectable society.*

love story, as the success of *Shakespeare in Love*, *The English Patient* and *Captain Corelli's Mandolin* show.

BELOW Manhattan, *along with* Annie Hall, *may ultimately be seen as Woody Allen's major achievements in the cinema. With a wonderful score of George Gershwin tunes,* Manhattan *is not only about the love stories of the characters, but a hymn of love to the city itself.*

MELODRAMAS, WEEPIES OR WOMEN'S PICTURES

Hollywood took over melodrama from the "penny dreadfuls" and 19th-century theatre. Melodrama has always been viewed as the poor relation of tragedy and realism, but the works of important novelists such as Dickens and Dostoevsky contain plenty of melodramatic incidents and climaxes. Silent movies lent themselves to melodramatic excess; when only the image and gesture communicated meaning, then actors and directors had to hook into the melodramatic tradition to tell their stories and express feeling. Acting

ABOVE *Jane Wyman makes all the usual female sacrifices in the melodramatic weepie* The Blue Veil *(1951).*

ABOVE *The 1949* Little Women *is quintessentially a women's picture as seen through the eyes of Hollywood. The important characters are all female, it is based in the family and concerns the loves and aspirations of the female characters. Here, June Allyson gives advice to Margaret O'Brien.*

styles in the silent movie era borrowed from the tradition of acting in stage melodramas (and from mime).

Hollywood producers thought largely in stereotypes when considering audiences, so it was at the female audience that most melodramas were directed because of

the appeal that the subject matter was thought to have for women. These movies came to be known as "weepies" or "women's pictures" because of the excessive emotion they supposedly provoked in the largely female audience. However, they provided the opportunity for powerful female characters to be represented on the screen, and some independent-minded stars were created by the genre: Davis, Crawford, De Havilland and Stanwyck. These were the female stars that women were expected to identify with, the stars who acted out on screen the kind of challenges and anxieties experienced by most women – according to the ideas of Hollywood scriptwriters, at least.

The term "women's picture" can embrace several genres, from melodrama to love story to romantic comedy. However, to the traditional Hollywood producer, a women's picture meant tears shed by the

audience because of the sacrifices made by the women characters and the courage shown by these representations of womanhood in adverse circumstances – whether those were brought about by the perfidious male sex, social conditions, personal blights such as the sudden onset of illness or even lack of attractiveness, familial oppression, ungrateful children, broken or hopeless love affairs, or a combination of all of those factors. All of the afore-mentioned stars made serious sacrifices on screen for the sake of

ABOVE *Ann Sheridan was a regular in women's pictures of the 1940s. Here she is in* Nora Prentiss *(1947), playing a singer who ruins a doctor's life.*

ABOVE *The MGM star Greer Garson was closely identified with the women's picture genre. Here she dallies with Leo Genn in* The Miniver Story *(1950).*

husbands, lovers, children, parents, friends or society in general. "We know", these films seemed to be saying to the female audience, "how hard your life can be and how undervalued you are, and we are bearing testimony to that!"

There were several subgenres within the genre of melodrama: two were the maternal melodrama in which a mother figure was variously scorned, neglected or sacrificed for her children, and the family melodrama in which the institution of the family was put under strain and finally reinforced. There was also the melodrama of romantic love, in which the female protagonist was wooed, abandoned, tricked or seduced but usually ended up with the man of her choice. The ideological purpose of these movies was to reinforce female roles. But, by making women the pivotal figures in the story, they also raised questions about what women should do with their lives, and created powerful role models for millions of cinema-goers. Katharine Hepburn, Bette Davis and Barbara Stanwyck were early versions of the liberated women on our screens today.

Bette Davis and her ilk occasionally had to resort to guns and murder to get their way, but generally they never went so far as Susan Sarandon and Geena Davis in *Thelma and Louise*, who leave their partners, take to the road, shoot guns off, become the target of a police chase across the country and end up driving off a cliff to their deaths. *Thelma and Louise* was a merger

ABOVE *A classic women's picture of the 1960s is* The VIPs *(1963), which starred Elizabeth Taylor and Richard Burton. Liz is seen here with Louis Jourdan.*

of the female buddy movie with the melodramatic thriller and the road movie that showed women contemplating a future without men – indeed, what they were escaping from was men. It was hugely popular, so it must have struck a chord with a lot of people.

The traditional women's picture may have vanished, but movie producers know that it is very often the woman in a partnership who chooses which movie a couple go to see. When more than half of the cinema audience is composed of women, then whatever producers think will appeal to this female audience will determine what movies get made.

LEFT *Patricia Roc was a star of the 1940s and 50s in Britain, starring in love stories such as* Something Money Can't Buy *(1952). Here she is with co-star Anthony Steel.*

223

WAR MOVIES

All major movie-producing nations have made war movies to attract a mass audience who either perceive them as a kind of adventure yarn or as an authentic attempt to reproduce the experience of war on the screen. War movies have been used as propaganda by all nations, especially in times of war, or in the aftermath of wars, when morale has to be kept high or national pride and mythology have to be celebrated. As a result, too many war movies in the past have been exercises in jingoism or self-congratulation; too few have represented war authentically. "War is hell!" is a plea made by intensely patriotic and anti-

LEFT *One of the better Hollywood war movies was the 1949* Twelve O'Clock High, *which showed war as hell, avoided false heroics and represented the cost in individual terms.*

war movies alike. Many movies, while pointing to the horror of war, simultaneously indulge in the most dishonest heroic posturings and simplification of the issues and of who the good and bad guys are. Such films are really westerns under a different guise.

However, there have been honourable exceptions to this jingoistic rule. *All Quiet on the Western Front* (1930) and *A Walk in the Sun* (1945) were both directed by Lewis Milestone and both concentrated on the realities of war and not on false heroics. The 1949 *Twelve O'Clock High* was of the war-is-hell school, but managed to show the ravages that the strain of military life in wartime can lead to in even the strongest of men. The 1957 *Paths of Glory*, directed by Stanley Kubrick, is one of the finest

ABOVE *Richard Attenborough's 1977 movie about the debacle of the 1944 Arnhem parachute drops,* A Bridge Too Far.

and most powerful of all war movies. Strictly speaking not an anti-war movie, it still manages to indict the military mentality that can blithely send men to their certain deaths in the name of glory. Robert Aldrich's *Too Late the Hero* (1970) has a refreshingly cynical anti-war tone, which does not quite erase the memory of that other Aldrich-directed movie *The Dirty Dozen* (1967), which in the final analysis glorifies killing. Most Hollywood war movies have been too similar to the objectionable John Wayne-produced *The Green Berets* (1968), propagating a facile patriotism and mindless love of militarism.

ABOVE *John Wayne made many war movies. Here in* The Longest Day *(1962), he relaxes on the Normandy beaches before taking on the whole German army.*

KENNETH MORE

Vainqueur du ciel

"REACH FOR THE SKY."

MURIEL PAVLOW   LA VIE DE DOUGLAS BADER   PRODUCTEUR   DANIEL M. ANGEL
LYNDON BROOK · LEE PATTERSON   d'après le livre de Paul Brickhill   MISE EN SCENE   LEWIS GILBERT

ABOVE *Kenneth More starred as Douglas Bader, the flying ace who lost both his legs but who climbed back into the cockpit, in the 1956* Reach for the Sky.

This mindset changed somewhat in the 1990s with World War II epics such as *The Thin Red Line* and *Saving Private Ryan*. In *Saving Private Ryan* Steven Spielberg pulls no punches with a searing, stomach-churningly realistic depiction of the physical and mental trauma of battle. In a powerful, visceral opening sequence, the audience experiences all the tension and adrenaline rush of the US infantry as they launch into the D-Day assault on Omaha Beach. Using first-hand accounts from actual survivors, Spielberg does not flinch from showing graphic scenes of carnage and devastation, bringing home all the senselessness of war – rather than the glory. Spielberg's *Empire of the Sun* and *Schindler's List* also hammered home the idiocies and cruelty of war.

RIGHT *Oliver Stone's 1986 movie about Vietnam,* Platoon, *packs a lot of emotional power and communicates the horror of the Vietnam war almost viscerally.*

If the American cinema had the mythology of the opening of the western frontier to feed off and add to, the British cinema seemed to find its central myths in World War II when Britain stood alone against the power of Germany and Japan. Post-war British cinema was obsessed with recreating the "finest hour" and reinforcing the myths surrounding "the Dunkirk spirit", the Battle of Britain, the struggle on the home front, the battle at sea and the defence of the British Empire by its loyal subjects. A large proportion of British films in the 1940s and 50s starred John Mills, Jack Hawkins, Richard Attenborough, Bryan Forbes, Peter Finch, John Gregson, Donald Sinden and Anthony Steel in a variety of uniforms showing the world and themselves how Britain did it. It was as though British film-makers were stuck in a time warp and were drawn irresistibly to the tales of POW escapes ("My turn for the tunnel, sir"), submarine warfare (Richard Attenborough turning yellow below the waves), dog-fights in the air ("I bagged a couple of gerries, Flight!") or espionage behind the enemy lines ("Your job is to convince those krauts the Normandy landings are going to take place in Spain").

225

PLATOON

SOCIAL PROBLEM MOVIES

Every so often the cinema deals with a "social problem" such as racial prejudice, political unrest, alcoholism, drugs, poverty and unemployment, sexual inequality and violence towards women, or mental illness. The movies are meant to appeal to a mass audience, but because of this need to attract millions of people, the tendency has been to emphasize the personal problems of the characters at the expense of the general social issue that is ostensibly being represented. In the heyday of the studio era, Hollywood was careful not to alienate sections of public

ABOVE The Best Years of Our Lives (1946) *dealt with the problems of returning GIs after World War II. Here Dana Andrews confronts errant wife Virginia Mayo.*

opinion, and thereby endanger box-office returns; studios had to contend with multifarious pressure groups such as the Catholic Legion of Decency, the American Legion, the Daughters of the Revolution and frequently bigoted local censorship boards, all of which might put a seal of disapproval on a film – a move that could have a major impact on how well it did at the box office. The powerful Legion of

RIGHT *In the 1947 movie* The Beginning or the End, *Hollywood took on the subject of the development of the atomic bomb. Was it OK because it was in the hands of the good guys or had a genie been unleashed from the bottle that would not go back in?*

Decency's telling Catholics not to see a film because of its sexual explicitness, politics or perceived blasphemy was the stuff of producers' nightmares. Thus, many of the movies that dealt with "explosive" issues had to be so kid-gloved in their treatment that they lost credibility as serious social documents.

From the 1930s through to the 50s, the Production Code Administration, or Hays Office, which had the job of imposing censorship on all movies that aspired to being shown in American cinemas,

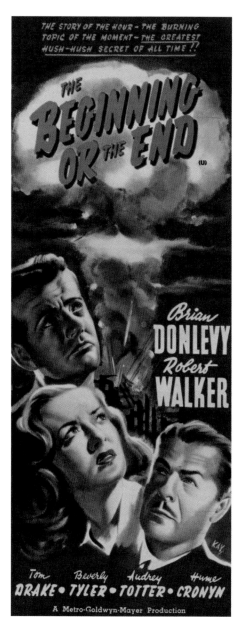

ABOVE *Hollywood producer and director Stanley Kramer tackled a big theme in his 1961* Judgment at Nuremberg, *which represented the trial of former Nazi leaders for war crimes. Spencer Tracy played a judge, Burt Lancaster a troubled ex-Nazi, Richard Widmark a prosecuting counsel, and Marlene Dietrich the widow of a German general.*

was a very conservative organization that saw its function as the defence of "Americanism" and the American Way of Life. Any movie that implied, for example, that racial prejudice was rife in the States would be frowned upon, so producers and writers learned to portray such manifestations as isolated examples rather than the rule. For example, in the *film noir Crossfire*, one of the themes is anti-semitism in post-war American society, but the film had to imply that the anti-semitism portrayed was merely a prejudice of one psychotic individual, played by Robert Ryan,

ABOVE The Blackboard Jungle (1955) dealt with juvenile delinquency and had the first rock 'n' roll soundtrack in any Hollywood movie, Rock Around the Clock played by Bill Haley and the Comets. Conservatives blamed the movie for encouraging delinquency by using such arousing music in the movie.

rather than a widespread social phenomenon. When Ryan is shot dead at the end of the film, the implication is that the problem disappears with him. Another 1940s film, Gentleman's Agreement, again deals with anti-semitism, but instead of showing a Jewish person coming up

ABOVE From time to time, Hollywood has examined the American political system. In one of the best movies about politics, Henry Fonda played a presidential contender with integrity – in The Best Man (1964), scripted by Gore Vidal.

against actual prejudice, audiences saw Gregory Peck as a journalist pretending to be a Jew to find out the extent of anti-semitism in America. The film manages to be reassuring and self-congratulatory by individualizing the issue and suggesting simplistic solutions. It is a familiar ploy.

Movies nowadays deal more authentically and frankly with social problems, although the tendency to exonerate societies and institutions by showing the occasional sinner being punished for his transgressions is still prevalent. In Wall Street, Gordon Gekko, the character played by Michael Douglas, is shopped by his former disciple and the implications are that he will go to jail for his illegal junk bond dealing, that Wall Street is shown to be capable of cleaning itself up, and that all it takes is for one good individual to stand up for morality for things to change. Most Hollywood films dealing with social issues are melodramatic and fairly simplistic – the narrative almost inevitably seeks an ending that resolves the problem in favour of a consensus solution. However, Hollywood is now willing to deal with sensitive issues such as

Aids: Philadelphia, for all its sentimentality, had Tom Hanks, one of its top male stars, playing a homosexual dying of Aids. Think of the possibility of James Stewart playing such a part and you can see how things have moved on. Yet Hollywood will inevitably put a coating of sugar over even the grimmest of subjects. Even social problem movies have to have happy endings in Tinsel Town.

ABOVE The dangers of the uncontrolled development of nuclear power stations was explored in the 1979 The China Syndrome, starring Jane Fonda as a concerned television reporter, Michael Douglas as her sidekick, and Jack Lemmon as a whistle-blowing employee at a nuclear power station.

BELOW Oliver Stone made JFK (1991) about a district attorney's investigation into the Kennedy assassination. It starred Kevin Costner as Jim Garrison, who pieces together a conspiracy theory about the case.

227

THRILLERS

LEFT *Hitchcock adapted* The Birds *(1963) from a Daphne Du Maurier story and turned it into a tense psychological drama centred on man–woman relationships and the family.*

Suspense thrillers were, and are, standard products for the Hollywood studios: murder mysteries, chase thrillers, women-in-peril movies and private-eye yarns. The thriller format was often used by writers and directors to explore aspects of society and human psychology within a recognizable formula of unravelling a mystery or situating the main protagonist in danger and mayhem. Some thrillers can be classed as *film noir*, but while *film noir* crossed generic frontiers, many thrillers had no discernible *noir* elements at all.

The acknowledged master of the thriller was Alfred Hitchcock. He used the genre to manipulate his audience by means of suspense, while exploring his personal obsessions about guilt and punishment, sexuality and voyeurism, and the darker sides of human nature. For Hitchcock, plots were the means of hooking an audience. He then manipulated the members of the audience to feel as he wanted them to feel, to switch allegiances and sympathy for the characters as he wished them to do and, generally, to react on cue to the

stimuli that he controlled through the images on screen. Hitchcock seemed to be haunted by a fear of punishment and a sense of guilt – he often talked about his Catholic childhood and the fear that any authority figure, such as a priest or a policeman, would generate in him. The French critics and directors of the New Wave of the 1950s were perhaps the first to analyze seriously the thematic

ABOVE The Man from U.N.C.L.E. *television series was translated to the big screen in a number of films. Here Robert Vaughan and David McCallum star in* One Spy Too Many *(1966).*

concerns of Hitchcock the director. Francois Truffaut, for example, did a whole series of interviews with Hitchcock that were published in book form.

Does this kind of analysis treat Hitchcock with too much seriousness? After all, the man made movie thrillers, which he claimed were merely entertainments aimed at manipulating the fears and emotions of the audiences who flocked to see them. Should they not just be enjoyed for the ephemeral entertainments they

ABOVE *Director Brian De Palma has made several thrillers that pay direct homage to Hitchcock. This one,* Body Double *(1984), seemed to take its inspiration from Hitchcock's* Rear Window.

are and not over-intellectualized? This is the age-long argument about commercial movies: do critics and intellectuals make far too much of dissecting what popular movies mean to the detriment of just enjoying them? Specifically, can movie thrillers really be worth discussing in depth?

Well, does a Hitchcock movie such as *Vertigo* have deeper resonance than its labyrinthine storyline and plot twists seem to imply? I would say it has, but that any meaning it has, the

LEFT *Michael Caine starred in the Ken Russell-directed* Billion Dollar Brain *(1967). Caine played the character of Harry Palmer, the awkward undercover agent conceived by author Len Deighton.*

viewer has to bring to it. Hitchcock weaves the tapestry; the patterns we choose to see in that tapestry are up to us. It is a similar story with Hitchcock's other masterpiece *Psycho*. On one level it is a piece of outrageous schlock, a horror movie that goes for the jugular. On another level it deals with deeper psychological issues in a highly emotional and disturbing style. The same argument can be made for a number of Hitchcock thrillers, including *Rebecca, Notorious, Strangers on a Train, Rear Window* and *North by Northwest.*

There have been many imitations of Hitchcock's films, notably by the American director Brian De Palma and the French director Claude Chabrol, but few have achieved the same mastery of audience manipulation that he did. Most cinema is manipulative in the sense that films seek to draw you, the viewer, into their representation of reality so that you suspend your disbelief. Thrillers depend on that suspension and on suspense as well; if you are, metaphorically, to be on the edge of your seat, you have to believe that the heroine is genuinely going to fall off the cliff or that the hero has been fatally wounded and will not recover. You have to feel the danger the protagonists are feeling, you have to want desperately for them to escape and for the villains to be defeated. To enjoy a thriller fully, your fears have to be engaged, you have to care, you have to go through agonies and suspense before relief is granted. If you are detached from the action on the screen, you might be able to admire clinically how the formula is constructed, but you are unlikely to gain much more from the experience.

BELOW LEFT AND BELOW The Thomas Crown Affair *has been made twice: in 1967 with Steve McQueen and Faye Dunaway, and in 1999 with Pierce Brosnan and Rene Russo. The two characters play a cat-and-mouse game as each tries to keep one step ahead of the other.*

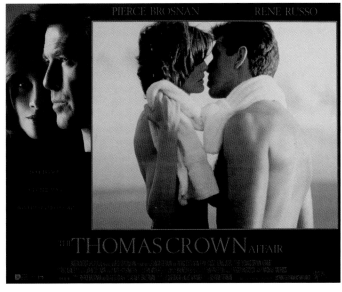

COMPUTER-GENERATED FILMS

from the creators of "toy story"

WALT DISNEY Pictures
Presents
A PIXAR Film
a bug's
life

LEFT A Bug's Life (1998) is a computer-animated feature produced by Pixar, the same company that produced the Toy Story movies.

Special effects have become ever more sophisticated since the early days of cinema. Nowadays, film-makers dispense with models, sets, automation, blue screens and such like crude tricks. The computer rules in the movies, just as it does in many other walks of life. Computer-generated effects are here to stay – or at least until they are themselves displaced by some advanced technology that hasn't even been thought of yet.

The new whizz-kids of special effects are the children of the computer age. They work for George Lucas's Industrial Light and Magic in California or for the Disney studios, where old-fashioned animation is still alive and kicking in movies such as *Beauty and the Beast* and *The Lion King*, although animated films have become ever more complex and spectacular in the images and sounds they create.

We have to get our heads around the idea that much of what we see on screen nowadays is not real in the physical sense – the "realities" we see exist only because a computer has generated them. For example, the scenes in *Gladiator* in the Roman arena were largely computer-generated. Only a partial set was built and a relatively small crowd used to people it; there was no amphitheatre as in, say, *Spartacus* or the 1959 *Ben-Hur*, where the movie-makers had to go to the expense of constructing arenas and peopling them with hundreds of extras. Now the whizz-kid on the computer summons all of this up with an intricate knowledge of how computer graphics work.

Yes, Hollywood has new toys and the danger is that the effects will swamp the end-product and that movies will try to outdo themselves in the audacity of the special effects produced. Yet perhaps this is just the complaint of a writer on film wedded to the old ways of doing things. Proponents of computer-generated effects would argue that movies such as *Toy Story* and *Toy Story 2*, far from being swamped by the special effects, are greatly enhanced by them because the story, characters and humour still shine through all the technological wizardry. Some serious people rate the two *Toy Story* movies as being among the best movies produced over the whole of the 1990s.

Similarly, the *Lord of the Rings* movies use an avalanche of special effects. Do these swamp the basic story of the search for the Ring? Or can the full impact of Tolkien's story only be communicated because of the wealth of special effects at the movie-makers' disposal? Is nothing to be left to the imagination of the audience by these spectacular effects? Should the audience be made to work harder to envisage for themselves the wonders of Tolkien's story? Are the special effects in essence the movie: a merging of style with meaning, so that the special effects are the meaning, the ultimate message of the film?

But I hear the cry that movies are just harmless entertainment. The intention behind movies such as *A Bug's Life*, *Antz*, *Shrek*, *Dinosaur* and *Stuart Little* is to provide an amusing entertainment for a couple of hours,

BELOW Antz (1998) is another computer-animated movie about an ant called Z with the voice and personality of Woody Allen.

Every ant
has
his day.

ANTZ

COMING SOON

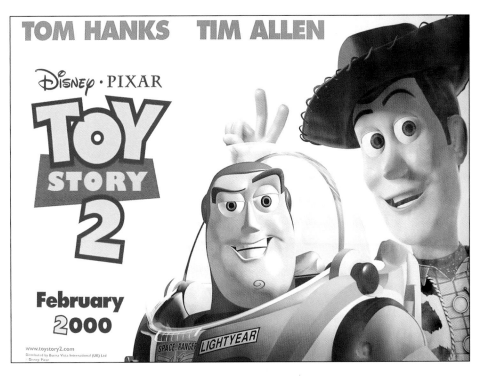

ABOVE Toy Story 2 (1999) is generally regarded as being even better than the 1995 Toy Story, and is also rated as the best of the new crop of computer-animated cartoons.

which will take the audience out of themselves and make them forget mundane reality for the period of time they are watching the screen. This is the way it has always been in the world of the cinema, and the advent of computer-generated effects has not really made any difference to that central aim of movies; it has merely expanded enormously the range and complexity of special effects that can be summoned up to keep an audience in that state of wonder that has been the aim of producers from the time of the nickelodeons onwards.

Well, perhaps. There will always be niche markets in world cinema and an audience for movies such as those of Ingmar Bergman and Krzysztof Kieslowski. Not all movies need to be festooned with special effects. The danger is that mainstream Hollywood movies, because of the enormous box-office receipts garnered by movies such as *The Lord of the Rings* and the *Harry Potter* series, all go for the same market and the same ingredients. There has always been a sort of territory between the extremes of the totally populist blockbusters and the art-house movies, inhabited by well-made, entertaining movies that are not insulting to the intelligence. Perhaps it is those kinds of movies that are threatened with extinction if everyone goes after the stupendous special-effects movie and their attendant big bucks. Meanwhile, computer-generated special effects movies are here to stay, and let's hope the movie-going public demand some sustenance for the brain while watching them and eating their popcorn. Mentally grazing while food-grazing is not to be recommended.

ABOVE Shrek (2001) had a sophisticated script, great computer-generated animation, together with the voices of Mike Myers, Eddie Murphy and Cameron Diaz, among others.

ABOVE The Lord of the Rings: The Fellowship of the Ring *was an immense box-office hit and was generously rewarded with Oscars. The computer effects were even more sophisticated in the two sequels with the creation of the "CG" character, Gollum.*

HOLLYWOOD SCANDALS AND TRAGEDIES

It is a hoary old cliché that Hollywood, and show-business in general, extracts a heavy price for its prizes of stardom and fame, but the history of the American film industry does seem to be littered with the dead bodies and ruined reputations of many of its most famous personalities. It may be that the movie industry extracts no higher price for success than, say, the profession of accountancy does, but suicides and murders among movie stars tend to reach the front pages rather more often.

Another matter of debate is how much these unfortunate stars were victims of an uncaring, exploitative system and how much they contributed to their own downfall through their own self-destructive natures. What is undoubtedly true is that people living under the glare of the Hollywood spotlights are at high risk of succumbing to egomania, self-destructive patterns, delusions, feelings of unworthiness and media hounding. "Ah, well," as the man said, "if you have the fame, you have to take the heartaches that go with it."

However, almost all spheres of endeavour in which the rewards are high in terms of fame, power and wealth cause casualties. In the world of politics, for example, reaching for the highest pinnacles of power means an individual lays himself or herself open to incredible scrutiny, and many a politician has crumbled under that gaze. But not many people weep over the corpses of politicians, so why should movie stars and film people gain more of our sympathy? Most people's attitude to the stars they admire are ambivalent: they admire from a distance, but some part of star

ABOVE *Rob Lowe's early exploits in his private life caused a stir in Hollywood, but they did not affect his film or television career.*

worship involves envy and the unconscious wish to destroy the loved one. The tabloid newspapers sell very well when they expose the scandals surrounding these gilded creatures who seem to have it all. Many people

feel a certain guilty satisfaction in seeing the famous toppled. "See," they say, "they're just like the rest of us after all!" Well, of course they are. Movie stars are just actors elevated to almost mythical status, but they remain essentially Joe Bloggs from Idaho or Norma Nobody from Essex. And they make a mess of their lives just like you and me.

THE FATTY ARBUCKLE AFFAIR

In the very early days of Hollywood, Roscoe "Fatty" Arbuckle became a famous Mack Sennett slapstick comedian. He was a fat man with a moon face, and he had something on screen that made people laugh. He made two-reel silent comedies with titles such as *Fatty and Mabel's Simple Life*, *Mabel and Fatty's Married Life*, *Fatty's Flirtation* and *Fickle Fatty's Fall*. In other words, Arbuckle was a professional fat man, but he was a great box-office attraction and very well paid, until events that took place in 1921 put an end to his meteoric career.

The events that led to Arbuckle's downfall happened at a weekend-long party organized by Arbuckle in the St Francis Hotel in San Francisco. During the course of the party, a young starlet, Virginia Rappe, was severely injured around the abdomen: injuries that led to her death five days later from peritonitis. How she came to be seriously hurt was never finally established, but Arbuckle had been in a bedroom alone with her just before she was discovered in a state of severe pain and with her clothing torn. Rumours spread that Arbuckle had used a bottle on Rappe in a perverse and bizarre sexual attack.

Subsequently, Arbuckle was charged with rape and murder. The newspapers were full of the case and Arbuckle was tried and found guilty in the public consciousness before the case got anywhere near a court. The scandal rocked Hollywood, and the nation's moral guardians, eager to attack the film colony, labelled it a modern-day Sodom and Gomorrah. Further rumours circulated that Arbuckle had used a Coca-Cola bottle on Rappe in an attempt at unnatural penetration. Three trials ensued and, after two hung juries (one opting for acquittal, the other for conviction), the third jury cleared Arbuckle of all charges. But his film career was over. Despite his acquittal, his erstwhile friends and the film studios turned their backs on him. He made a couple of two-reelers in the 1930s. The mighty had fallen and no one seemed to care very much. He had been found guilty by association. Arbuckle became an alcoholic and died at the

ABOVE *Fatty Arbuckle was a major star before his encounter with Virginia Rappe at a Hollywood party. Although he was never found guilty of any crime, the bad publicity effectively finished his movie career.*

age of 46 in 1933. Whether or not he was guilty (and after all he was innocent in the eyes of the law), Arbuckle's fall is a cautionary tale of excess and indulgence: sudden fame and riches can play havoc in the lives of ordinary people suddenly elevated to heights of fame and success that they had hitherto only dreamt of.

233

PAUL BERN AND JEAN HARLOW

Paul Bern was a top MGM executive in the 1930s. He was a small, unattractive man, hardly the type to be thought of as a likely husband for blonde star Jean Harlow, whose screen persona was brassy and promiscuous. However, Harlow had married Bern in July 1932. Perhaps she believed that a top executive such as Bern would help to protect her career at MGM; perhaps Bern, 22 years her senior, represented some kind of father figure for her. Whatever the reasons for the marriage, the couple appeared to be happy and the union seemed as likely to last as any other marriage in Tinsel Town, where even then the divorce rate was high.

But marital happiness, if they ever tasted any, did not last very long. Two months after the marriage Bern was found shot dead in their home. A suicide note was left in his handwriting, referring to his "abject humiliation" and to the previous night as "only a comedy". It seemed that Bern was so ashamed of his inability to make love to his wife that he took his own life. Whether this was because of Bern's homosexuality or some inadequacy in his sexual equipment has never really been clarified. It seemed, however, an open-and-shut case: little Paul Bern had taken his own life because he could not make love to his screen goddess wife.

Louis B. Mayer and Irving Thalberg, who ran MGM at that time, were on the scene before the police, giving rise to the rumour that some kind of cover-up had been put into operation. What did Mayer and Thalberg cook up between them to protect their star? Harlow was then a very "hot" property for the studio. Her pictures were making the studio millions of dollars, and she was young and seemed likely to remain a big star for a number of years. A lot was at stake.

The official story began to come out. It was stated that Harlow had been staying with her mother at the time of Bern's death. She had, of course, nothing to do with her husband's death. The couple were in love, but Bern had taken his own life while the balance of his mind was disturbed.

But was there more to this affair than met the eye? Could the suicide note have been forced out of Bern to make it look like suicide? Was Harlow actually there in the house at the time? Rumours abounded about Bern having found out about an affair that Harlow was having. The same rumours marked her down as her husband's killer and Mayer and Thalberg as perverting the course of justice to hide the real facts. Whatever the truth, Harlow herself did not survive her husband that long; by 1937 she too had died, from uremic poisoning.

BELOW *Jean Harlow was the epitome of sexual allure for 1930s audiences, so it was odd that insignificant-looking Paul Bern, an MGM executive, should be the man she chose to marry.*

ERROL FLYNN

Errol Flynn was a renowned womanizer on and off the screen, but his promiscuous ways landed him in deep trouble in 1942 when he was charged with statutory rape under a Californian law that made it illegal to have sex with anyone under the age of 18. At the Grand Jury hearing, Flynn was acquitted because the girls involved told conflicting stories. However, the authorities pursued the case and Flynn had to stand trial. Flynn had made some enemies in Hollywood, his lifestyle outraged the puritans and he was probably the most famous movie actor of his time: he had these three strikes against him, so there were lots of people out there gunning for him.

Jerry Geisler, a top-notch criminal lawyer, defended Flynn and managed to tear the girls' stories to shreds. Flynn was again acquitted. The real puzzle was: who or what was behind this campaign to get Flynn? A whole can of worms involving Warner Bros. and Flynn's studio paying kickbacks to politicians and the police could have been opened if anyone had spilled the beans. In other words, Flynn was almost certainly set up as a fall guy: his scalp would have been a feather in the cap of the investigating authorities. The possibility arises that the case collapsed because the authorities allowed it to collapse when his studio came to terms with the people who feared exposure. It was a grimy, corrupt mélange with powerful interests ranging up on both sides, and Flynn just happened to be the pinball being struck from side to side.

As it happened, Flynn's reputation as a lover and star was only enhanced by the trials. Unfortunately, his own self-destructive instincts saw to it that he departed this life at a comparatively young age without the help of outside agencies, apart from booze, drugs and a lifestyle that practically invited death. But, even after his death in 1959, they were still trying to pin something on old Errol: he has been variously accused of being a Nazi spy and an IRA supporter. Perhaps Flynn wasn't the only one who had difficulty in telling the difference between reality and the movies.

BELOW *Errol Flynn on location with co-star Olivia de Havilland during the shooting of the western* Dodge City *(1939).*

FRANCES FARMER

The story of Frances Farmer raises the issue of responsibility: was her steep fall from Hollywood grace largely self-inflicted, was she the victim of a vindictive system, or was it six of one and half-a-dozen of the other? Farmer was never a major star, but hers is an interesting case because she acquired a reputation for being a rebel within the Hollywood system. The question was: was she destroyed by that system or did she do it all herself?

Like other Hollywood luminaries such as John Garfield and Elia Kazan, Farmer had emerged from New York's Group Theatre, which had a reputation for being left-wing and challenging in theatrical terms. She was signed up by Paramount, but was used largely in extremely mediocre movies such as *Rhythm on the Range* (1936) and *South of Pago Pago* (1940). This may have been part of the

problem: she had come from the Group Theatre which had tried to mount meaningful plays with politically committed content; in Hollywood she was the love interest in Bing Crosby musicals.

Along the way she married a Hollywood actor, Leif Erickson, who, according to her, beat her up regularly. In 1943 she had a couple of dust-ups with the Los Angeles Police Department over traffic violations, then subsequently broke her parole. At her trial, she threw an ink-pot at the judge and slugged a police officer. She was put in a straitjacket, served some time in jail and a private sanatorium, then was committed for ten years to a state asylum where she was systematically abused and humiliated. Finally, she had a lobotomy, which left her stable but unrecognizable. When she was released from the asylum she even

ABOVE *Frances Farmer looking relaxed and composed: a publicity photograph taken before her breakdown. The Hollywood publicity machine ignored the reality of stars' lives.*

fronted a television show for a while. Her story was filmed in 1983 with Jessica Lange playing her.

Farmer was undoubtedly a strong-minded, independent woman with left-wing sympathies. This combination probably accounts in part for the horrific treatment that was doled out to her. Had she been star in Hollywood in the 1960s rather than in the 30s, her form of spirited independence might have been accommodated. As it was, in the 40s when her real troubles began, the powers-that-be were unaccustomed to dealing with young women who refused to conform and who were not over-grateful for getting trashy parts in tenth-rate movies.

LANA TURNER AND THE HOOD

As a young 17-year-old Hollywood hopeful, Lana Turner had supposedly been discovered by a press agent sitting in Schwabs Drugstore on Sunset Boulevard. Like many of the myths surrounding this actress, this was complete hogwash. Nevertheless, Turner quickly became a star for reasons that leave some of us bewildered. She couldn't act, sing or dance, and her looks were of the plastic variety. By the time she became headline news again because of a murder case, her career was in decline, but along the way she had been a major box-office star.

In 1958, Lana Turner's daughter Cheryl stabbed to death her mother's lover, Johnny Stompanato, in her mother's bedroom in the Beverly Hills mansion that the three of them shared. Stompanato, a psychopath with gangland connections, had repeatedly threatened Turner during the course of their relatively brief relationship. Cheryl, 14 at the time of the killing, had overheard the "gigolo-type" Stompanato threatening to cut her mother up. She then took a long kitchen knife and plunged it into his stomach.

At the subsequent trial, Turner reputedly gave one of her best performances: as the distraught and contrite mother fighting for her daughter. The jury returned a verdict of justifiable homicide. However, the details of Turner's private life were splashed over every front page in America. Some vindictive people released her love letters to Stompanato to the press. The strong rumour started that it had been Turner herself who had stabbed Stompanato in a lovers' quarrel and that her daughter had taken the rap because of the certain knowledge that she would be acquitted. The irony is that, after all this bad publicity, Turner's career

had an upsurge and she continued to make films, one of which – *Imitation of Life* – was her greatest success. The connections between Hollywood and organized crime have never been a secret as such, but the Turner–Stompanato affair brought some of those tawdry connections to the fore.

ABOVE *Life imitated the movies when Lana Turner was involved in a real-life murder case. Her Hollywood career did not suffer, however, and she later starred in Sirk's appropriately titled* Imitation of Life *(1959).*

237

GEORGE CUKOR, CLARK GABLE AND *GONE WITH THE WIND*

In 1939 George Cukor was assigned to direct *Gone with the Wind* by producer David Selznick. It was a dream assignment because even before it came in front of the cameras *GWTW* was the most talked-about movie ever. Cukor, one of Hollywood's most discreet homosexuals, had made his reputation by directing female stars (Hepburn, Garbo and Crawford) in *Dinner at Eight, Little Women* and *Sylvia Scarlett.* Insiders in Hollywood and in the Hollywood press corps must have known about Cukor's homosexuality, but there was a code of silence about it. Nowadays, no one would raise an eyebrow in Hollywood if a director announced to the world that he was gay, but those were different times. As long as Cukor remained discreet, so would the press. (However, Cukor was himself a notorious gossip.)

Shortly after filming on *Gone with the Wind* commenced, Selznick replaced Cukor with Victor Fleming, a journeyman MGM director. Seemingly, Clark Gable – Rhett Butler in the film – had insisted that Cukor be replaced because the star felt that Cukor was too much of a woman's director and was giving undue attention to Vivien Leigh in her role as Scarlett O'Hara, and too little to Gable and the male side of the story. That was the official reason given for replacing Cukor. It says much about the power of a major star like Gable that he could pull strings to replace a director in the middle of a shoot and on such a major, major production as *GWTW*. But when it came down to it, in a battle of wills, there was no contest between Gable and Cukor. Selznick and MGM needed Gable; they did not need Cukor as much.

ABOVE *Clark Gable in his most famous role as Rhett Butler. Could the most masculine of Hollywood stars really have had a spell as a rent-boy, as director George Cukor claimed?*

Near the end of his life, however, Cukor gave quite a different explanation for his replacement. According to Cukor, before Gable had become a star, he had been an up-market rent-boy for Hollywood's homosexual colony. Gable was aware that Cukor knew this sordid detail about him and could not bear to be directed by the man. Thus, he insisted that Cukor be given the push. By the time Cukor made these allegations, Gable had been dead nearly 30 years, so it may have been the act of a vindictive old queen, getting his own back on the star who had had him sacked all those years ago by making up nasty stories about Gable's youth.

THE STRANGE OBSESSIONS OF ALFRED HITCHCOCK

Hitchcock's obsession with cool, blonde women, such as Grace Kelly, Kim Novak and Ingrid Bergman, was well known, but the extent to which he carried this neurotic attachment with another of his stars, Tippi Hedren, was disturbing to say the least. Hedren starred in two of Hitchcock's movies, *Marnie* and *The Birds*, the latter being about the sudden inexplicable onslaught by our feathered friends on a small fishing village. An ex-model, Hedren was perhaps a surprising choice to take the female lead in these two movies, because both parts demanded a range of emotional acting skills she had given no evidence of before on screen. At best she is barely adequate in both movies.

For some of the scenes in *The Birds*, Hitchcock insisted that real birds be used to peck away at Hedren while she was pinned down by invisible bonds. She was protected by a net that would not show up on film, but clearly the scenes involved more than a little risk to Hitchcock's new star. After a week-long shooting of a particular scene, things got wildly out of hand. Hedren was reduced to hysteria after remorseless attacks by crazed birds, and she also suffered a severe injury to one of her eyes.

The evidence suggests that Hitchcock was undoubtedly strongly sexually attracted to her, a feeling that was not reciprocated. Perhaps the director represented his anger at being repulsed by the actress in these

elongated scenes of ornithological assault. It seems that Hitchcock was eaten up with self-loathing because of his obesity and took it out on blonde actresses who aroused his hopeless passions. If this is the case, it is all rather sad. In Hitchcock's defence, he went to meticulous lengths to achieve the effects he wanted to put on celluloid. He saw his job as making the audience squirm with anxiety. Perhaps his zeal in setting up the bird attack scenes on Hedren was more to do with the director's pursuit of screen perfection. I would say the jury is still out on this one.

BELOW *Alfred Hitchcock had a thing about cool blondes. Eva Marie Saint starred in his excellent 1958 thriller,* North by Northwest.

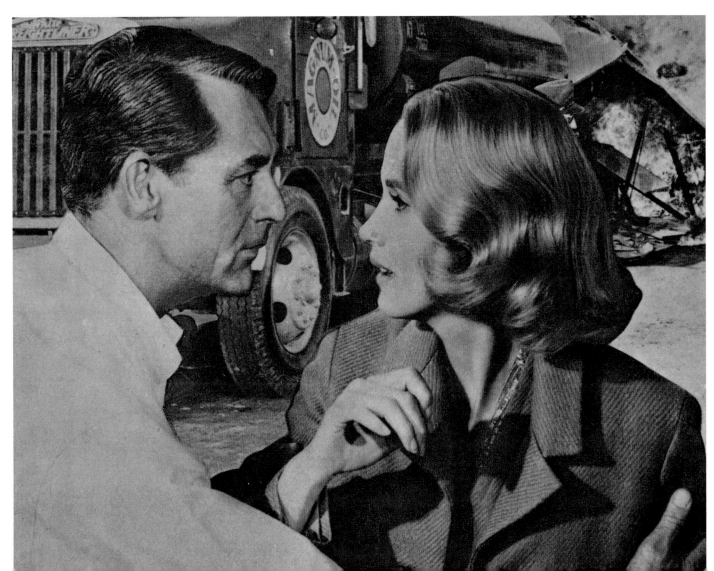

GIG YOUNG

No screen persona belied the reality of an actor's life more than that adopted by Gig Young. Young had a long movie career as a light comedian, playing the hero's best friend, the charming rival of the star and the second lead who never seemed to get the girl in movies such as *Old Acquaintance, Young at Heart, Desk Set, Ask Any Girl, That Touch of Mink* and *Strange Bedfellows*. On screen, he seemed to be the eternal philandering bachelor without a care in the world and living the life of Reilly. His features revealed an inner soul untroubled by anxieties. In real life, however, Young was an alcoholic, and in the latter part of his life he suffered from skin cancer. Many actors are like Young: on the surface they are happy-go-lucky, affable, seemingly making their way through life like blessed children. Under this superficial front, however, they are a mass of insecurities. Acting is their way of covering up their distress.

In 1978 at the age of 64 and with his screen career in decline, Young married a woman of 31. Only three weeks later both of them were found dead in his New York apartment. Young was clutching a revolver. The obvious conclusion was that Young had first shot his wife in the head, then turned the gun on himself. Whether his wife was party to a suicide pact or not remains in doubt.

The carefree actor in some of Hollywood's lightest confections had faced up to the desperation of his own life and put an end to it, taking his new wife with him. Movies create illusions: about ourselves, about the stars we see on the screen, and about what is perceived as reality. In the case of Gig Young, the escape he found in the illusions of the screen was no longer enough of a safety net. He ended those illusions with a bullet to his head.

LEFT *In this studio pose Gig Young is the debonair actor the world saw on screen, but behind that carefree air was a deeply insecure man. When the aging process caught up with him, he could not face his life any more.*

240

THE LOVING MOTHER

In 1977 Christina Crawford, Joan Crawford's adopted daughter, wrote a memoir about her mother entitled *Mommie Dearest*. It chronicled a story of the Crawford family life as vicious and uncaring. Up there on the silver screen Joan Crawford so often played the sacrificial mother fighting her way to the top to give the good things of life to her children. In real life, Crawford seemingly acquired her two adopted children because it would help her image as a caring star and hence her film career, which had gone into decline. She imposed severe discipline on the kids, beating them with coathangers amongst other things, and expecting absurd levels of obedience and regimentation.

Crawford had always worked hard at her career in her younger years, seeking sugar daddies who were in a position to land her the small parts that were essential if she was to climb the stairway to stardom. Eventually, by sheer determination rather than talent, she became a featured player, then an MGM star. Stories abound in Hollywood about her legendary bitchiness, especially to other female stars such as Norma Shearer, Greta Garbo and Bette Davis. When she could no longer play ambitious secretaries, she turned to playing suffering matrons. Throughout her career she pandered to the fan magazines and in public played the role of the star to the hilt.

Crawford's adopted children were forced to pose with her for loving family publicity pictures, which disguised the hell they were living through. The final straw for daughter Christina was when her mother took over her role in a television soap opera when she (Christina) was lying ill in hospital. Seeing her mother play a part – her part – that was meant for an actress 40 years younger probably

finally prompted Christina to write *Mommie Dearest*. It was filmed in 1981 with Faye Dunaway playing Crawford. As someone who courted fame and publicity assiduously all her life, Crawford might not have been too unhappy at this late burst of fame. In 1938 she had been one of the stars dubbed "box-office poison" in an

ABOVE *Joan Crawford, at the height of her phenomenal success as a movie star, in* The Shining Hour *(1938).*

ad placed by exhibitors in The Hollywood Reporter. She fought her way back from that nadir and would have clawed her way back after *Mommie Dearest*, had she not died in 1977.

241

COLLECTING MOVIE MEMORABILIA

The collecting of movie memorabilia expanded spectacularly in the 1990s, once the major auction houses realized there were people out there willing to pay good money for vintage movie posters, costumes and props, star autographs and a whole range of other collectables. What had been a small niche market for avid movie fans who frequented movie jumbles and scoured "collectables" shops suddenly burgeoned into a collecting area that rivalled other similar pastimes such as acquiring rock memorabilia or modern first editions of novels.

There are all sorts of reasons why collectors want movie "trash". Vintage movie posters are the main target for most collectors and they may want to build a collection around a genre (westerns, *film noir*, musicals, British comedy, sci-fi and horror). Or some people collect on a particular star or director, so they will want to acquire

every movie poster relating to their idol. What they want are the first-release movie posters that were issued at the time of the movies' initial screening. Whether or not a movie poster is from a first release or a later reissue makes a great difference to the value of a poster, just as the first edition of a novel is worth more than subsequent reprints. And, of course, these are genuine movie posters, not the kind of commercial reprints that are sold by poster shops, which have no intrinsic value. Each country produces their own posters for individual movies, so a keen collector of the Orson Welles movie *Touch of Evil*, say, would want to acquire the original US, British, French, Italian, German, Polish, Spanish, Argentinian, Belgian and other countries' posters for that movie.

Original movie props from films such as the *Star Wars* series or Universal horror movies go for a tidy sum, and costumes that stars have worn on screen also fetch high prices. What people are buying is a part of screen history, and acquiring a prop or costume brings them closer to the movie world that fascinates them. Original stills, lobby cards, the press books that the studios sent out to exhibitors and journalists, autographs, movie

ABOVE *Sci-fi movie posters from the 1950s are highly valued by collectors. This poster for* The Day the Earth Stood Still *(1951) typifies the quality of graphic art that is most prized by collectors.*

magazines, ads and flyers: these are some of the other collecting areas that fuel the market.

So how valuable are some old vintage movie posters, for example? The world record for a movie poster sold at auction belongs to an original US one sheet of the 1932 *The Mummy*.

LEFT *An original US movie poster for* The Mummy *holds the world record for a movie poster sold at auction. Its rarity explains the price.*

RIGHT *Original* James Bond *movie posters have shot up in value since the 1990s, and the Bond craze shows no sign of abating.*

ABOVE Breakfast at Tiffany's *is a favourite target for movie poster collectors. This is one of the original Italian posters for the movie.*

It was bought by one happy collector for $453,500 in 1997. Indeed, 1930s Universal horror posters figure prominently in the all-time record lists. Anything original on the 1933 *King Kong* also fetches very high prices: $244,500 in 1999 for an original US one sheet. Fritz Lang's *Metropolis* is also highly sought after: $357,750 in 2000 for an original German poster. *Casablanca, Gone with the Wind, Citizen Kane,* very early Disney or RKO musicals, and the *James Bond* movies (the Sean Connery titles) are other areas that invariably attract high prices.

So, with prices like those around, it is clear that the unwary could get their fingers burnt by buying the wrong

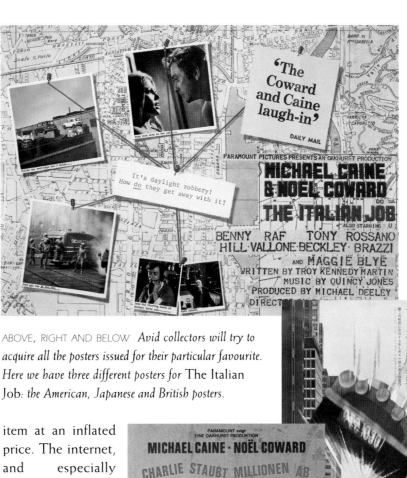

ABOVE, RIGHT AND BELOW *Avid collectors will try to acquire all the posters issued for their particular favourite. Here we have three different posters for* The Italian Job: *the American, Japanese and British posters.*

item at an inflated price. The internet, and especially auction sites such as *eBay*, have thrown fuel on the craze for collecting movie memorabilia. On any given day, there are hundreds of thousands of items of movie memorabilia for sale on *eBay* alone. And then there are dealers in movie memorabilia from many countries who advertise items for sale through their websites. Specialist galleries have sprung up in major cities such as London, New York, Los Angeles and Paris. Auction houses such as Christie's and Sotheby's hold regular sales of movie items, and some auction houses also sell through internet bidding. If you really want to start a collection, then there is an Aladdin's Cave out there to feast on.

A very useful guide to the value of movie posters is provided by *The Movie Poster Price Almanac*. Edited by John Kisch, it is updated annually and gives inclusive lists of the price of posters of almost every film ever made, as recorded from sales at auction, through dealers' websites or via *eBay*. Information about this invaluable guide is available from *info@posterprice.com*. Good hunting!

THE OSCARS

The Academy Awards! Every year around January the ballyhoo begins when the nominations for the multifarious categories are announced. Then the studios' publicity machines go full-blast in support of the actors or movies they have a vested interest in seeing win. This onslaught of publicity does not relent until the awards ceremony itself in March, when nowadays the event is televised around the world to billions of interested fans. Even after the event is over, the publicity machine keeps working, covering the post-Oscars parties, analysing for the Great Unwashed out there which party is the hot ticket of the year, who went where and with whom, who was over the moon and who was sick as a parrot, and with endless interviews with the winners and losers. It is one big jamboree for the American film industry and for the television channels and entertainment press.

But why should anyone care? From the point of view of the film-makers and the actors, they have a lot to gain from winning a coveted Oscar. An actor who wins an Oscar for Best Performance or Best Supporting Role will see their asking price shoot up. For the producers, an award for their movie can immediately translate itself into added millions at the box office. If they sweep the board of the Oscars – winning five or more Oscars for the same movie – then that means that they can retire. So people in the industry take the Oscars seriously for very pressing commercial reasons. But what about the rest of us? Should we really care which actor wins or which movie the members of Academy of Motion Picture Arts and Sciences happen to vote for in any particular year? Perhaps we shouldn't give a damn, frankly, my dear, but millions seem to, otherwise the Oscars ceremony wouldn't have the viewing figures it gets and movies that can advertise "Winner of so many Oscars" wouldn't do so well at the box office.

I watch the Oscars hoping to see some actor making an over-the-top speech when they receive their award (there should be an annual Sally Field Oscar in honour of such an achievement). I watch to be able to shake my head while some incredible mediocrity mounts the podium to get an Oscar. And occasionally, I can clap my hands when someone of real talent is recognized and rewarded. I suspect other people watch the Oscars in exactly the same frame of mind.

1920s AND 30s

1928

Best Picture: *Wings*
Best Director: Lewis Milestone (*Two Arabian Knights*) and Frank Borzage (*Seventh Heaven*)
Best Actor: Emil Jannings (*The Last Command* and *The Way of All Flesh*)
Best Actress: Janet Gaynor (*Seventh Heaven, Street Angel* and *Sunrise*)

1929

Best Picture: The Broadway Melody
Best Director: Frank Lloyd (*The Divine Lady*)
Best Actor: Warner Baxter (*In Old Arizona*)
Best Actress: Mary Pickford (*Coquette*)

1930

Best Picture: *All Quiet on the Western Front*
Best Director: Lewis Milestone (*All Quiet on the Western Front*)
Best Actor: George Arliss (*Disraeli*)
Best Actress: Norma Shearer (*The Divorcee*)

1931

Best Picture: *Cimarron*
Best Director: Norman Taurog (*Skippy*)
Best Actor: Lionel Barrymore (*A Free Soul*)
Best Actress: Marie Dressler (*Min and Bill*)

1932

Best Picture: *Grand Hotel*
Best Director: Frank Borzage (*Bad Girl*)
Best Actor: tie between Fredric March (*Dr Jekyll and Mr Hyde*) and Wallace Beery (*The Champ*)
Best Actress: Helen Hayes (*The Sin of Madelon Claudet*)

1933

Best Picture: *Cavalcade*
Best Director: Frank Lloyd (*Cavalcade*)
Best Actor: Charles Laughton (*The Private Life of Henry VIII*)
Best Actress: Katharine Hepburn (*Morning Glory*)

1934
Best Picture: *It Happened One Night*
Best Director: Frank Capra (*It Happened One Night*)
Best Actor: Clark Gable (*It Happened One Night*)
Best Actress: Claudette Colbert (*It Happened One Night*)

1935
Best Picture: *Mutiny on the Bounty*
Best Director: John Ford (*The Informer*)
Best Actor: Victor McLaglen (*The Informer*)
Best Actress: Bette Davis (*Dangerous*)

1936
Best Picture: *The Great Ziegfeld*
Best Director: Frank Capra (*Mr Deeds Goes to Town*)
Best Actor: Paul Muni (*The Story of Louis Pasteur*)
Best Actress: Luise Rainer (*The Great Ziegfeld*)

1937
Best Picture: *The Life of Emile Zola*
Best Director: Leo McCarey (*The Awful Truth*)
Best Actor: Spencer Tracy (*Captains Courageous*)
Best Actress: Luise Rainer (*The Good Earth*)

1938
Best Picture: *You Can't Take It with You*
Best Director: Frank Capra (*You Can't Take It with You*)
Best Actor: Spencer Tracy (*Boys' Town*)
Best Actress: Bette Davis (*Jezebel*)

1939
Best Picture: *Gone with the Wind*
Best Director: Victor Fleming (*Gone with the Wind*)
Best Actor: Robert Donat (*Goodbye, Mr Chips*)
Best Actress: Vivien Leigh (*Gone with the Wind*)

1940s

1940
Best Picture: *Rebecca*
Best Director: John Ford (*The Grapes of Wrath*)
Best Actor: James Stewart (*The Philadelphia Story*)
Best Actress: Ginger Rogers (*Kitty Foyle*)

1941
Best Picture: *How Green Was My Valley*
Best Director: John Ford (*How Green Was My Valley*)
Best Actor: Gary Cooper (*Sergeant York*)
Best Actress: Joan Fontaine (*Suspicion*)

1942
Best Picture: *Mrs Miniver*
Best Director: William Wyler (*Mrs Miniver*)
Best Actor: James Cagney (*Yankee Doodle Dandy*)
Best Actress: Greer Garson (*Mrs Miniver*)

1943
Best Picture: *Casablanca*
Best Director: Michael Curtiz (*Casablanca*)
Best Actor: Paul Lukas (*Watch on the Rhine*)
Best Actress: Jennifer Jones (*The Song of Bernadette*)

1944
Best Picture: *Going My Way*
Best Director: Leo McCarey (*Going My Way*)
Best Actor: Bing Crosby (*Going My Way*)
Best Actress: Ingrid Bergman (*Gaslight*)

1945
Best Picture: *The Lost Weekend*
Best Director: Billy Wilder (*The Lost Weekend*)
Best Actor: Ray Milland (*The Lost Weekend*)
Best Actress: Joan Crawford (*Mildred Pierce*)

1946
Best Picture: *The Best Years of Our Lives*
Best Director: William Wyler (*The Best Years of Our Lives*)
Best Actor: Fredric March (*The Best Years of Our Lives*)
Best Actress: Olivia de Havilland (*To Each His Own*)

1947
Best Picture: *Gentleman's Agreement*
Best Director: Elia Kazan (*Gentleman's Agreement*)
Best Actor: Ronald Colman (*A Double Life*)
Best Actress: Loretta Young (*The Farmer's Daughter*)

1948
Best Picture: *Hamlet*
Best Director: John Huston (*The Treasure of the Sierra Madre*)
Best Actor: Laurence Olivier (*Hamlet*)
Best Actress: Jane Wyman (*Johnny Belinda*)

1949
Best Picture: *All the King's Men*
Best Director: Joseph L. Mankiewicz (*A Letter to Three Wives*)
Best Actor: Broderick Crawford (*All the King's Men*)
Best Actress: Olivia de Havilland (*The Heiress*)

1950s

1950
Best Picture: *All About Eve*
Best Director: Joseph L. Mankiewicz
  (*All About Eve*)
Best Actor: José Ferrer (*Cyrano de Bergerac*)
Best Actress: Judy Holliday (*Born Yesterday*)

1951
Best Picture: *An American in Paris*
Best Director: George Stevens (*A Place in the Sun*)
Best Actor: Humphrey Bogart (*The African Queen*)
Best Actress: Vivien Leigh (*A Streetcar Named Desire*)

1952
Best Picture: *The Greatest Show on Earth*
Best Director: John Ford (*The Quiet Man*)
Best Actor: Gary Cooper (*High Noon*)
Best Actress: Shirley Booth (*Come Back,
  Little Sheba*)

1953
Best Picture: *From Here to Eternity*
Best Director: Fred Zinnemann (*From Here to Eternity*)
Best Actor: William Holden (*Stalag 17*)
Best Actress: Audrey Hepburn (*Roman Holiday*)

1954
Best Picture: *On the Waterfront*
Best Director: Elia Kazan (*On the Waterfront*)
Best Actor: Marlon Brando (*On the Waterfront*)
Best Actress: Grace Kelly (*The Country Girl*)

1955
Best Picture: *Marty*
Best Director: Delbert Mann (*Marty*)
Best Actor: Ernest Borgnine (*Marty*)
Best Actress: Anna Magnini (*The Rose Tattoo*)

1956
Best Picture: *Around the World in Eighty Days*
Best Director: George Stevens (*Giant*)
Best Actor: Yul Brynner (*The King and I*)
Best Actress: Ingrid Bergman (*Anastasia*)

1957
Best Picture: *The Bridge on the River Kwai*
Best Director: David Lean (*The Bridge on the River Kwai*)
Best Actor: Alec Guinness (*The Bridge on the River Kwai*)
Best Actress: Joanne Wooward (*The Three Faces
  of Eve*)

1958
Best Picture: *Gigi*
Best Director: Vincente Minnelli (*Gigi*)
Best Actor: David Niven (*Separate Tables*)
Best Actress: Susan Hayward (*I Want to Live*)

1959
Best Picture: *Ben-Hur*
Best Director: William Wyler (*Ben-Hur*)
Best Actor: Charlton Heston (*Ben-Hur*)
Best Actress: Simone Signoret (*Room at
  the Top*)

1960s

1960
Best Picture: *The Apartment*
Best Director: Billy Wilder (*The Apartment*)
Best Actor: Burt Lancaster (*Elmer Gantry*)
Best Actress: Elizabeth Taylor (*Butterfield 8*)

1961
Best Picture: *West Side Story*
Best Director: Jerome Robbins and Robert Wise
  (*West Side Story*)
Best Actor: Maximilian Schell (*Judgment
  at Nuremberg*)
Best Actress: Sophia Loren (*Two Women*)

1962
Best Picture: *Lawrence of Arabia*
Best Director: David Lean (*Lawrence of Arabia*)
Best Actor: Gregory Peck (*To Kill a
  Mockingbird*)
Best Actress: Anne Bancroft (*The Miracle
  Worker*)

1963
Best Picture: *Tom Jones*
Best Director: Tony Richardson (*Tom Jones*)
Best Actor: Sidney Poitier (*Lilies of the Field*)
Best Actress: Patricia Neal (*Hud*)

1964
Best Picture: *My Fair Lady*
Best Director: George Cukor (*My Fair Lady*)
Best Actor: Rex Harrison (*My Fair Lady*)
Best Actress: Julie Andrews (*Mary Poppins*)

1965
Best Picture: *The Sound of Music*
Best Director: Robert Wise (*The Sound of Music*)
Best Actor: Lee Marvin (*Cat Ballou*)
Best Actress: Julie Christie (*Darling*)

1966
Best Picture: *A Man for All Seasons*
Best Director: Fred Zinnemann (*A Man for All Seasons*)
Best Actor: Paul Schofield (*A Man for All Seasons*)
Best Actress: Elizabeth Taylor (*Who's Afraid of Virginia Woolf?*)

1967
Best Picture: *In the Heat of the Night*
Best Director: Mike Nichols (*The Graduate*)
Best Actor: Rod Steiger (*In the Heat of the Night*)
Best Actress: Katharine Hepburn (*Guess Who's Coming to Dinner*)

1968
Best Picture: *Oliver!*
Best Director: Carol Reed (*Oliver!*)
Best Actor: Cliff Robertson (*Charly*)
Best Actress: tie between Katharine Hepburn (*The Lion in Winter*) and Barbra Streisand (*Funny Girl*)

1969
Best Picture: *Midnight Cowboy*
Best Director: John Schlesinger (*Midnight Cowboy*)
Best Actor: John Wayne (*True Grit*)
Best Actress: Maggie Smith (*The Prime of Miss Jean Brodie*)

1970s

1970
Best Picture: *Patton*
Best Director: Franklin J. Schaffner (*Patton*)
Best Actor: George C. Scott (*Patton*)
Best Actress: Glenda Jackson (*Women in Love*)

1971
Best Picture: *The French Connection*
Best Director: William Friedkin (*The French Connection*)
Best Actor: Gene Hackman (*The French Connection*)
Best Actress: Jane Fonda (*Klute*)

1972
Best Picture: *The Godfather*
Best Director: Bob Fosse (*Cabaret*)
Best Actor: Marlon Brando (*The Godfather*)
Best Actress: Liza Minnelli (*Cabaret*)

1973
Best Picture: *The Sting*
Best Director: George Roy Hill (*The Sting*)
Best Actor: Jack Lemmon (*Save the Tiger*)
Best Actress: Glenda Jackson (*A Touch of Class*)

1974
Best Picture: *The Godfather Part II*
Best Director: Francis Coppola: (*The Godfather Part II*)
Best Actor: Art Carney (*Harry and Tonto*)
Best Actress: Ellen Burstyn (*Alice Doesn't Live Here Any More*)

1975
Best Picture: *One Flew Over the Cuckoo's Nest*
Best Director: Milos Forman (*One Flew Over the Cuckoo's Nest*)
Best Actor: Jack Nicholson (*One Flew Over the Cuckoo's Nest*)
Best Actress: Louise Fletcher (*One Flew Over the Cuckoo's Nest*)

1976
Best Picture: *Rocky*
Best Director: John G. Avildsen (*Rocky*)
Best Actor: Peter Finch (*Network*)
Best Actress: Faye Dunaway (*Network*)

1977
Best Picture: *Annie Hall*
Best Director: Woody Allen (*Annie Hall*)
Best Actor: Richard Dreyfuss (*The Goodbye Girl*)
Best Actress: Diane Keaton (*Annie Hall*)

1978
Best Picture: *The Deer Hunter*
Best Director: Michael Cimino (*The Deer Hunter*)
Best Actor: Jon Voight (*Coming Home*)
Best Actress: Jane Fonda (*Coming Home*)

1979
Best Picture: *Kramer vs. Kramer*
Best Director: Robert Benton (*Kramer vs. Kramer*)
Best Actor: Dustin Hoffman (*Kramer vs. Kramer*)
Best Actress: Sally Field (*Norma Rae*)

1980s

1980
Best Picture: *Ordinary People*
Best Director: Robert Redford (*Ordinary People*)
Best Actor: Robert De Niro (*Raging Bull*)
Best Actress: Sissy Spacek (*Coal Miner's Daughter*)

1981
Best Picture: *Chariots of Fire*
Best Director: Warren Beatty (*Reds*)
Best Actor: Henry Fonda (*On Golden Pond*)
Best Actress: Katharine Hepburn (*On Golden Pond*)

1982
Best Picture: *Gandhi*
Best Director: Richard Attenborough (*Gandhi*)
Best Actor: Ben Kingsley (*Gandhi*)
Best Actress: Meryl Streep (*Sophie's Choice*)

1983
Best Picture: *Terms of Endearment*
Best Director: James L. Brooks (*Terms of Endearment*)
Best Actor: Robert Duvall (*Tender Mercies*)
Best Actress: Shirley MacLaine (*Terms of Endearment*)

1984
Best Picture: *Amadeus*
Best Director: Milos Forman (*Amadeus*)
Best Actor: F. Murray Abraham (*Amadeus*)
Best Actress: Sally Field (*Places in the Heart*)

1985
Best Picture: *Out of Africa*
Best Director: Sydney Pollack (*Out of Africa*)
Best Actor: William Hurt (*Kiss of the Spider Woman*)
Best Actress: Geraldine Page (*The Trip to Bountiful*)

1986
Best Picture: *Platoon*
Best Director: Oliver Stone (*Platoon*)
Best Actor: Paul Newman (*The Color of Money*)
Best Actress: Marlee Matlin (*Children of a Lesser God*)

1987
Best Picture: *The Last Emperor*
Best Director: Bernardo Bertolucci (*The Last Emperor*)
Best Actor: Michael Douglas (*Wall Street*)
Best Actress: Cher (*Moonstruck*)

1988
Best Picture: *Rain Man*
Best Director: Barry Levinson (*Rain Man*)
Best Actor: Dustin Hoffman (*Rain Man*)
Best Actress: Jodie Foster (*The Accused*)

1989
Best Picture: *Driving Miss Daisy*
Best Director: Oliver Stone (*Born on the Fourth of July*)
Best Actor: Daniel Day-Lewis (*My Left Foot*)
Best Actress: Jessica Tandy (*Driving Miss Daisy*)

248

1990s

1990
Best Picture: *Dances with Wolves*
Best Director: Kevin Costner (*Dances with Wolves*)
Best Actor: Jeremy Irons (*Reversal of Fortune*)
Best Actress: Kathy Bates (*Misery*)

1991
Best Picture: *The Silence of the Lambs*
Best Director: Jonathan Demme (*The Silence of the Lambs*)
Best Actor: Anthony Hopkins (*The Silence of the Lambs*)
Best Actress: Jodie Foster (*The Silence of the Lambs*)

1992
Best Picture: *Unforgiven*
Best Director: Clint Eastwood (*Unforgiven*)
Best Actor: Al Pacino (*Scent of a Woman*)
Best Actress: Emma Thompson (*Howards End*)

1993
Best Picture: *Schindler's List*
Best Director: Steven Spielberg (*Schindler's List*)
Best Actor: Tom Hanks (*Philadelphia*)
Best Actress: Holly Hunter (*The Piano*)

1994
Best Picture: *Forrest Gump*
Best Director: Robert Zemeckis (*Forrest Gump*)
Best Actor: Tom Hanks (*Forrest Gump*)
Best Actress: Jessica Lange (*Blue Skies*)

1995
Best Picture: *Braveheart*
Best Director: Mel Gibson (*Braveheart*)
Best Actor: Nicolas Cage (*Leaving Las Vegas*)
Best Actress: Susan Sarandon (*Dead Man Walking*)

1996
Best Picture: *The English Patient*
Best Director: Anthony Minghella (*The English Patient*)
Best Actor: Geoffrey Rush (*Shine*)
Best Actress: Frances McDormand (*Fargo*)

1997
Best Picture: *Titanic*
Best Director: James Cameron (*Titanic*)
Best Actor: Jack Nicholson (*As Good As It Gets*)
Best Actress: Helen Hunt (*As Good As It Gets*)

1998
Best Picture: *Shakespeare in Love*
Best Director: Steven Spielberg (*Saving Private Ryan*)
Best Actor: Roberto Benigni (*Life is Beautiful*)
Best Actress: Gwyneth Paltrow (*Shakespeare in Love*)

1999
Best Picture: *American Beauty*
Best Director: Sam Mendes (*American Beauty*)
Best Actor: Kevin Spacey (*American Beauty*)
Best Actress: Hilary Swank (*Boys Don't Cry*)

2000s

2000
Best Picture: *Gladiator*
Best Director: Steven Soderbergh (*Traffic*)
Best Actor: Russell Crowe (*Gladiator*)
Best Actress: Julia Roberts (*Erin Brockovich*)

2001
Best Picture: *A Beautiful Mind*
Best Director: Ron Howard (*A Beautiful Mind*)
Best Actor: Denzel Washington (*Training Day*)
Best Actress: Halle Berry (*Monster's Ball*)

2002
Best Picture: *Chicago*
Best Director: Roman Polanski (*The Pianist*)
Best Actor: Adrien Brody (*The Pianist*)
Best Actress: Nicole Kidman (*The Hours*)

ENDQUOTES

"I started at the top
and worked down."
ORSON WELLES

"To put it bluntly, I seem to
be a whole superstructure
without a foundation, but I am
working on the foundation."
MARILYN MONROE

"I never hear anyone say, boy,
I must see that film, I hear it
came in under budget."
BILLY WILDER

"The thing about Larry was he was
jealous of everyone, whatever they
did, if he felt they did whatever
they did better than he could. This
gnawing dissatisfaction made him
terribly unhappy all his life."
*ROBERT STEPHENS ON
LAURENCE OLIVIER*

"To make a film is to improve on
life, to arrange it to suit oneself, to
prolong the games of childhood,
to construct something which is at
once a new toy and a vase in which
one can arrange in a permanent way
the ideas one feels in the morning."
FRANÇOIS TRUFFAUT

"I was the only star they allowed to
come out of the water looking wet."
BETTE DAVIS

"I never go out unless I look like
Joan Crawford, the movie star.
If you want to see the girl next
door, go next door."
JOAN CRAWFORD

"I'm revered like an old building.
Yet I still seem to be master of
my fate. The boat may only be
a canoe, but I'm paddling it."
KATHARINE HEPBURN

"I don't use any particular
method. I'm from the let's
pretend school of acting."
HARRISON FORD

"The tougest three pictures I ever
made. It was shot in a state of
emergency, shot in confusion,
and wound up in blind panic."
JOSEPH L. MANKIEWICZ ON CLEOPATRA

"I sometimes think I'm impersonating
the dark unconscious of the whole
human race. I know this sounds
sick, but I love it."
VINCENT PRICE

"I've got a very good left profile
and a very bad right profile. I was
the Loretta Young of my day.
I was only ever photographed
on the left-hand profile."
DIRK BOGARDE

"I've never been through psycho-
analysis. I solve my problems
through the pictures I make."
STEVEN SPIELBERG

"At heart Larry was what the French
call a *cabotin*. Not exactly a ham:
a performer, a vulgarian, someone
who lives and dies for acting."
*DIRECTOR TONY RICHARDSON ON
LAURENCE OLIVIER*

"I have life rage. What am I going to
do with it? I can't kick the shit out of
someone. I have a therapist on each
coast. I've had a different personality
when I go to each one."
CHRISTINA RICCI

"I'M NO ACTOR AND I'VE 64 PICTURES TO PROVE IT."
VICTOR MATURE

"I DON'T ASK QUESTIONS. I JUST TAKE THEIR MONEY AND USE IT FOR THINGS THAT REALLY INTEREST ME."
GEORGE SANDERS

"Hollywood, like Midas, kills whatever it touches."
CLIFFORD ODETS, DRAMATIST AND SCREENWRITER

"Can you imagine being overpaid for dressing up and playing games?"
DAVID NIVEN

"He's about as likely a candidate for stardom as the neighbourhood delicatessen man."
TIME MAGAZINE ON WALTER MATTHAU

"She moves rigidly on to the set, as if wheels were concealed under the stately skirt; she says her piece with flat dignity and trolleys out again, rather like a mechanical marvel from the World's Fair."
GRAHAM GREENE ON BRITISH ACTRESS ANNA NEAGLE

"The number one book of the age was written by a committee, and it was called the Bible."
LOUIS B. MAYER

"Motivation is a lot of crap."
DEAN MARTIN

"I don't care to belong to any social organization which would accept me as a member."
GROUCHO MARX

"I do not believe the public will want spoken comedy. Motion pictures and the spoken arts are two distinct arts."
HAROLD LLOYD, SILENT ERA COMEDIAN

"My acting range? Left eyebrow raised, right eyebrow raised."
ROGER MOORE

"I've been to Paris, France, and I've been to Paris, Paramount. Paris, Paramount is better."
ERNST LUBITSCH, WRITER AND DIRECTOR

"I live by a man's code designed to fit a man's world, yet at the same time I never forget that a woman's first job is to choose the right shade of lipstick."
CAROLE LOMBARD

"Strip the phoney tinsel off Hollywood and you'll find the real tinsel underneath."
OSCAR LEVANT

"Acting has been good to me. It has taken me to play golf all over the world."
BORIS KARLOFF

"The days at MGM were marvellous. Everyone was pitching in. We had real collaboration. It was fun. We didn't think it was work."
GENE KELLY

"Writing a good movie brings a writer about as much fame as steering a bicycle."
BEN HECHT

"Charlie Chaplin is no businessman – all he knows is he can't take anything less."
SAMUEL GOLDWYN

"I am paid not to think."
CLARK GABLE

251

"IF I'M WORKING WITH FRIGHTENED PEOPLE, I DO TEND TO DOMINATE THEM. I'M NO DOLL, THAT'S FOR SURE."
BURT LANCASTER

INDEX

ACKNOWLEDGEMENTS

The publisher would like to thank the following for the use of their pictures:

Cine Art Gallery
759 Fulham Road
London SW6 5UU

Vertigo Gallery
29 Bedfordbury
Covent Garden
London WC2N 4BJ

Moviedrome
moviedrome@ntlworld.com